The Divine Rider in the Art
of the Western Roman Empire

Marjorie Mackintosh

BAR International Series 607

1995

Published in 2019 by
BAR Publishing, Oxford

BAR International Series 607

The Divine Rider in the Art of the Western Roman Empire

© Marjorie Mackintosh and the Publisher 1995

ISBN   9780860547860   paperback
ISBN   9781407349114   e-book

DOI   https://doi.org/10.30861/9780860547860

A catalogue record for this book is available from the British Library

This book is available at www.barpublishing.com

BAR Publishing is the trading name of British Archaeological Reports (Oxford) Ltd.
British Archaeological Reports was first incorporated in 1974 to publish the BAR
Series, International and British. In 1992 Hadrian Books Ltd became part of the BAR
group. This volume was originally published by Tempvs Reparatvm in conjunction
with British Archaeological Reports (Oxford) Ltd / Hadrian Books Ltd, the Series
principal publisher, in 1995. This present volume is published by BAR Publishing,
2019.

BAR
PUBLISHING

BAR titles are available from:

BAR Publishing
122 Banbury Rd, Oxford, OX2 7BP, UK
EMAIL   info@barpublishing.com
PHONE   +44 (0)1865 310431
FAX   +44 (0)1865 316916
www.barpublishing.com

Acknowledgement

It is almost impossible to express the debt of gratitude I owe to Dr. Martin Henig for the time, encouragement and guidance he gave me as I worked on this project. Thank you.

Thanks also for support and patience to my husband Ray and my son Ethan.

The work on this thesis was done during the 1980s and completed in 1991. The relationship of more recent finds to the material discussed here may form the basis of future publications.

Contents

Chapter 1

The Background

It is stating the obvious to say that one of the most common images in Roman Imperial iconography was the horseman. Rider figures have been preserved for us in large numbers. Human and divine, arrayed in armour, dressed in plain tunic or simply nude, they sit astride horses which gallop, rear or stand still. Riders appear in sculpture in the round, in relief, painting and the minor arts. And yet the horseman image, despite its popularity and virtual ubiquity, occurs in only a very few variations. Artists, it would seem, when faced with a commission involving the representation of horsemen, turned to a few stock types that could be manipulated to suit each new set of conditions. The extent to which this approach was the norm can be observed in the new iconographical types, or rather the paucity of really new types, invented to represent rider gods during the Roman period. These new images were created in response to the wish of those inhabitants of the Empire whose gods had hitherto been largely aniconic to give their deities tangible form.

The device of identifying non-Greek and non-Roman gods with the Graeco-Roman pantheon solved, for the most part, the problem of the visualization of aniconic deities, so long as the foreign deity could be presented satisfactorily in a standard Graeco-Roman guise with the addition of a few attributes to individualize the representation. Many of the models that were still being copied in the second and third centuries AD had first been created during the high Classical period in Greece, like the Zeus and Athena of Phidias. The transformation of the enthroned Zeus of Olympia into a seated Celtic Jupiter, for example, could be effected with little difficulty in sculptural terms although, in the process, it is possible that Celtic characteristics of the god — a distinctive costume or hairdressing, perhaps, described in myth but not visualized before Roman times — may have disappeared behind the Roman façade.

What makes the development of rider-god iconography in the Imperial period distinctive is that, in contrast to standing or seated deities, there was no clear earlier divine prototype, in particular no earlier Classical Greek prototype, to which the artist could turn. So when asked to represent deities like Epona or the rider gods of the Celts and Thracians who were not easy to provide with tidy Graeco-Roman counterparts, artists were forced to look for new forms. Yet, here again they did not invent afresh but coped with each new problem by drawing upon what had gone before, transforming it into something, at the same time, different from its Greek and Roman prototypes but recognizably derived from them.

The object of this study is to look at the rider deities of the western Empire including both those whose Graeco-Roman identities are clear and those, by far the majority, for whom the new hybrid forms were introduced. Also we seek to show how the artists adapted old, mainly Greek, forms to represent the deities of the Imperial period. To understand why it was

Greek forms that dominated, we need first to examine the development of the horse image in early Greece.

The Earliest Greek Rider Representations

One of the characteristics of the Graeco-Roman pantheon was the near absence of mounted deities. Chariotry, not riding, was the mode of locomotion most favoured by the gods, with the exception of the Dioscuri who were often mounted. This does not, however, imply that the gods never rode — rare examples of mounted gods in the Classical period and earlier do exist — nor that horses were not valued. On the contrary, several deities, notably Poseidon and Athena, had close associations in myth and cult with horses, as we shall see below, but this relationship is not usually represented pictorially by showing the gods mounted. There are exceptions however, especially in the case of Poseidon. A silver coin from Potidaea dated to about 500 BC, for example, has on its obverse the figure of a mounted Poseidon, clearly identified by the large trident he is carrying.[1]

The question arises as to why the Greek gods of the Classical period were not represented as riders. One clue may lie in the likelihood that the art of riding itself was little practised, particularly in warfare, during the formative period of Greek religion and religious art, that is, in the Bronze and early Iron Ages. The earliest representations of horses from the Greek mainland are on the stelae from Grave Circle A at Mycenae[2] and these are horses drawing chariots. The scenes on the stelae appear to cover the major occupations of a chariot-owning upper class: racing, hunting and war, although, alternatively, they may represent the contests taking place at the funeral games of those buried beneath them.[3] In either case, owning horses and chariots was costly and obviously the preserve of the rich and powerful, the richest and most powerful of whom were the gods.

Mycenaean relief and painting[4] and the information about Bronze Age (or early Iron Age) life supplied by the epics offer very little testimony for contemporary riding.[5] As J. K. Anderson remarks, "riding seems to have been unimportant and uninteresting to the artists of the period".[6] Nevertheless, it is certain that riding was known. The evidence comes in the form of a small clay figure of a horseman found at Mycenae in a deposit with a quantity of LH III pottery.[7] The horse has an elongated body which is painted with vertical stripes. The rider is seated toward the rear of its long back. He has rudimentary arms and legs and wears a conical helmet. He carries a sword and, presumably, is meant to be a warrior.

Egyptian reliefs of the New Kingdom also show horsemen among the armies in battle, but there is no evidence for an organized cavalry. The chief vehicle for the royal warrior as shown in the art of both Egypt and Mycenae was the chariot.[8] Thus the situation reflected in the Mycenaean remains and echoed in the epics suggests that the highest warriors, those worthy of notice in art and literature, drove or were driven in chariots; those socially and financially in the second rank owned and perhaps rode their horses while the vast majority of the army were foot-soldiers. The gods naturally emulated the highest level of society and travelled by chariot.

The primacy of the chariot can also be seen from the relatively late introduction of the race for ridden horses into the Olympic Games in 648 BC, thirty-two years after the introduction of the four-horse chariot race in 680, the two-horse chariot having been raced for considerably longer.[9] The result of the continued prestige of the chariot meant, therefore, that although mounted figures began to appear on vases before 700 (probably implying an enhanced social and military position for the rider) and became particularly popular during the Orientalizing period,[10] the gods, as a rule, were still depicted travelling in chariots.

Early Greek Female Riders

The male figure riding astride was not the only equestrian type known from the Bronze Age. Another, also appearing first during the Mycenaean period, was the mounted female who rides side-saddle. A small terracotta now in Athens represents a female figure seated on a high-sided saddle on what seems to be a horse or some other equine creature. Her arms are raised like the little figurines of the *psi* type, so-named because of their resemblance to the shape of that letter. If these little *psi* figurines, found in tombs and house deposits, are goddesses, as scholars believe,[11] then the mounted lady is most probably also a goddess.

Similar statuettes are known from the Geometric period. Examples have come from Arcadia, from Olympia and also from Samos. The Samian figure was found in the sanctuary of Hera,[12] further supporting a divine identification for the mounted woman. The origins and identities of these figures are uncertain, but very likely they represent offerings to goddesses with equine associations. They certainly foreshadow the Celtic representation of Epona. But they cannot be thought to have influenced it because the side-saddle representation seems to have disappeared from the list of acceptable epiphanies for goddesses during the Classical period.

Gods and Heroes Associated with Horses

The Greek god who was most closely associated with horses was Poseidon. A god who was truly Greek, Poseidon's name appears in both the Pylos and Knossos Linear B texts. At the latter site, he is already known by his epithet, Earth-Shaker,[13] but the limited information to be gleaned from the tablets makes no mention of horses. However, mythological sources that most likely have their origin in Mycenaean times associate Poseidon quite clearly with horses. Indeed he is the progenitor of horses, the most famous of these being Pegasus who was the son of Poseidon by the Gorgon Medusa. Pegasus was tamed for riding but never, it seems,

for chariotry.[14] Moreover, Bellerophon, the hero who rode Pegasus, was unable to subdue him without the divine help that he received from Athena who herself had close associations with horses.

In artistic terms, Bellerophon and Pegasus became the prototype for the heroic horse and rider. It is not the god who rides but the heroic youth. It is worth remembering here also that the Dioscuri who seem to inhabit a half-way world between the Olympian and heroic are also usually represented as youthful riders rather than as divine charioteers.

An early representation of the chimera story on a plate from Thasos of about 660 BC shows the young Bellerophon mounted on his horse whose wings spread wide. The horse has raised his front legs as if rearing because beneath him is the chimera all of whose heads — lion, goat and snake — turn toward the horse and rider. Unusually, the group faces left so that Bellerophon's right hand holds the reins and he aims his spear toward the back of the beast with his left.[15] The style of the groups reflects the Orientalizing phase of Cycladic vase painting, but the composition itself, except for its leftward orientation, already shows the developed image of the heroic rider.

Pegasus was not the only equine offspring of Poseidon. The god was also the father of a stallion called Areion by the goddess Demeter. In order to avoid Poseidon's advances, Demeter changed herself into a mare. Poseidon proceeded to match her transformation by changing himself into a stallion and mated with the goddess in that guise.[16] The incident was said to have taken place in Arcadia (although the same myth appears in Boeotia[17]) and at many places in that region, Poseidon was worshipped as Poseidon *Hippios*, the horse-Poseidon with an equine element in the rites. At Mantineia, for example, his temple lay near a race-course and during his festivals, races were held.[18]

At Corinth, too, Poseidon was worshipped as the god of the horse and among the votive tablets offered to him were some which showed the god as a rider.[19] But the mounted Poseidon more commonly occurs as rider of a sea horse (hippocamp), as on a fourth century BC hydria in New York where the bearded god is seated on an animal whose front parts are those of a horse but whose body ends in a long curling fish tail. The god holds his identifying attribute, the trident.[20] It seems that, however close his associations may have been with the horse, pictorially, at least, his link with the sea was still stronger.

Several other deities were, like Poseidon, closely associated with horses. Athena, Demeter and Hera were all worshipped as *Hippia*,[21] but none of these seems to have contributed to the iconography of the rider.

Athena's connection with horses appears to have been related to their control. If, in their famous contest, Poseidon sired the horse and offered it to the Athenians, it was Athena who made the bridle and built the chariot.[22] Similarly it was she who helped Bellerophon to control Pegasus, an association commemorated by the addition of two winged horses to the helmet she wears on Phidias's statue.[23] On Panathenaic amphorae, Athena's shield sometimes shows Pegasus as a device and sometimes a wheel, indicating her association with chariotry.[24] But there is no evidence that Athena was ever thought of as a rider on any animal, even though other goddesses, like Artemis and Aphrodite, were occasionally represented riding side-saddle. The latter, for example, is shown riding a goose on a white-ground cup by the Pistoxenos Painter dated about 470 BC.[25]

The Rider Image in Archaic and Classical Greece

The development of the rider figure in Greece depended not on divine iconography but on the human and heroic. On current evidence, horsemen began to appear on vases from the middle of the eighth century BC.[26] A neck-handled amphora in New York of Attic late Geometric style, for example, shows a horse and rider moving toward the right in a procession behind two light chariots each drawn by two horses. The rider's left hand is raised holding the reins, and his right arm is also raised.[27]

Fighting horsemen appeared slightly later. On a plate-fibula from Thebes in the National Museum in Athens, a group of two fighting men on one side of the plate is balanced by a horseman trampling a fallen enemy on the other. The fibula is dated to the second quarter of the seventh century BC and is an early example of the important motif of the victorious rider above his conquered enemy.[28] The Bellerophon plate, discussed above, is also a variation on this same horseman and enemy motif of about the same date.

During the Archaic period, riders started to be seen in relief on funerary monuments. One of the earliest scenes is of a horseman accompanied by his servant and dog. It is carved on the back of a stele from Dorylaion in Phrygia. The front of the stele shows a winged goddess wearing a *polos* and carrying a lion.[29] Despite its Anatolian origin, the style of the relief is late Archaic Greek. From the Greek mainland, from Lamptrai in Attica, comes a low relief stele with the image of a man riding a walking horse carved on the front with mourners on the two sides.[30] Both of these stele are dated to the sixth century BC and stand at the beginning of the development of the tranquil rider motif in relief sculpture.

The horseman in combat, on the other hand, seems to have made his appearance in funerary relief only during the fifth century BC.[31] Of particular interest is a relief, now in the Villa Albani in Rome, which shows a rider who has just jumped from his horse in order to strike a fallen enemy. The style of the work suggests that it dates from a decade or so after the Parthenon frieze[32] on which such a variety of horsemen were represented. Like the riders of the Parthenon frieze, the Albani horseman belonged to a state monument, in this case, most probably a grave monument erected for those who died in battle against the Spartans on behalf of the city.[33] It is likely that the horseman motif was used just for cavalry dead and not only referred to the actual form the military service of the deceased had taken, but also symbolized their courage and bravery.[34] The image of the fighting horseman with its resonances of mounted heros of myth was here used as a vehicle for representing the heroism of those who died in battle.

The next step in the development of the rider image is preserved in the stele of Dexileos of 394 BC which shows a horseman mounted and attacking his fallen enemy. This is a private monument, but the mounted figure almost certainly has the same significance as the dismounted cavalryman of the Albani relief. The dead man is celebrated for his horsemanship and courage, and again, the form of the composition must have brought to mind a mythical hero-rider such as Bellerophon making his attack on the chimera.

Turning to sculpture in the round, the Archaic and Classical periods have left little firm evidence of large scale rider statues. The most famous of Archaic horsemen is the Rampin rider found on the Acropolis in Athens. His head and torso are preserved along with the head of his horse. Fragments suggest that he was one of a pair but the identities of the two are uncertain.[35] The reconstruction produced by Harald von Roques de Maumont shows a pair of nude riders on walking horses. The riders face outward and carry spears in their outside hands. The outward turning of the riders' heads is balanced by the inward-looking horses.[36] Other examples of free-standing horse and rider groups found on the Acropolis suggest that, like the Rampin rider, the typical composition was a standing horse balanced on all four legs with perhaps a support under the belly.[37]

The Classical period, despite the richness of the rider reliefs of the Parthenon and the fighting horsemen of the Athena Nike temple, has left no examples of rider statues in the round in Attica. In terms of human riders this may indicate, as has been suggested, that the idea of honouring individuals with rider statues ran counter to the democratic spirit of the age.[38] But at the same time, the lack of Classical divine rider statuary may also be related to the fact that during the period which saw the creation of the definitive forms for the major gods, chariotry was still considered the main mode of divine transport and therefore there was no incentive to produce an image of a god mounted. Even the Dioscuri, rarely parted from their horses, do not seem to have inspired significant rider statues. The favoured composition, which may have had its origin in the Classical period, was a standing Dioscurus holding the reins of his horse.

Alexander and Rider Imagery

It remained for the Hellenistic period to elevate the rider to divine status. Or rather, it was the influence of Alexander the Great and the art and iconography that were developed for him which appear to have changed and raised the status of the rider. Even before Alexander, horsemanship seems to have been particularly highly valued by the Macedonians. Horses and riders began to appear on Macedonian coinage in the fifth century BC, a reflection, most likely, of the importance of horse breeding to that country.[39] On coins of the early fifth century, an unnamed god whom Herodotus identified with Ares can be seen represented as a horseman walking beside his horse and holding a pair of spears.[40] A rider armed with two spears also appears on Macedonian coins of the early fifth century and perhaps is to be identified with the same deity.[41] We have already seen that Poseidon too was depicted as a rider on early Macedonian coinage, and this suggests that the prestige of riding was very much greater in Macedonia than in Greece from an early period.

The conquests and legends of Alexander and his horse Bucephalus naturally enhanced the value of riding. But in artistic terms, it was the series of famous works of art in which Alexander was represented mounted that contributed so greatly to the development of the horse and rider theme in the succeeding centuries. The great importance of the works of art created for Alexander, beyond their worth as artistic creations, lies in the fact that these were the first monuments to have as their subject a living and identifiable individual as opposed to a generalized ideal.

State and private monuments before Alexander were usually erected to the heroic dead and were neither portraits nor personalized representations. The image on the stele of Dexileos tells us nothing about the young man himself. It is not meant as a portrait. The same is true of the state monuments for the mass graves of the heroic military dead. The battles and their participants are generalized and homogenized and the individual suppressed. Tonio Holscher has called this characteristic the *Ethos of Anonymity*.[42]

Alexander, on the other hand, is clearly represented as an individual with his own attributes. These make him easy to identify, even where the quality of the portrait is poor, in much the same way that the gods can be differentiated one from the other through their attributes. The development of this special iconography can perhaps be credited to Lysippos who produced the most famous statues of Alexander, both in standing and riding poses. The nude standing statues of Alexander recall the standing statues of the gods (Figures 1 and Plate 1, for example) and the equestrian statues are the first rider statues to represent a man who was living and not yet one of the heroized dead when the statue was made.[43]

Moreover, even in painting, as represented by the Alexander mosaic, a new conception of the place of the individual in the composition can be seen. The famous mosaic, found at Pompeii and now in the Naples Museum, is believed to be a copy of a painting which Philoxenos of Eretria made for the Macedonian King Cassander in about 300 BC.[44] Tonio Holscher has drawn attention to the way in which the composition of the Alexander mosaic revolves around the two figures of the Macedonian and Persian kings with other fighting figures given a lesser role. This is a radical departure from the Classical arrangement of battle scenes into small groups where all figures are accorded equal weight in the composition.[45] The new grouping reflects the emergence of a hierarchical way of thinking in which a singular individual of more than human dimensions dominates the rest. The hierarchical arrangement of figures in art had a long history in the Near East. However, in Greece its introduction signaled the beginning of profound changes in the way the world and society were perceived.

Also with Alexander, the distinction between gods and humans began to be blurred. The deification of Alexander at Siwa by the Egyptians may not have been taken seriously by educated Greeks and Alexander's associates, but was probably accepted by the majority of ordinary people and was put to political use by Alexander.[46] In addition, Alexander, or perhaps Alexander and his father, commissioned the sculptor Leochares to produce chryselephantine statues of himself, his parents and his paternal grandparents for the Philippeion at Olympia which

Philip built after he won the battle of Chaironeia.[47] Statues of gold and ivory had hitherto been reserved for the gods.[48]

Two small heads made of ivory were found in the main chamber of Tomb II among the royal tombs at Vergina. Both are under 4 cm. in height. They were part of the relief decoration of a bier. The heads are incomplete, ending at the hairline, which suggests that the hair was of another material, perhaps gilded metal. They have been identified by the excavator of Vergina, Manolis Andronikos, as portraits of Alexander and his father on the grounds of their resemblance to known portraits of both Macedonian kings.[49] It may be that they are based on the full-size statues in ivory and gold which were created by Leochares. But even if they are not, they confirm that precious materials were now being used for portraits of mortal men.

Alexander, it would seem, introduced the practice of erecting statues of living leaders in a semi-idealized and also semi-divine form. The statues were portrait statues but idealized to the extent that they represented their subjects in handsome, vigorous manhood, no doubt, handsomer and more vigorous than nature had made them even in their prime. One of the favoured forms that these statues took was the rider. It was also the form that Alexander used to commemorate his companions who died at the battle of Grannicus. This monument included twenty-five figures which were produced by Lysippus's workshop.[50] The group itself was taken to Rome as booty by Caecilius Metellus in the second century BC. It is possible that the statuette from Herculaneum showing a rider on a rearing horse is not, as some suggest, Alexander himself, but one of the fallen companions from this Grannicus memorial group.[51]

That the practice of erecting ostentatious rider statues was continued by Alexander's successors can be seen from the fragments of an equestrian statue of Demetrios Poliorketes that was found during excavations in the Athenian Agora. Demetrios's father was an associate first of Philip and then of Alexander. Demetrios himself imitated Alexander in a number of ways including the erection of a life-size, or slightly over life-size, equestrian statue which was gilded.[52]

The numerous statue bases that have survived at Olympia and other sanctuaries give evidence that the practice of erecting such monuments became especially common during the Hellenistic period when not only statues of kings but other individuals of note were placed at important sites in Greece.[53] Inscriptions on the bases show that Romans too erected portrait statues at the major Greek sanctuaries.

The Roman Rider

The Romans may have borrowed the idea of the equestrian statue from the Greeks as early as the sixth century BC to commemorate Cloelia,[54] although as we have seen, there is only little evidence for rider statues in Greece at that time. According to Livy, Cloelia was a young girl who helped bring about peace between the Etruscans and Romans and who was honoured for her courage by the erection of a statue, set up at the top of the Sacred Way, showing her on horseback.[55] The Romans also borrowed much of their divine iconography from the Greeks, and like the Greek gods, the major Roman gods were not normally represented mounted. Nevertheless, heroic rider imagery of the period before Alexander would have been known from a variety of sources including the art of the Greek colonies to the south of Rome, as well as the Greek-influenced art of the Etruscans and also of other Italic people outside Rome and Latium.[56] The Hellenistic practice of erecting statues to famous living men was also adopted by the Romans although these statues were usually sited not in sanctuaries but in civic areas.

The general tendency, seen in the evolution of equestrian statuary, for the prerogatives of gods and heros to be usurped by living leaders is also reflected in other arts, very clearly, for example, in the imagery on Roman coins. The introduction of new images, particularly of living men, in coin iconography bears witness to the same desire to redefine the relationship between men and gods, that we saw in the rider statues of Alexander and his successors.

Alexander's own coinage followed the accepted usage with the head of a deity on the obverse and a full figure, heroic or perhaps divine, on the reverse. Herakles was often the god honoured on the obverses while a number of subjects, including horsemen, were depicted on the reverses.[57] But some of Alexander's successors put the conqueror's portrait with the horn of Ammon in his hair on their coins.[58] The horn symbolized Alexander's divine origin as proclaimed by the Egyptians and, thus, confirmed his right to the dominant position on the coin. But at the same time, the use of Alexander's portrait on their coins probably reflected the desire of his successors to present themselves as the heirs of the god-king while not actually claiming divine honours for themselves.

In the case of Demetrios Poliorketes, however, there was no such subtlety. He issued coins with his own portrait on them wearing bull's horns in obvious imitation of Alexander but associating himself with Poseidon whom he claimed as his father.[59] It was Demetrios, we may recall, who had himself represented as a rider on a gilded statue in Athens, a further indication of his divine pretensions. Interestingly, some of his coins retain a traditional armed Macedonian rider on the reverse but not a mounted Poseidon. When Poseidon does appear, he is portrayed in one of his more typical poses either hurling his trident or standing leaning on it.[60] The choice of the canonic Greek iconography for Poseidon rather than a distinctively Macedonian one makes it clear that Demetrios is speaking to the whole Greek world and beyond in making his claim of divine paternity. Moreover, as a divine son, he has as much right as Alexander or Herakles to appear on a coin. Here we have an early appearance on coins of Greek-speaking people of the Near Eastern concept of the divine ruler. The move from the representation of sons of gods to sons of men (but successful men and therefore divinely favoured) on coins was not long in coming.

In Rome the earliest coins were influenced by Greek forms and tended to represent divinities, particularly Dea Roma and the Dioscuri. By the late second century BC, newer types showed gods on the obverse with a narrative scene, sometimes having political implications, on the reverse. Coins began to have a more personal meaning for the moneyer. A coin of M. Sergius Silas in 115 or 114 BC had a reverse on which a galloping rider was represented holding aloft a severed human head. The rider was an ancestor of Silas.[61] The individual moneyer with no claim to divinity still felt able to present his personal agenda on his coins. So the coins, like the equestrian statues, show two parallel developments: the divinization of rulers and the secularisation of art forms previously reserved for the gods. The coin, statue or relief becomes the vehicle for personal propaganda and aggrandisement. For, not just the divine ruler, but the worthy nobleman or soldier feels able to appropriate the old forms to satisfy his own vanity.

But, if the Hellenistic period saw a greater degree of freedom in the use of hitherto divine imagery, under the Roman Empire, the process began to reverse and the rider statue and the coin obverse became the preserve of that new divine figure, the emperor. According to Niels Hannestad, the central theme of the Principate from its beginning was the emperor as Jupiter's proxy.[62] In artistic representation, at least, the distinction between deity and proxy soon began to break down. Claudius, for example, had himself portrayed as Jupiter on several statues, one of which was erected in the Imperial cult temple at Olympia.[63]

The equestrian statue became a favoured type of monument for Roman rulers just as it had been for Hellenistic leaders, no doubt on account of its association with Alexander the Great, its links with the semi-divine heros of old and its potential for sheer, dominating size.[64] The colossal equestrian statue of Domitian which was erected in the Forum Romanum in AD 91 was the subject of a poem by Statius[65] extolling its virtue as the visualization of Imperial invincibility.[66]

Thus the Imperial rider combined the attributes of a Bellerophon or Castor of the Classical Period and an Alexander of the Hellenistic. Even when he was fighting, the Imperial horseman was represented as more than human. The mounted Trajan on the Great Trajanic frieze incorporated into the Arch of Constantine is shown riding helmetless as he strikes down the enemies below and in front of him. This certainly would not have been the case if the scene were meant to be realistic. Rather the emperor is shown as the divine rider who has no need for such mortal accoutrements as a helmet.[67] The same observation has been made regarding the Alexander of the Alexander mosaic who also rides bareheaded into the battle.[68] While the obvious reason for this convention is that the leader must be recognised, it also reminds us that a superior force protects the king or emperor in his exertions which allows him to fight without the encumbrances so necessary to mere mortals.

Horse and Rider in Celtic Art

The third constituent, along with the Greek and the Roman, in the mix that leads to the mature art of the Western Roman Empire, is the Celtic. Unlike the Greeks and Romans, the Celts were expert riders as well as charioteers, the legacy of their semi-nomadic history.[69] The settled, urban Romans, who preferred to fight on foot, recruited members of their mounted auxiliary units from among the Gauls and other equestrian nations. It would therefore not be surprising to find that the horse and horse imagery have a long history in Celtic art.

The question arises, however, as to how far back the Celtic *ethnos* can be traced. Horse imagery can be found from Neolithic times among the artefacts of peoples believed to be Indo-Europeans.[70] The appearance of such early objects representing horses as well as the discovery of horse burials[71] hints at the importance of the horse within the emerging Indo-European society. But while this may set the Celtic material into the context of a very ancient tradition, it is too far distant to be useful in analysing Celtic art on the brink of the Roman conquest (and the Romans, of course, were also inheritors of this tradition). To investigate the pre-Roman background of Romano-Celtic art, we must look to the La Tène Celts and also to their immediate predecessors and in some areas, ancestors, the people of the Hallstatt culture in Western Europe whose characteristic artefacts belong to the first half of the first millenium BC.[72]

Horse images, especially models, have been found on sites with Hallstatt occupation. The site of Hallstatt itself has yielded a bronze ceremonial axe on which a horse and rider have been cast on the handle end of the blade (Figure 2). The figures of both horse and rider are very crude with thick, stubby arms and legs and a minimum of detail. The rider may once have carried a weapon. The axe was found in a grave and is dated about 600 BC, Hallstatt C.[73] Another axe of similar type from the same site has a horse of less crude design standing on the shaft of the axe. This too was discovered in a grave[74] suggesting a cultic association for these objects as divine images, amulets or apotropaia.

The Strettweg Wagon

A particularly interesting example of horsemen from the Hallstatt period is found on the famous cult vehicle from Strettweg in Austria.[75] The flat-bedded wagon is the platform for a tall figure of a woman who holds a shallow bowl on her head. Male and female figures less than half her height stand below her. Some of the males are ithyphallic. At the front and back of the wagon, two female figures stand by a stag, and at the sides are four riders. The nude riders sit on thin, long-legged horses (Figure 3). They wear pointed caps and carry long oval shields over one arm and raise short sticks, perhaps standing for spears, with the other. The features of the faces are very simple. The vehicle is variously dated to the sixth century BC and circa 700 BC.[76]

Nancy Sanders sees a close relationship between these figures, particularly the goddess, and Greek Geometric period bronze figurines. Indeed, she believes that the Strettweg goddess was actually made by a Greek craftsman or a Celtic one trained in a Greek workshop.[77] For example, the goddess wears a belt which is similar to those worn by many Greek figures. The apparently boneless curves of her arms with no suggestion of the angle of the elbow can also occasionally be found among Greek examples.[78] On the other hand, this trait is not common. The majority of Greek bronzes have an indication of the elbow in the modelling of their upraised arms. There are also other differences which shed doubt on a Greek creator for the figure. The curvature of the buttocks on Greek statuettes of the Geometric period is generally more pronounced than that of the Strettweg

goddess and all the figures on the wagon show this same weak modelling of contours. The horses too are distinct from the Greek types. The join between their heads and necks is a curve rather than an angle, analogous to the 'boneless' arms of the goddess. Here we may be seeing a preference on the part of the artist for curvilinear forms, a characteristic which appears more Celtic than Greek.

Looking at the other figures on the wagon, it does not seem likely that they were made by an artist other than the one who made the goddess. There are enough differences between the Greek examples and this group to leave it open to question as to whether a Greek artist was in any way involved, although Greek influence or a Greek-trained artist may be a possibility. A similar iconographical group comes from Gemeinlebarn, also in Austria, in the form of a pot with a horseman and other figures standing on the shoulder. Like the Strettweg riders, this horseman has a shield, but his is round while the wagon riders hold oval shields. The Gemeinlebarn rider is accompanied also by a stag and other figures including a female with a large bowl on her head distinctly reminiscent of the Strettweg goddess.[79] The figures are considerably cruder than the Strettweg group and it is possible that here we have an allusion to the same theme as the larger work but in a less costly medium.

One significance of these early monuments, however, is that they link riders to cult in the early Celtic and perhaps pre-Celtic populations of Europe. The Strettweg vehicle shows that armed horsemen were in some way (as protectors?) connected ritually with a female deity. Whether they were meant as worshippers or as companion gods is impossible to say, but the juxtaposition of the armed male rider and a female power is a common occurrence in the finds of the Roman period in the Celtic world. The Hallstatt riders may be early examples of the armed rider deity who, under the Romans, is often interpreted as the mounted Mars or even possibly the mounted Jupiter. Or we may wonder if there is not some relationship with the mounted Dioscuri and their goddess sister Helen to be discussed in Chapter Five. A goddess and attendant riders is also to be found in the Danubian Rider cult considered in Chapter Seven. Given the geographic diversity of this concept, one possibility is that the association of protector gods or heros and a central goddess may have its roots in Indo-European culture (although it appears in the Near East as well). That the male associates of the goddess became riders when riding became identified with the role of warrior — a role which the male figures in the Strettweg wagon clearly fill — would be consistent with their protective function.

Numbers of small horse and horsemen figurines have been found from both Hallstatt and La Tène sites. Many were probably ex-votos and some were clearly pendants with bronze loops attached to their backs. The pendants illustrated by Ferdinand Maier are all dated to the La Tène period. In several cases the distinctively long necks and tiny heads of some Hallstatt C horses are repeated in the La Tène types.[80] The comparisons suggest a continuity of tradition which also goes on into Roman times. But under Rome, in some cases, continuity of function is accompanied by changes in style owing to replacement of traditional forms by Roman models. For it does not seem possible that the sophisticated rider figures of the Roman period could have developed out of these very simple and stylized Hallstatt and La Tène forms, as there is no evidence of intermediate developmental stages. Rather, the iconographical tradition remained alive during the Roman period but, among the more Romanized populations, its artistic form was often borrowed from contemporary Roman models as we shall discuss further in Chapter Two.

Sources of Mediterranean Influence

If it could be shown convincingly that the Strettweg wagon was indeed influenced by Greek types, it would, in fact, not be too surprising because the development of Celtic art was not isolated from Mediterranean forms. The Greeks were actively exploring during the seventh century. The foundation of Massalia in circa 600 BC by the Phocaeans, and then that city's own daughter colonies which dotted the Mediterranean coast of Gaul, brought the Greeks into close trading contact with the late Hallstatt peoples of the interior. The result appears to have been not just the importation of luxury goods,[81] but also the borrowing of motifs and the beginning of an interest in larger scale figural representation by the host communities. An early example of this interest may have survived in a standing warrior figure wearing a torque from Hirshlanden in Germany dated to about 500 BC. This figure could well depend, in its upright stance and particularly in the heavily muscled legs, on the contemporary Greek *kouros* type.[82]

Trade was bringing Mediterranean objects into the chieftain societies of Gaul. The burial at Vix of a woman, perhaps a princess, contained not only the biggest bronze volute krater known, but other examples of Greek art including a Droop cup which can be fairly precisely dated to between 530 and 520 BC and a second undecorated cup placed at 520–510.[83] According to René Joffroy, the source of the wealth needed to acquire these objects and other treasures found at Vix may well have been the position of the settlement on the trade route between Italy and Britain which provided the Mediterranean world with tin.[84] The Greek objects would have come by way of Etruria. The Celts, therefore, especially those in favoured geographical positions, were familiar with the products of Mediterranean civilization already in the first half of the first millenium BC, long before the advent of the Romans.

During the subsequent La Tène period, the continuing presence of the Greeks at Massalia, the fifth century movement of the Celts into the Po Valley and consequent close contacts with Etruria, the attempts at conquest of rich Mediterranean cities like Rome itself in the fourth century or Delphi in the third and, during the course of the third century, the push of groups of Celts into Asia Minor, all represent points of contact, in addition to trade, where Mediterranean art became available to the Celts.[85] J.-J. Hatt characterizes the relationship between Mediterranean art and Celtic during the La Tène period as being one of alternation between the predominance of external influences, mainly from the Mediterranean, transmitted principally by Italy, and a counterbalancing indigenous reaction.[86] Other scholars also see evidence for Scythian, Anatolian and Persian influences.[87] In the decorative arts, many have seen the relationship between the spiral and curvilinear Celtic designs and Greek and Etruscan motifs, borrowed and broken down

to be reconstituted in new, distinctively Celtic, form.[88] It is perhaps worth repeating Nancy Sanders's comments on the borrowings by Celtic art from the Mediterranean cultures it met as it expanded. Speaking of the early La Tène Celts she says:

> Their artists knew well what they were about when they sifted the foreign gauds, accepting some and refusing some. There was no one yet to impose acceptance, as happened so disastrously when Roman conquered Celt. Classical stereotypes — palmette, lotus, lyre, tendril — were taken, naturalistic figures rejected, elements of composition were taken, narrative rejected and so on.[89]

The Gundestrup Cauldron

The great variety of influences absorbed by pre-Roman period Celts has been nowhere discussed in greater detail than in studies of the Gundestrup cauldron. The bowl was found by peat cutters in Jutland, Denmark in 1891 a few kilometres from the site of an Iron Age fortified village. It had been dismantled and consisted of five curved rectangular inner plates and seven out of eight original outer plates which would have been attached to the sides of a shallow silver bowl that formed the lower portion of the cauldron. It also had a round base-plate.[90] There were no contextual clues to its date.

Iconographically the work is extremely complex, being made up of a series of mythological scenes worked in relief. The outer plates consist of large figures represented only to the waist, males and females, who dominate each plate while smaller figures surround them. Some of the inner plates are more clearly narrative, but all are difficult to interpret. Despite its Danish find-site, internal clues point to Celtic connections, perhaps origins, for the cauldron. Torques, for example, those distinctively Celtic ornaments, are clearly to be seen around the necks of most of the major figures, whose unquestionable dominance suggests they are divinities.[91] Similarly, on one of the inner plates, three figures carry a carnyx, the typically Celtic wind instrument.[92] Garrett Olmstead has looked closely at the details of dress and weaponry and has shown how well these, in general, match with what is known of pre-Roman Celtic usage.

In artistic terms too, the work is very complex. Graeco-Roman motifs, transformed, appear in the winged horse on the plate designated 'plate (a)' according to Ole Klindt-Jensen's scheme[93] and in the boy on a dolphin on plate (A), the plate with the figure of a horned god.[94] On plate (g), the man wrestling a lion is identified as Herakles but the motif is so old and widespread that the Classical world need not be its only source.[95] Much has also been made of the various types of un-Celtic elements on the bowl, especially the 'hanging feet' of some of the animals, which have given rise to suggestions of Oriental links particularly with Thrace or the Scythians of Central Asia where this motif is common.[96]

Despite the clearly Celtic objects and possible Celtic iconography, a comparison of the cauldron plates with material from Thrace, in particular, yields a wealth of correspondences. Not only the hanging feet but the taste for fantastic winged animals like those that appear on Gundestrup plate (B) below the two elephants, and on plate (C) below the bust of the wheel god,[97] has Thracian analogies. A phalera found in a tumulus of circa first century BC at Stara Zagora in Bulgaria illustrates the similarities.[98] It shows Herakles and the Nemean lion, a subject already noted on the cauldron, although the two craftsmen treat the subject differently. On the bowl, Herakles is standing and holding the lion by the neck while its legs hang free. On the phalera, the hero, this time considerably more Classical in style, kneels while he grasps the lion about the neck. Around him parade a group of animals: two fantastic winged lions, two griffins and two walking lions whose punched coat decorations are very similar to that of the Nemean lion on the Gundestrup bowl.

The organization of the groups on the phalera has a good deal in common with the organization of several of the plates from the Gundestrup cauldron. The phalera is composed so that the central scene of Herakles and the lion is surrounded — framed — by the six animals already mentioned placed symmetrically in pairs facing inward. Plate (B) from Gundestrup has the same composition but in a rectangular setting: the bust of a goddess is the central focus with an inward-facing elephant on each side of her and below, two inward-facing griffins. A third wolf-like creature fills the space below the deity. Plate (C) is similar but with the animals in the upper half on either side of the wheel god facing right while the griffins below him face left.

The placement of animals above the central figure, found on the phalera but not on plates (B) and (C), is to be seen on plate (D) where three bulls are being attacked by three men.[99] Animals run above and below the triple central group. In addition, the roundel from the base[100] of the Gundestrup bowl shows the main figure — an enormous bull — surrounded by other elements including a man above, knees flexed like those of the phalera Herakles, about to kill the giant animal. Like the composition on the phalera, this scene shows a strong sensitivity on the part of the artist to the circular shape of his picture field. The limbs of the bull, like the limbs of the phalera lions, curve to echo the shape of the frame.

Comparing the Gundestrup bowl with Thracian metalwork in terms of details of style,[101] we can point to the way in which the legs of some animals on the cauldron, including the bull on the base medallion, have a second line of border along the backs of their legs — the fill of horizontal striping representing fringes of hair. The horses on a series of plaques from the Letnitsa treasure (see Chapter Six and Figure 83) have the same markings.

A recently discovered treasure from Rogozen in Bulgaria, more clearly Greek-influenced than some of the other Bulgarian treasures, includes a silver jug on which winged centaurs, depicted with frontal heads, exhibit the same strong chins and thin slit mouths as the major figures on the Gundestrup cauldron.[102] The Rogozen treasure is believed to have been assembled between the last quarter of the fifth and the mid-fourth century BC[103] and thus, like so many other Thracian comparisons, to antedate the Gundestrup cauldron

by several centuries. T.G.E. Powell addresses this problem and considers the conservatism of provincial metalsmiths and the use of ancient pattern books as possible reasons for the anomaly.[104] However, we may note that the Stara Zagora phalera has been dated as broadly contemporary with the currently accepted date for the cauldron and it shows quite clear stylistic affinities to the bowl.

One of the inner cauldron plates, designated (E), includes a group of riders (Figure 4). There are four and they face right. Behind them on the left is a figure of a god, more than twice their size, who draws a man down into a bucket or cauldron.[105] Suggested interpretations of this scene are as a sacrifice to Teutates[106] or an illustration of the stories preserved in Irish myth.[107]

Comparison of these riders with Thracian horsemen seems to indicate that the cauldron riders are more Celtic than Thracian. The Gundestrup horsemen whose feet nearly touch the ground are echoes of the Letnitsa riders in this detail. However, all Thracian horsemen — only some of whose feet reach the ground — ride horses whose four legs can be seen. The Gundestrup horses show only two. In Thracian metalwork, other creatures are occasionally represented with only a single front and back leg visible,[108] but not horses. The long narrow head shape of the Gundestrup horses can be found on a cheek piece from Agighiol showing a mounted figure,[109] but the rider himself is quite different from the Gundestrup type.

The Gundestrup horses are, in fact, quite similar in style and conception to other Celtic horses. Olmstead compares these horses to the La Tène cast horse from Freisen[110] in the body and head shape — long and narrow. However, other comparisons also come to mind. Some of the small rider brooches found in Britain (Figure 21) are similar in many ways to the Gundestrup horsemen.[111] The horses are, like those on the cauldron, two legged, and the particular disposition of the brooch horses' legs is strikingly like the Gundestrup animals. In both cases, the rear legs have a pronounced inward slant so that the hooves appear well beneath the belly of the horse. The front legs are bent as if at a gallop although they stand squarely on the ground. The heads are elongated on most brooches and the necks sometimes curve gracefully, although the manes are often more fully indicated than on the cauldron, giving the brooch horses a less slender appearance. The riders on the brooches, however, have a tendency to lean backward toward the horse's rump, a trait not found among the Gundestrup horsemen.

The horses on the Marlborough bucket, which was found in Wiltshire, share some of the same characteristics in the representation of the horse as the Gundestrup cauldron, but exaggerated so that the attenuated body, neck and head become even longer and more curvilinear — the effect being more decorative than narrative.[112]

The diversity of influence represented on the Gundestrup cauldron suggests a place of manufacture where a variety of styles, some quite ancient, were still current. T. G. E. Powell has suggested that it should be a place where "Thracian versions of ancient Orientalizing art were still executed by craftsmen who were perhaps not exclusively

Thracian or Celtic, and so their home can be narrowed down to those parts of Carpatho-Danubian Europe where archaeology must continue to explore the interrelations of these people".[113]

An estimate of the cauldron's date can only be made from internal evidence, as for example, the carnyx appears to have been in use from the second century BC to the first century AD,[114] thus providing at least a limit on either side. N. K. Sanders[115] and T. G. E. Powell[116] see the end of the second to the beginning of the first century as most likely while Garrett Olmstead prefers a date within the first century.[117]

The place of the Gundestrup cauldron in the Celtic world is difficult to define as its origins may well be among the fringes of Celtic culture. In terms of the horses on the bowl, however, these do appear to be closer to Celtic rather than to known Thracian types, an echo of what we have seen of La Tène and Hallstatt horses.

This brief survey of early La Tène and Hallstatt horses and horsemen shows that although the horse image was represented often and in many forms by the Celts, there was no interest in the natural or realistic representation of horse or horse and rider as we saw developed particularly in Greece during the sixth and fifth centuries BC. The conception of the horse in late La Tène differed little from the simple conception of the Greek Geometric age except that Celtic artists were happy to enhance the simple, inherited form by unrealistic elongation and graceful curves for decorative purpose, while the Geometric artist was at the beginning of a slow transformation which culminated in the horses of the Parthenon, the statues of Alexander and his comrades and the gigantic mounted figure of Domitian which inspired Statius to poetry. Indeed, the Gundestrup cauldron, as a very late work and an intrinsically valuable one, shows how acceptable to Celtic eyes a quality work of older, or perhaps better, unchanging, style could be.

But the Roman conquest caused enormous changes. The impact of Roman ideas about art and the works themselves which were the source of developments and alterations in artistic form in the conquered territories of the western Roman Empire are the subjects of the chapters that follow.

Chapter 2

Mars and the Horse

The Nature of the Roman Mars

Mars was the Roman god of war and the progenitor of the Roman people through his sons Romulus and Remus. Although he was not represented as a rider by the Romans, he was closely associated with horses particularly through the rites that were practiced in his name.

In the months of February and March, chariot races were run on the Campus Martius during a ceremony called the *Equirria* (horse-festival). Its purpose seems to have been to get cavalry mounts ready for the new season of military campaigns.[118] Such a ritual accords well with the notion of Mars as a deity of war. But the other major rite which connects Mars with horses reveals another, agricultural, aspect of his nature and this has been the subject of scholarly controversy for many years.[119] This festival, the rite of the October Horse, has elements which indicate that it was both very old and unrelated to military concerns. It too began with a chariot race on the Campus Martius like the *Equirria*. But when the race was finished the right-hand horse of the winning team was sacrificed to Mars and its tail and head removed. By the first century BC the original practice of fighting over the head seems to have died out, but the tail was still taken, dripping blood, to the *Regia*, the king's house, where it was allowed to drip onto the ash of the sacred hearth. The mixture of ash and blood was collected for use in the spring in an agricultural festival called the *Parilia*.[120]

The rite of the October Horse, which preserved a role for the ancient royal dwelling and which today evokes ideas of fertility magic and resonances of Indo-European horse sacrifice, has convinced many that Mars was originally more than a war god and that his concerns extended to agriculture and fertility of the land. Other corroborating evidence includes the prayer to Mars with the epithet *Silvanus* for the health of cattle in the *de Re Rustica* of Cato,[121] the prayers in the *Carmen Arvale*, and the testimony, although only in the form of an epitome, of the Augustan writer Verrius Flaccus to the effect that the rite of the October Horse was performed in order to secure a good harvest.[122] Thus Mars offered protection not only against the assault of human enemies but against the depredations of nature as well.

But despite his ritual association with the horse, the image of Mars which is most familiar does not include any indication of this relationship. The Roman Mars was rarely represented in proximity to horses. An exception is a coin which was minted in Naples in 320 BC which showed the helmeted head of Mars on the obverse with a horse-head on the reverse.[123]

Two elements may have acted to suppress the pacific side of Mars's nature: first, the identification of Mars with the Greek Ares and secondly, the changes brought about by the religious reforms of Augustus who put strong emphasis on Mars as a god of war. Mars was the protector of the Imperial family.[124] Augustus built a temple to Mars Ultor, Mars the Avenger, both to commemorate the death of his adoptive father and to celebrate the return of the standards captured by the Parthians.[125] The statue of Mars Ultor was a standing, cuirassed figure holding a patera in his extended right hand while his left hand rested on his shield.[126]

Both the form of the standing statue of Mars and the special emphasis on his warrior character owe much to the influence of Greece. Mars was identified with the Greek god Ares who was also a god of war, but one whose nature was very much simpler than that of the Roman god. He was one of the lesser Olympians who had a temple cult in only a few places and represented the destructive and hateful in war as against Athena who stood for the skill of tactics and the glory of victory.[127] Ares does not seem to have had a special connection with horses although an altar at Olympia included Ares *Hippios* in its dedication.[128] An example of a mounted Ares, clearly marked with the god's name, is found on a Boeotian lekane dated to the fourth quarter of the fifth century BC. Ares, wearing a petasos and carrying a spear, is riding toward Herakles who has slain Ares's monstrous son Kyknos. But this representation is exceptional and may illustrate a local Boeotian version of the story.[129]

The Standing Mars and its Models

With a few unusual exceptions, like the Ares on horseback just described, the war god was not a rider for the Greeks and Romans. He was represented as a standing figure with certain identifying attributes. We shall look first at the development of this standing figure in the form of the Roman Mars and then at some of its appearances in the Celtic world as the Celtic Mars. This will give us an idea of the tradition that Romano-Celtic craftsmen would have had before them when they were looking for ways to create images of their own deity who was identified with Mars, but whose character as a rider they wished to emphasize.

The most famous statue of Ares, artistic prototype for the standing Mars, is probably the one made by Alkamenes around 430 for the temple of Ares in the Athenian Agora and mentioned by Pausanius.[130] The 'Ares Borghese' may be a copy of this statue (Figure 1). The god is nude with his head slightly turned to the right. His right arm is lowered, presumably to rest on a shield, while his left arm is raised to grasp a spear.[131] The type is, in fact, rather similar to the Doryphoros of Polycleitos which is well known from copies.[132] In this latter, the head is raised slightly and the weight is placed on the right leg rather than on the left but there is little difference otherwise. The image of the nude Ares was borrowed for representations of Mars. It appears on money coined by the Triumvirs about 38 BC; the nude god wears a helmet and stands with his weight on his right foot and his right hand raised to hold a lance.[133]

Alexander with the Lance by Lysippos might also have been a prototype for the Roman Mars.[134] Although the statue no longer exists, it has been recognized in small bronze copies as, for example, a statuette in the Louvre or one in the Fogg Art Museum at Harvard (Plate 1).[135] The two figures are unlike in detail but both have the left arm raised parallel to the body rather than held in front of it with the hand poised at waist height like the Doryphoros. These differences, however, are minor and we can say that the figure of the spear-carrying youth originated in the fifth century BC in Greece, continued to develop in the hands of the great artists of the fourth century and would have been widely known through the Graeco-Roman world in copies.

The standing Mars was also familiar in Etruria. An example was discovered at Todi in Umbrian territory (Figure 5). Although there is an inscription in Umbrian on the god's corselet, the technical finish of the statue is Etruscan. It is bronze and under life-size and was probably made in the late fourth century BC. Of the head, only the face survives. The helmet which the figure must have worn has disappeared as has the lance which would have fitted into the curved fingers of the left hand.[136]

The Todi Mars already shows the adaptation of the Greek type to the iconographical requirements of Mars. Indeed among the major deities, Mars appears to be the only one whose image was not taken over as a whole from the Greek repertory, but modified. In Rome, Mars was normally represented in armour and it is interesting to note in this regard that, according to Stephanie Boucher, small bronzes of the nude Mars, although common in the western Empire, were not popular in Rome itself.[137] Their place of origin has been suggested as Greece.[138] The discovery of Athenian workshops which made bronzes of various sizes during the Roman period supports the possibility that some bronzes including figures of the nude Mars were imported directly into Gaul from Greece.[139]

Nude figures obviously present problems of identification. The standing male nude based on the Alexander of Lysippos or another statue of that compositional type is also the prototype for the standing Dioscurus. Therefore, the identification of a standing figure as Mars must be based on the attributes which form part of the representation. Mars, naked or cuirassed, is usually represented with his helmet, spear and shield but not necessarily all together. The problem of identification can be come difficult when a nude figure has lost its identifying attributes as was the case with the life-size figure from Coligny. This figure, which is lacking the back of its head, was thought at first to be Apollo because the missing section was believed to be a rayed crown. Mercury's petasos was also suggested. However, the most likely restoration appears to be a helmeted figure grasping a spear or lance and, therefore, Mars.[140] The helmet is a particularly good indicator of Mars since other deities in military dress, like the mounted Celtic Jupiter on a column or the Dolichene Jupiter, do not, as a rule, wear it.[141] Similarly Mars carries a shield which the others normally lack although he shares both these attributes with Athena/Minerva.

Mars in the Celtic World

If Mars as he often appears in Roman state art was a deity concerned mainly with warfare, the gods identified with Mars in the Romano-Celtic world seem to have had numerous other concerns. Although the standard iconographical type was generally adhered to, as in the Coligny statue, the powers attributed to the deity or deities named as Mars in Celtic lands were quite different from Ares/Mars of Imperial Rome and closer to the Mars of Cato or the *Equus October* ceremony in their concern for domestic welfare and fertility. Several examples will serve to indicate the nature of the Celtic god or gods who were called "Mars" under the *Interpretatio Romana* by the Roman conquerors of Gaul.

Lenus Mars

One of the deities who was identified with the Roman Mars and whose cult has been studied in detail is Lenus, a god whose main centre was in the tribal area of the Treveri. Among the Treveri, Mars was the most important god and in this, the Treveri showed affinities with Central Gaul rather than the Rhine area.[142] The temple site at Martberg has yielded artefacts clearly connected with the Mars cult. The only god to be identified from inscriptions at the Martberg is Lenus Mars. One of the most interesting inscriptions is a bilingual Greek and Latin one thanking Ares/Mars for healing the dedicant Tychicus, indicating that for this individual, at least, Lenus is clearly to be identified with the Graeco-Roman god of war — as the naming of Ares shows — who here also heals. It dates from the mid-second century AD.[143] The statuette of a nude, helmeted, youthful Mars in bronze of the type favoured in the western Empire was also found on the site.[144] It is a likely assumption that this represents the god of the cult.

At another site, Irmenenwingert near Trier on the Mosel River, is a temple complex also revealing the presence of Lenus Mars and perhaps giving a clearer picture of the nature of the Celtic god identified with Mars. Here an inscription shows that Mars was worshipped with the female deities called Xulsigiae. They may have been healing deities who healed with the aid of spring water.[145] The whole complex appears to have been built over a pre-Roman cult site.[146] Among the finds at Irmenenwingert were nineteen terracotta mother goddesses, two figures of Epona and four Venus figures, all concerned with fruitfulness and prosperity. There were also thirty-nine busts of small boys and girls and a swaddled baby. These latter were most likely addressed to another Mars, Mars Iovantucarus, who looked after the well-being of children.[147]

Intarabus

The Roman name of Mars was also given to yet another god honoured at Irmenenwingert — Intarabus — a fine bronze of whom was found in Luxembourg along with a statue base (found separately) identifying him.[148] The figure is of a standing youth dressed in a tunic with a wolf-skin draped around his shoulders. His right arm is raised as if grasping a lance or staff. The sanctuary which housed the statue was in the territory of the Tungri not far from the borders of Treveran lands.[149] The Roman Mars too was connected with the wolf, particularly in the foundation myth of the city of

Rome in which a she-wolf suckled his twin sons Romulus and Remus. On a second century gem in the Karthago Museum, Mars sits side-saddle on a wolf[150] and on a glass intaglio he rides the wolf while his sons sit below its belly.[151]

Whether the three epithets of Mars at Trier represent the identification with the Roman Mars of three Celtic gods or of one god called by several names, the functions which can be deduced for the Celtic Mars among the Treveri are unrelated to the Roman warrior except by the very loosest definition of his role as protector.

The Altbachtal Rider

The archaeological evidence from Irmenenwingert and from the great cult complex of the Altbachtal, where Lenus Mars was also worshipped, shows that at both places the Roman period temples were built over pre-Roman religious sites and that water, particularly associated with healing, played a significant part. Indeed, the Altbachtal complex is sited between two water courses, the Altbach and the Weverbach.[152] Investigation of the site produced a standing life-size figure of Mars in armour which still showed traces of paint.[153] Also noteworthy is the fact that the Altbachtal site yielded a single terracotta figure of a rider in the region of the 'Aveta Chapel' so-called after a dedication found there to the goddess Aveta.[154] Similar figures have been found at Metz, Drohnecken, Bertrich and Heddernheim.[155] The rider is a young man dressed in a tunic and wearing what appears to be a helmet with a crest running vertically down to the nape of the neck. He wears a sword and carries a round shield.[156] Emil Krüger has identified the figure as one of the Dioscuri (Figure 6).

Krüger's identification of the rider as a Dioscurus is open to question. The Dioscuri are occasionally represented wearing helmets, particularly on gems, for example, on a gem from Magdalensberg where a standing nude Dioscurus holds his horse by the bridle — the stance most commonly used to represent the twins.[157] Despite the helmet, the stance clearly identifies the figure as one of the Dioscuri. However, in another example, a relief from La Horgne-au-Sablon, the two nude helmeted figures bearing shields and lances were identified, also by Emil Krüger, not as Dioscuri but as 'Martes', the amalgamation of the Dioscuri with a double form of Mars (Figure 7).[158] If the helmet and shield suggested to Krüger that the relief from La Horgne was to be identified with a form of Mars rather than the Dioscuri, the clay riders who not only wear helmets but full military gear seem even more likely to represent Mars rather than the Dioscuri. Moreover, this group of statuettes represented by the Altbachtal rider is probably best seen in relation to other rider figures in military gear, to be considered below, which have been found in Gaul and Britain and who may represent a Celtic form or forms of Mars.

The Altbachtal rider was the only male in a large find of terracotta figures, but as we have already seen, Mars, especially Lenus Mars, appears to have had ties with mother and fertility goddesses. The rider is the only, and somewhat tenuous, link between Lenus Mars and horses. However, the coinage of the Treveri shows that the horse was an important symbol for them as for all the Celts. Treveran coins which belong to the period before and during the Gallic wars shows a striking number of horses in many variants and styles on their obverses. Horses alone and with riders are common.[159] The horse was the commonest animal represented on Celtic coins in all areas where Celtic coinage is found and remained the dominant motif through some three centuries of coining.[160] It is possible that the horse on the obverse of a Celtic coin was like the horse on the obverse of that Roman coin from the fourth century BC mentioned above: a symbol or attribute of the god Mars or in this case, a sign of the tribal god identified with Mars. There is indeed some evidence, to be discussed shortly, from Gaul and Britain that horse figurines and horse and rider groups were offered by worshippers to Mars. The apparent lack of equine associations for Mars among the Treveri may be an accident of archaeology or it may be the result of the high degree of Romanization which characterized the Imperial city of Trier and influenced the way local deities were represented toward a greater Roman iconographical orthodoxy.

Evidence for the Celtic Mars and Horses

That a Celtic deity, or perhaps several, identified with the Roman Mars was worshipped as a rider or in horse form may be inferred from a large body of often circumstantial evidence.

In southern Gaul the earliest of the known sanctuaries, that at Mouriès, which is of late Hallstatt or early La Tène date, has revealed a series of crudely incised horses and horsemen.[161] Although these images have no special artistic merit, they are of interest because of their subject matter. The later sanctuaries of Nages, Roqueperteuse and Entremont all have produced horse or horse and rider reliefs. Horses without riders decorate lintels at Nages and Roqueperteuse. At Nages a lintel was carved showing horses alternating with severed heads.[162]

At Entremont where the occupation of the site can be reliably dated as extending from the fourth century BC until its destruction by the Romans in the second century BC, a relief carving of a horsemen was discovered on a pillar. The Greek influence seems evident in spite of the worn state of the relief. The condition of the work leaves details unclear but the Hellenistic date given by Fernand Benoit, the excavator of the site, does not seem out of place.[163] The horse stands with the front off-leg raised. The horseman holds an object in his raised right hand which Fernand Benoit has suggested is a pick[164] although his reasoning is unclear. The rider wears a sword and perhaps a helmet. Although the raised leg of the horse and the posture of the rider argue for a Mediterranean prototype, the elongation of the horse's body suggests a local artist.

These few examples serve to show that the Languedoc sanctuaries preserved a tradition involving veneration of horses and riders going back at least to the end of the Hallstatt period and surviving in many cases beyond the Roman conquest.

The earliest evidence for the Celtic horse and rider cannot be linked specifically with Mars. The artefacts and remains of the southern Gaulish sanctuaries show the cultic importance of the horse and rider but not the rider's (or riders') identity. However, sites with post-conquest remains and inscriptional evidence connect a Celtic god addressed as Mars with horses alone and with horses and riders. At Les Bolards at Nuit-St. Georges (Côte d'Or) there are remains of a vast sanctuary where three temples have been found superimposed one upon another, the first dating from the end of the period of Gaulish independence.[165] One of the early finds at the site was a bronze figure of an equine (horse or perhaps mule), now lost, standing on a base. An accompanying inscription dedicated the animal to *Deus Segomo*.[166] Among the more recent finds was a votive inscription dedicated specifically to Mars Segomo.[167] Mars Segomo is also known from other sites: Mars Segomo Cuntinus at Contes and Mars Segomo Dunalis at Culoz,[168] and from Germania Superior among the Helvetii-Sequannes.[169]

The significance of the identification of Mars Segomo at Les Bolards is that the lost bronze was not the only equine found on the site. Other figures of horses have also been discovered. These include clay horse figurines of Allier type and a fragment of a horse and rider group.[170] The pipe clay horses often appear in temple-site excavations and may be a common dedication to the Celtic Mars. The fact that some of the votive objects are horsemen suggests that unlike the Roman Mars, this Mars was a rider.

At the sanctuary of Sougères-en-Puisaye (Yonne) several fragments which may be riders have been found, including the torsos of two statues, probably of life-size, one of which is in armour. Other fragments of the horses' legs seem to be on the same scale, so the human and horse fragments may belong to equestrian groups. The human figures may have been mounted or dismounted beside their horses. The fragments are not easy to interpret. Small stone horse statuettes were also found which bear a strong resemblance to those made in the workshops of the Allier. There is no indication as to which god the sanctuary at Sougères was dedicated. A female head was also discovered on the site, so it is possible that several gods were worshipped there. The cuirassed figure and the horses suggested to Émile Thevenot that one of the gods worshipped at Sougères was Mars.[171] Identification with Mars was deduced by Thevenot mainly because the fragments of the large horse brought to mind the bronze horse found at Neuvy-en-Sullias (Loiret).[172]

At Neuvy, not far from Orleans, a bronze horse statue of excellent quality was discovered. The base was provided with rings which were probably used as aids in carrying it during ceremonies. Like the lost animal from Les Bolards, this horse was inscribed on the base. Its two donors offered the figure to Rudiobus.[173] The name Rudiobus has been equated with that of another god known from inscriptions, Mars Rudianos, found at Rochefort-Sanson and Saint-Andeol-en-Quint.[174] On the second of these inscriptions the donors describe themselves as *curatores* as do the donors of the Rudiobus horse.[175] And at one site where Rudianus was venerated, St. Michel de Valbonne, a stone in the shape of a menhir was found on which the archaic and crude figure of a horseman set above five disembodied heads had been carved.[176] Moreover, the choice of St. Michael as the main object of veneration by the Christianized population of St. Michel de Valbonne suggests that the image of the mounted warrior still clung to the site — an example of religious continuity from pre-Roman times through Christian.[177]

Another continental site where Mars had likely links with horses is Magdalensberg in Carinthia, ancient Noricum. In the sanctuary there, a large statue of a horse was discovered (but now lost) equipped in a manner analogous to that of the Neuvy horse.[178] The chief god of Magdalensberg was Mars Latobius, referred to in an inscription as Mars Latobius Marmogius Toutatis Sinatis Mogetius. Some of the epithets are transparently Celtic, e.g., Mogetius, 'the great' or Toutatis, 'father of the tribe'.[179] The statue which is thought to represent Latobius is known as the Helenenberg or Magdalensberg youth. It is a standing figure of a nude young man of the Polycleitan type. But the slenderness of the figure and the treatment of the hair in thick waves suggest perhaps a fourth century Praxitelian model.[180] The figure possesses no identifying attributes. An inscription on the right thigh, while not naming the god, dates the work to the last decade of the Republic. Along with the statue, a small shield was also found. This does not belong to the figure but may have been dedicated to him as Mars. An 'M' in the inscription has been tentatively completed as 'M[ARTI]'. The right arm of the statue is raised but the fingers are spread with the palm turned outward and, therefore, it is unlikely that the youth held anything in it originally. The left arm hangs at the side. He may have held a lance loosely in the lightly curled fingers.[181]

Despite the Graeco-Roman style of the cult statue, there is some indication of a connection between Latobius and horses. The relationship has been deduced from a fragment of mosaic at Magdalensberg on which the figure of a horse standing in the centre of a simple boat is preserved.[182] Finds from the Latobius temple connect the god closely with water, as is often the case with the Celtic Mars. In addition, his sanctuary at Bergstall itself was known as the *Navale*, the 'shiphouse'.[183] The horse on the ship may, therefore, represent Latobius, the 'shiphouse' being his shrine.

Although we cannot always make a direct association between the Celtic Mars and horses, the evidence is such that it can be satisfactorily interpreted as showing, even where Mars was represented standing in the Graeco-Roman manner, that, as with Latobius, he had some connection with horses.

Horse and Rider Figurines

The horse and rider figurines that have come to light are often quite tiny and hence, easily portable. Some of these statuettes of riders have been found in proximity to standing figures of Mars as at the Altbachtal or they have been connected with Mars through other evidence. However, horse and rider figures have also been found on sites with no known association with Mars. These present bigger problems of identification. Indeed, it is possible to question whether they represent divine figures at all, for they do not share with the standing Mars an easily recognizable divine prototype within the Graeco-Roman artistic repertory and little is certain about their Celtic identity. We shall see, however, that an investigation of the prototypes of these figures also leads to the conclusion that they too represent gods.

Votive Figurines from Britain

A number of the most important finds of horsemen and horse-related cult and votive objects have come from Britain. The site of Brigstock in Northamptonshire has over a period of time yielded the largest number of small rider figures in the country although it is not the only site at which such figures have been found. The first of the Brigstock figures was ploughed up in 1957 within 300 metres of what turned out to be a Roman temple. The horse and its rider were found separately. Under the horse's belly is a fragment of a pin for attachment to some object. The right arm is broken off at the elbow and the left arm is broken slightly higher. Originally the figure held a spear or a shield or perhaps both. He wears a short cloak and a helmet.[184]

A year later a horse without a rider was found, and in 1963 another horse and rider of slightly larger size than the first was discovered (Figure 8). This rider's right arm is intact but the object he held, perhaps a spear, is missing. His left arm is also largely gone. Like the earlier horseman, he wears a helmet. There is no trace of a hole in the horse's belly.[185] Again in 1981, a horseman was found at Brigstock but without a horse. This figure also wears a helmet and, while the hands are missing, the arrangement of the arms suggests that, like the earlier horsemen, he too carried a spear and shield.[186]

Excavation has revealed that Brigstock was the site of two temples which the excavators date to between the mid-third century and AD 380 on the basis of coin evidence.[187] The ground plans of the buildings showed them to be respectively circular and polygonal in plan. The horse and rider unearthed in 1963 were found near the centre of the circular shrine.[188] A Coritanian stater of approximately AD 25 was found along with a large number of Roman coins of the first to the fourth centuries as well as pottery of third and fourth century date. Beneath the polygonal temple lies a penannular ditch, the shape of which suggests an Iron Age date[189] and thus, analogies with other sites where Romano-British temples have been superimposed on Iron Age circular ditches such as Frilford or Maiden Castle.[190] Coins and pottery show that the Brigstock temple was built within the Roman period, but the Iron Age ditch and also pre-Roman small finds suggest continuous occupation of the site predating the building of the temple. So it appears that, like the continental sanctuaries, the Brigstock site was sacred before the building programme of the Roman period.

Another bronze horse and rider group was found in a grave in an inhumation cemetery at Westwood Bridge, north of Peterborough (Figure 9). The horse is fastened to a circular stand, convex in section.[191] The rider is notable for the elaborately plumed helmet he wears which puts one in mind of the nude, helmeted, standing figures of Mars from Barkway in Hertfordshire and Fossdike in Lincolnshire.[192] He holds a decorated shield on his left arm while his extended right arm may have held a spear.

Two more horse and rider statuettes were found in a box at Willingham Fen in Cambridgeshire. One, which is small and squat, still holds his shield and raises his right arm presumably to grasp his missing spear (Plate 2). The second figure, longer and thinner, is missing the major portions of both arms.[193] The other items in the hoard included remains of a bronze sceptre or club with a representation of the wheel god on it, a bust of Antoninus Pius, the fragment of another horseman, birds and busts of deities, one possibly identifiable as Mars.[194]

A horseman found at Cave's Inn in Warwickshire differs from the others in being considerably larger and hollow-cast. He is 20.5 cm. tall and wears a helmet and and a tunic and mantle rather than body armour. Both hands have fingers curved as if they were holding equipment. The right arm is raised for a spear thrust while the left arm is poised at waist level indicating that he held a shield or possibly the reins of his horse. He was found at the bottom of a well. Pottery and a sestertius of Faustina I of c. AD 141 date the deposit. No horse was found, but a bronze disc, also discovered there and of 7.6 cm. in diameter, may have been the rider's shield.[195] The deposition of the figure in the well was perhaps accidental, but examples of sacred wells with apparent votive deposits can be cited.[196]

The size of the Cave's Inn rider is interesting. If the rider were mounted on a horse, the group would measure about 30 cm. high. Such a group could have been the centre-piece of a small shrine, possibly even of a domestic shrine of the type discussed by George Boon.[197] Indeed, any of the smaller horsemen may also have served in this way, placed in a niche or alcove with other figurines.[198] This is one way to explain the single finds of riders not associated with clearly recognizable shrines, temples or graves.

One such single find is the horse and rider from Canterbury (Figure 10). It is of the same type as the series from Brigstock but cruder and more Celtic in conception particularly in the elongated body of the horse. Like the first Brigstock rider found, this one has a hole in the lower side, in this case in the base, for the pin to pass into. Part of the pin is, indeed, broken off inside the base. E. J. W. Hildyard has suggested that these figures were attached to a pole or wand.[199]

Continental Votive Horse and Rider Figurines

Although Britain has produced a larger number of these complete rider groups of the Roman period than continental sites, there are, nevertheless, examples known from the continent and there is no doubt that some of the horse figurines found there did at one time have riders.[200] Compared with the numbers of horses, very few unattached horsemen figurines have been preserved from continental sites. Those that have been, are often quite different from the British examples. One found in Gaul at Bavai, for instance, is dressed in a tunic. He wears a cap with a button at its centre and holds a patera in his right hand.[201] He seems unrelated to the armoured British riders.

Possible Prototypes for the Rider Figurines

Some of the few complete rider groups preserved on the continent, however, may serve to suggest prototypes for the little bronze riders found in Britain and perhaps also for the lost riders of the continental sites who must have belonged to the numerous horses found there. Two poses for these horses are most frequent encountered.

The Rearing Horse

A group in the Landesmuseum für Kärnten in Klagenfort and found at Tigring in Kärnten consists of a rider in armour on a galloping or rearing horse (Figure 11).[202] The horseman is believe to be Alexander and the bronze a copy of a full-sized Hellenistic original.[203] The statuette of Alexander makes a good starting point from which to discuss the antecedents of the provincial bronze rider figurines of the Roman period.

As indicated in Chapter One, the evidence suggests that the Greeks of the Classical period did not erect rider statues to men they wished to honour[204] and it was only at the end of the fourth century BC that equestrian monuments were dedicated in Greek sanctuaries. Mounted statues of Philip, Alexander and Seleukos are known to have existed at Olympia and these very likely had a significant influence on the acceptance of the concept of the rider as a royal, then Imperial, symbol. The statues at Olympia were probably erected after 305 when Seleukos took the royal title.[205]

The statuette of Alexander from Austria represent the hero sitting on a horse whose hind legs alone touch the base. At Olympia three statue bases were found on which traces of horses' hooves show that these horses too were rearing.[206] This dynamic stance for horses seems to have been a favourite during the Hellenistic era.[207] Among the small bronzes of the Roman period found on the continent, other examples of rearing horses are known.[208] These may perhaps, like the Alexander statuette, go back to Hellenistic prototypes, although, based on coin evidence, statues of Roman emperors on rearing horses existed as well.[209]

The Hellenistic rearing horse usually carried a rider engaged in battle or other vigorous activity. A rider now lacking his horse, who may be Alexander, was found in Begram in Afghanistan.[210] This armoured figure holds his right arm aloft with fingers closed over a spear, now missing. His left hand probably held the reins. A horseless rider found at Athribis in Lower Egypt may also be Alexander, in the opinion of Ariel Herrmann,[211] or one of the Ptolemys, according to Harald von Roques de Maumont.[212] The figure is nude except for an elephant head and skin worn over the rider's own head and knotted over his chest. Like the previous figure, this rider raises his right arm to brandish a weapon while holding the reins in his left. The slight tilt of his body suggests that he was also riding a rearing horse.

A cursory examination of riders wielding spears on both Greek and Roman reliefs shows quite clearly that as a rule, the rearing or galloping horse was the vehicle of the embattled rider. Riders who are not in the midst of battle or the hunt are represented on walking horses, most of which have one leg bent and poised above the ground. It is worth noting that the small British riders are anomalous in holding weapons while mounted on walking horses.

The Walking Horse

The walking action is commoner than the rearing posture among continental Roman bronzes as well as among British.[213] It too has a Greek origin. Statues of horsemen on walking or resting horses appeared in the Hellenistic period along with the more vigorous rearing type. It is possible that among the spoils which Caecilius Metellus bought back to Rome from his victory over Perseus of Macedon in 148 BC was the bronze equestrian group celebrating the companions of Alexander at the battle of Grannicus.[214] A bronze horse in the Palazzo dei Conservatori in Rome may be a survivor of this group of riders. It stands on three legs with the front left leg raised.[215] The extreme angle at which the rear legs are bent suggested to Harald von Roques de Maumont that this was a Greek and not a Roman animal.[216]

Another example of the Hellenistic walking horse occurs on a monument to King Attalos I of Pergamon who, on the evidence of the surviving base, was riding a horse which stood on three legs.[217] Although the statue no longer exists, a possible reconstruction shows the king holding the reins with one hand while his other arm rests at his side.[218] A small bronze in the Museum Calvet at Avignon, but of unknown origin, reflects this composition. The now headless figure sits on a quiet horse, one hand holding the reins, the other resting on his thigh.[219] If the statue of Attalos I is not the prototype (assuming it is restored correctly), something similar must have been.

Of these two commonest equine representations, according to Harald von Roques de Maumont, it was the calm walking horse which was favoured by the Roman emperors who preferred to be represented making peaceful gestures of greeting rather than fighting. The rider statue became the exclusive preserve of the Imperial house and continued to be so until the end of the Empire.[220] Coin evidence corroborates this view.[221]

The rearing horse, however, remained popular in the provinces, particularly for cavalry gravestone reliefs during the first century AD as these were essentially battle scenes. It appears to have become less common as time went by. It did not die out completely but tombstones considered to be later than the first century AD, like the fragment from Chester depicting a barbarian seated beneath the horse's legs, show a standing horse.[222] So it is most probable that the bronze horsemen found at sites like Brigstock, dating perhaps to the third century, do not depend on Hellenistic models like Alexander, nor do they depend on reliefs like the cavalry tombstones. Their prototypes are works of the Imperial period.

Imperial Models

It is certainly possible that the immediate model for the little figures — which differ strongly one from the other in style but are strikingly similar in composition — was a cult statue which existed at one or more sanctuaries in Britain but is now lost. We can think of the rider fragments from Sougères fulfilling this role in Gaul, for example. However, the ultimate prototype was more likely to have been the Imperial statues which would have stood in the major centres of the Empire including Britain.[223] A link between the British figurines and Imperial statuary is provided by a statuette now in Rouen. Its origin is unknown. It is of relatively mediocre workmanship and represents a rider seated on a walking horse (Figure 12). The rider is dressed in a short-sleeved tunic. He is bearded, bare-headed and raises his right arm in a rhetorical gesture or in greeting. The group is mounted on a tall base which accounts for about one-third of its 10.5 cm. height.[224] An almost exactly similar horse is in the Museum Calvet in Avignon. Its rider, which was also found, has now disappeared but the description of him is almost identical to the Rouen example. Marcus Aurelius has been suggested as the rider's identity.[225]

In terms of composition, this statuette is virtually the same as the various British figurines. The raised right arm could be modified to hold a spear and the lowered left one could easily be covered by a shield. On the Westwood Bridge figure, the right arm is lowered slightly and this position can be found on the Imperial statues, most notably the famous rider statue of Marcus Aurelius in Rome (Figure 13).

That Imperial statues or figurines provided the model for votive horsemen from Britain can easily be explained by the fact that no model for a horseman god existed from the Graeco-Roman world except perhaps the Dioscuri and these seem to have been represented among the troops of Britain mainly in their standing form (see Chapter Five). A Dioscurus may, as Krüger suggested, be present at the Altbachtal in the form of an armed terracotta rider,[226] but this is by no means certain. Clay horsemen of the Altbachtal type have not been found in Britain and the bronze figurines are quite different in style from the terracottas. However, this need not indicate a difference of subject matter particularly when the iconographical elements are so similar.

The transformation of the Imperial rider into the armoured horseman is, as we have noted above, a simple one in technical terms. The Imperial horseman made a suitable model for the representation of a local rider god in Roman form since only the Imperial family, who were themselves objects of worship, could be represented thus. So the Imperial statues already had a sacred character. The fact that the adaptations consisted mainly of the additions of simple elements of military gear: helmet, shield and spear, suggest very strongly that the prototypes were being remodelled to represent not a simple horseman but the armed god Mars. Moreover, an inspection of the British bronze figurines show that they are all dressed differently. They are not either wearing body armour or nude, as Mars often was in Britain, but have a variety of costumes varying from cuirass to simple tunic. This may be related to the fact that the Imperial model was normally dressed in a tunic and cape and each artist adapted this costume for the military Mars as much as he wished or was able.

The Martlesham Base

Although there appear to be no mounted Mars groups on the continent comparable to the British figurines, there may be some evidence for continental works similar to the group originally cast on the bronze base found at Martlesham in Suffolk. The Martlesham base is a small shield-shaped statue base dedicated to the god Mars Corotiacus.[227] Of the original group only a supine figure and the stump of a horse's hoof remain. The most reasonable reconstruction of the lost elements is as a rider on a rearing horse trampling a supine enemy. But while no complete bronze groups with this subject have ever been found, the rearing horse figurine is not uncommon among continental finds. A rearing horse from Makkum in Friesland of relatively large size (length: 16.6 cm.; height: 14.4 cm.) has a circular depression in its underside which could have been made to leave space for an enemy crouching beneath. That the space was left for a support is less probable[228] since a support is unlikely to have been required for such a small bronze unless, of course, it was part of the model being copied.

Another example of a rearing horse, a fine looking animal found near Liège, was fixed to its base, now lost, by tenons which are still attached to its hooves. It rears high with its front legs well extended.[229] There would be room for an enemy underneath, but this must stay a conjecture. The Martlesham base remains the only example where the exact nature of the original group can be discerned.

Other Forms of the Rider in Britain

As on the continent, not all the evidence for a rider god in Britain is in the form of bronzes. An altar from Bisley in Gloucestershire is decorated with a figure in relief of an armed rider (Figure 14). The altar is small, only 61 x 33 x 15 cm. It was found with a second undecorated altar.[230] South central Gloucestershire has been rich in finds of sacred items, many of Mars. The neighbourhood of Bisley has yielded four altars dedicated to Mars[231] and not far away at King's Stanley, four more altars to Mars were found.[232] So an identification of the Bisley rider with a local Mars seems reasonable. The poorly preserved Bisley rider fills nearly the whole of one side of the altar. He is riding toward the right on a horse whose body is unrealistically large in comparison to its head and legs. Both the rider's arms are raised. He brandishes a weapon, a sword perhaps, in his right hand while holding his shield aloft in his left. There is no inscription.

Comparing this conception of the armed horseman with that of the bronzes, it would seem that the artist at Bisley had depended less on Roman models and more on Celtic forms indicating perhaps local artistic traditions. Both the thick-bodied horse and the arm gestures can be found on Celtic coins. A coin of Cunobelin struck at *Camulodunum* in the early first century AD shows a horse galloping to the right. Although the head and limbs are somewhat larger in proportion to the body than the horse on the Bisley altar, the heavy rump and thick neck and forequarters contrast strongly with the commoner slender and elongated Celtic horses.[233] The same taste for a heavy-bodied horse can be seen on a coin of the Dubonni found near Bibury in Gloucestershire on which the horse's body has become a rectangle with corners smoothed to a curve, the various divisions of the body indicated by volumes, swelling for hind and forequarters, receding again for the abdomen.[234]

In addition, there is the discovery made during excavations of the Roman villa at Frocester Court near Stonehouse in Gloucestershire of a small bronze horse (Figure 15). It is believed by the excavators to date from the first century BC although it was found in a later context.[235] This horse too, like the horse on the Bisley altar and the Bibury coins, is of stocky build with a short thick body. It is quite different in stance from the little Brigstock horses who lift one front leg in imitation of Imperial statues. This little animal stands with all four legs firmly on the ground, an example of local taste or a continuing local tradition.

Another characteristic of the group on the Bisley altar, which suggests local tradition rather than Roman influence, is the arm-raising gesture. It can be found on both British and continental Celtic coins. A gold coin of Tasciovanus, dated around the turn of the first century, shows a horseman brandishing a carnyx (Figure 16).[236] This single arm gesture can perhaps be described as a transformation of an original spear-throwing action on Greek or Macedonian rider coins. But on other examples, the raised-arm gesture is used for both arms. Two coins of the Redones of Gaul show the type. On one, a nude female figure rides to the right raising what appears to be a shield with her right hand and an unknown object with her left (Figure 17). A second coin shows a female figure riding left (Figure 18). She holds a shield in her left hand but with her right she holds up a severed head, its spiky hair splaying out in all directions.[237] For the second figure in particular, this gesture appears to be one of victory or self-congratulation.

A coin now in the Danicourt collection in Peronne in France, but of unknown provenance, depicts a male rider in virtually the same posture as the horseman on the Bisley altar. In his right hand, the figure on the coin holds a spear aimed toward the upper right. In his left hand, he holds his shield.[238] In none of these cases does the rider appear to be holding any sort of rein.

Whether the raised-arm gesture is the prerogative of deities alone is uncertain, although the two female riders must surely be goddesses. It may not be too much to see this same composition, or an attempt at it, on the crude rider plaque now in the University of Nottingham Museum (Figure 19). The rider's body is rectangular with tiny limbs. His arms are extended and end in a spear in his left hand and a shield in his right.[239]

Nor is the raised-arm motif confined to riders. A standing figure showing the same raised-arm pose has been found carved on a rock at Yardhope in Northumberland (Figure 20). This figure, a simple frontal figure with few details remaining, holds a shield in its raised right hand and a spear in its left. The discoverers would like to identify him with Cocidius who has been equated with Mars in dedications particularly on the northern frontier of Britain.[240]

Horseman Brooches

The Celtic character of the Bisley altar calls to mind the small horseman brooches which have been found at a number of mainly religious sites in Britain particularly in the South,[241] for they too show a style which owes more to local tradition than to Rome (Figure 21). The handling of riders' hair and the horses' manes on the rider brooches is similar to these elements on the Celtic coins particularly on the human-headed horse coins of Gaul (Figure 22).[242] The shape of the profile faces of these partly human animals is also reminiscent of the heads on the brooches. The other characteristic which shows these brooches to be of Celtic inspiration is the treatment of the horse. If the creator of the Bisley altar liked a thick-bodied horse, the producers of the brooches preferred the type whose body tapers sharply until it reaches the hind quarters. This body shape, along with the elongated head and stylized mouth which curves outward, can be seen even in horses of the Hallstatt[243] although it reaches perhaps its most extreme form on the Aylesford bucket.[244] The little horseman brooches show both these traits to varying degrees.

Whether the brooches are associated with Mars is difficult to assess. There is no clear evidence linking these objects to any deity. The recent excavation on Lamyatt Beacon, where brooches have been found, has uncovered a Romano-British temple where Mars appears at least twice, in stone and in bronze.[245] The stone figure is atypical, dressed in a tunic with his right arm at waist level crossing his body. The bronze statuette, however, is an orthodox nude, helmeted Mars, the position of whose arms suggests that he held a spear and shield. These figures were found with other statuettes of members of the Roman pantheon.[246] So the appearance of Mars need not be significant. On the other hand, it has also been suggested that a larger than life-size statue which probably stood in or near the temple may have been Mars,[247] the temple possibly being dedicated to him.

Other sites at which horseman brooches have been found are also associated with Romano-Celtic religious activity. At Woodeaton in Oxfordshire a square temple of Romano-British type has come to light.[248] The six rider brooches from Hockwold-cum-Wilton in Norfolk were found in an area where a series of ritual crowns has been discovered.[249] The summit of Cold Kitchen Hill, not far from Lamyatt Beacon, has produced horseman brooches along with quantities of other brooches and a variety of objects.[250] At Nor'nour in the Isles of Scilly, there was a single horseman brooch found among a vast number of other types of brooches. The site is considered likely to have been a shrine although there is no structural evidenced to confirm this.[251] Nor'nour has also yielded clay figurines, not horsemen, but of the 'pseudo-Venus' and *dea nutrix* type.[252] Several brooches have also come from Hayling Island, an established sacred site.[253] The evidence from all these sites, although often inconclusive, argues strongly for a religious significance for these brooches. Curiously enough, they have been found neither on the continent nor in association with bronze rider figures.

The Whitcombe Rider and His Antecedents

A horseman relief of quite a different type was found at Whitcombe in Dorset (Figure 23). The relief is not complete but consists of the centre portion of a slab on which an armed but helmetless horseman is riding toward the right on a horse whose lower legs are now missing. There is no inscription on the preserved fragment.[254]

Unlike the Bisley altar, this relief's antecedents are clearly Roman. At first glance it looks like a fragment of a cavalry tombstone, but this is questionable as there is no evidence for the presence in the area of a military installation to account for the discovery of a soldier's tombstone.[255] Moreover, a number of characteristics distinguish this figure from the common form of cavalry tombstone. For although it is hard to see the rider's garments in detail on account of the poor preservation of the piece, a lightly billowing cape falling in unbroken curves behind him is clearly part of his costume. While such a garment may have been painted in on cavalry tombstones, it is not to be seen on the stones as they are today although it is common on reliefs with divine and Imperial subjects.[256] It is difficult to determine exactly the action of the horse's legs, but it looks as if this was a walking and not a galloping horse in spite of the impression of wind-blown speed given by the billowing cape.

A second element also not found on the tombstones is the beard which can still be made out on the very worn face of the Whitcombe rider. The beard suggests a date no earlier than the second century for the relief, the period when beards became fashionable.[257] Scenes from Trajan's column show bearded legionaries.[258] If the tombstones do not record this fashion, it is no doubt because most of them date to the first century. Where they are later, very often the faces are too worn to show details. The fashion for beards seems to have died out with Constantine as can be seen from the coin portraits. So a date within the second and third centuries is likely for the Whitcombe relief on that basis. On the other hand, it was not unusual at any time for the Roman Mars to be bearded so the beard in itself, while suggestive, is not conclusive evidence for a date.

One other unusual aspect of this relief, however, does support a date within the period proposed above. The rider is holding his spear so that its point is in the upper right-hand corner of the relief. In virtually all other representations of riders holding spears, the weapon points downward as it is being thrust into a human enemy or hunted animal. Occasionally the rider hold his spear across his body and nearly parallel to the baseline of the relief as on a tombstone from Worms showing a rider on a walking horse[259] or on a sestertius in the British Museum showing Nero on a galloping horse.[260]

The closest parallel to the action of the Whitcombe horseman is on the reverse of one of the coins from the Arras treasure (Figure 24). This is a large gold medallion with a bust of Constantius I Chlorus on the obverse, and the same emperor on the reverse mounted on a standing or walking horse approaching the gates of London. The emperor is met by a kneeling Britannia behind whose back the walls of the city of London can be seen. The approaching emperor is bearded; his cloak billows only slightly behind him in a single unbroken curve. He carries his spear so that it points toward the upper right.[261] The compositional type appears again in the works of later emperors. A silver dish found at Kerch and now in the Hermitage shows Constantius II in virtually the same pose as his grandfather but with a victory in front of his horse.[262] A gold medallion of Justinian shows the same again (Figure 25). Harald von Roques de Maumont believes that this medallion is derived from a victory monument of Justinian.[263] It may be the case that the Arras medallion also reproduced a monumental horseman, a statue either of Constantius himself or one of his recent predecessors since the type only appears to have been popular in the later Empire.

The Whitcombe relief then could be an adaptation of a model associated with this late group of works. The difference, as far as it is possible to ascertain, lies mainly in the addition of shield to the left arm of the Whitcombe rider which none of the emperors carries. It is, of course, possible that the hypothetical prototype had a shield although extant Imperial statues and coins show no evidence that this was normal practice on Imperial monuments. What the Whitcombe rider's shield may indicate is that the horseman is meant to be the mounted Mars. The fact that he has no helmet is no bar to this interpretation. Examples of the Celtic Mars are known which are bare-headed.[264] The adaptation of an Imperial prototype would be fitting, as with the small bronzes, for the representation of the god as a rider.

The Stragglethorpe Rider

Closer to the common cavalry tombstone of the western Empire is the relief found at Stragglethorpe in Lincolnshire (Figure 26).[265] Here is a rider group where the horseman is riding down and spearing an enemy. The rider is dressed in a tunic and cape, the latter billows out behind the rider's raised right arm. He also wears a helmet and carries a shield. The standing horse lifts his front offside leg which he places on the head of a creature whose hair is dressed in thick straight locks around his head. The creature's body ends in a snakelike coil with a three-part finny tail.

The general composition of the Stragglethorpe relief is clearly derived from the cavalry tombstone although it differs from it in details. The rider in billowing cape and helmet, as observed above, is more likely to be Mars than the common soldier. Moreover, his loose, belted tunic also speaks against his being a cavalryman.

The Stragglethorpe rider's horse is walking rather than galloping. A spear-wielding cavalryman from the second century AD also rides a walking horse. This is the rider on a tombstone discovered at Stanwix.[266] Like the Stragglethorpe figure, this rider's horse has its leg placed over the head of the fallen enemy. But although this element is so similar to the Stragglethorpe composition, a work of the Stanwix type is clearly not the model for the Stragglethorpe relief as the horse on the Stanwix stone, most unusually, turns his head to face the viewer.

The Stragglethorpe group seems to depend for its model on a tombstone type on which a horseman is riding a standing horse seen in profile. This horseman raises his spear to thrust it at an enemy whose head is beneath the horse's front off leg. But not only has the craftsman who produced the Stragglethorpe relief changed the rider from a man to a god, he has also changed the nature of the enemy. The enemy here is a fish-tailed monster who is probably meant to be an anguipede, a snake-legged giant.

In the gigantomachies of Greece, particularly on the Great Altar of Pergamon, Ares fights snake-legged giants as do all the other gods, but Roman instances of Mars fighting a giant are rare. There is, for example, part of a relief column (or perhaps the middle pedestal of a Jupiter column) found at Hausen on the Zaber and now in Stuttgart which shows various gods engaged in battle with giants. Mars is seen from the back. He is nude but wears a helmet and carries a shield. He fights with a sword against a snake-legged giant.[267]

There are also other Mars and anguipede pairings where no active fighting is involved. The treasure found at Straubing, ancient *Sorviodurum*, included protective head coverings for horses, two of which have a figure of Mars supported by an anguipede. Both figures of Mars are of the standing Polycleitan type. Both wear helmets but, whereas one wears moulded body armour, the other has only a mantle over his shoulders and a baldric on which a sword is hung. The nude Mars is accompanied on either side by the Dioscuri represented on a smaller scale than he is. Above his head there is an eagle usually associated with Jupiter.[268]

The Stragglethorpe relief, then, probably represents the unusual theme of Mars fighting a giant but with Mars as a rider. The god seems more likely to be Mars than Jupiter who, as will be discussed in Chapter Three, is more usually associated in Celtic lands with an anguipede monster. It is not possible to be certain, of course, but the relatively ornate helmet and lack of beard suggests Mars as he was often represented in Britain rather than Jupiter. Support for this identification, albeit of a circumstantial nature, comes from the fact that at Stragglethorpe the local church, which is partly Anglo-Saxon, is dedicated to St. Michael and All Angels.[269] We may be seeing the same phenomenon already observed on the continent at St. Michel de Valbonne where the evidence suggests that Mars, probably the mounted Mars, was venerated and then replaced by the mounted Saint Michael when Christianity replaced earlier beliefs.

Furthermore, if the identification of the various riders discussed here as Mars is reasonable, it seems likely that the mounted Mars was a popular figure in Britain whereas the mounted Jupiter, so common on the Jupiter columns of the continent, was little known. It may be an accident of archaeology, but no Jupiter and giant groups have been found in Britain and it is possible that none existed. This may suggest a reason for the anguipede being turned into a triton-like figure rather than one with two snake-legs. The artist was perhaps not familiar with the snake-legged creature so chose instead a sea creature's tail for the god's monstrous enemy.[270] Animals whose bodies end in long fishy tails are a major element of a mid-second century mosaic at Fishbourne[271] while the pediment of the temple of Sulis Minerva at Bath has been reconstructed to include a pair of tritons with long convoluted fish tails.[272] Figures, human or animal, with a sea monster's tail were probably a good deal more familiar to the British craftsman than the anguipede since sea monsters were used decoratively in Britain. This type of figure was therefore substituted for an anguipede in the Stragglethorpe relief to represent the non-human character of the enemy.

It appears, then, that the iconography of the Roman Mars was insufficient as it was imported from Rome to represent the complexity of the Celtic Mars. Sometimes, particularly on continental temple sites, it seems that figures of standing Mars and of horses were worshipped side by side or as equivalents. But it also seems that artists, perhaps wanting to stress the god's very close association with horses in another way, looked for a different image and found it by transforming the Roman horseman, especially the Imperial horseman who was himself already revered as a god.

But Mars was not the only Roman god to be represented mounted in his Celtic form. Jupiter underwent the same kind of development and it is sometimes difficult to tell the two apart. As we have seen above, often only hints afforded by attributes can allow us to distinguish between the two.

19

Chapter 3

The Celtic Jupiter and Giant Column

If the evidence for Mars as a rider god depends largely on deductions made from inscriptions and tentative interpretation of votive offerings, the case for a Celtic god who takes the form of a mounted Jupiter is considerably more straightforward. Here the evidence comes from a group of relatively homogeneous monuments known as Jupiter-giant columns (Figure 27). The imagery is, in almost all its elements, Graeco-Roman. Prototypes for most of the features of these columnar monuments can be found within the Graeco-Roman repertory. But the sculptors have combined these features in a new way, unorthodox in terms of Mediterranean usage, and clearly meant to convey a meaning other than, or in addition to, that of a votive monument to Jupiter, the Roman god who is named in the inscriptions that often accompany the columns.

As was the case with the Celtic Mars, this form of Jupiter — as horse-riding victor over the giant — existed in the western Empire alongside the typical Graeco-Roman iconographical type. And again like Mars, it is the heterodox representation which tells us clearly that we are not dealing with the usual Roman deity. The Roman Jupiter and the Greek Zeus had no special association with horses and were normally bourne in chariots. The distinctive iconography of this Celtic figure belongs to a different tradition.

The typical Jupiter-giant column consists of a column standing on a double base made up of a square element below an octagonal one, both of which are decorated with relief figures of Roman deities. The column is crowned with a Corinthian capital to which four heads peering out of the foliage are sometimes added. Above the capital is a base supporting a group composed of a mounted, sometimes cuirassed, warrior whose horse is trampling a giant.[273] Most often the giant lies on his stomach raising his upper torso off the ground and supporting himself with his arms (Figure 28). His body is bent under the weight of the horse's front legs which rest on his shoulders. He faces away from the horse and rider and his features are often set in a grimace although some of the gigantic faces appear more benign.[274] Occasionally also, the giant is turned on his back in a half-sitting position so that he confronts the horse's raised front legs (Figure 29).[275] One of the most characteristic features of this type of rider group is that the giant's legs are replaced by two coiling snakes whose heads take the place of his feet and sometimes bite the rider or horse.

The rider is presented as a mature man (Figure 30). His thick, wavy locks and full beard conform to the type recognised as Zeus (or later, Jupiter or Serapis) after the statue at Olympia, the creation of Phidias in the fifth century BC. But on these equestrian statues of the Roman period, the god is often given a military cuirass to wear rather than the Phidian himation. He raises his right arm as if to throw a spear. Only rarely is any weapon preserved, but

thanks to a few fortunate finds where the original weapon accompanied the sculptural remains, as, for example, the rider from Saverne, we know that the god hurled a thunderbolt — a confirmation, if one is needed, of his identification with Jupiter/Zeus.[276] However, since the giant and rider series shows a certain degree of variation in the details of iconography, in type of costume worn by the rider and in number and position of giants, it is quite possible that other weapons were also put into the hands of some riders. In a few cases the god also holds a wheel in his left hand either gripped like a shield or with his hand between the spokes and grasping the rim.[277] The column on which the rider and giant are mounted is often accompanied by an altar to Jupiter.

Date and Geographical Distribution

This distinctive form of equestrian group raised on a column appears to have been erected mainly in the second and third centuries AD.[278] Its popularity can be gauged by the fact that Gerhard Bauchhenss records the remains of rider and giant statues from 173 sites in Germania Superior alone.[279] In addition, fragments from the carved sections forming the pedestals of columns have also been discovered on other sites but without traces of their crowning statuary. Some, at least, are likely to have had riders.[280] The rider groups which have been found were discovered almost exclusively within the territories of Gaul and Germania Superior (Map 1 shows the northern provinces). A few examples also come from Germania Inferior with possible outliers in Raetia and Pannonia in the east and Britain in the west.[281] In Britain only the lower parts of columns have been discovered, so it cannot be shown with any certainty that rider and giant groups actually surmounted columns in the British Isles.

Present archaeological evidence suggests that the main areas in which the columns were erected were the northern part of Germania Superior and the eastern part of Gallia Belgica.[282] The maximum density of finds is in the area of the northern Vosges mountains and in the valley of the Moselle and the middle Rhine.[283] These were regions of Celtic settlement. Outside these territories, the number of columns topped by the Jupiter-giant group drops sharply. In Germania Inferior isolated giant columns are found. But in Lower Germany in general, columns crowned with seated figures of Jupiter appear to have been more frequent.[284]

The Problem of the God's Identity

The columns have long been the subject of scholarly debate. Almost alone among the controversies which the monuments have engendered, those arguments which raged in the early decades of this century over whether they were Germanic or Celtic have been resolved to the satisfaction of most recent scholars. Few today deny a Celtic origin for the column and the deity represented.

While there is general agreement that the 'Jupiter' of the column as a Celtic deity, there is no consensus concerning his specific identity. The difficulty lies in the fact that all dedications on the columns are to Jupiter. Occasionally Juno is also addressed but there is never any associated Celtic name. Moreover, no ancient writer mentions the columns. So the columns themselves are the only witness to the beliefs or cult that they represent. Yet, considering the large number of monuments which have survived, it must be the case that the deity to whom the columns were raised was a Celtic god of great importance.

Although the column inscriptions only address the god as Jupiter, there have been attempts by scholars to discover the god's Celtic name. Some suggestion of an identity comes from the glosses made by the medieval Bern scholiasts to Lucan's *Pharsalia* in which the cruel sacrifices made to three Celtic deities: Teutates, Esus and Taranis, are described.[285] There are, however, two varying sets of identifications. The first scholiast equates Teutates with Mercury, Esus with Mars and Taranis with Dis Pater. The second has Teutates as Mars, Esus as Mercury and Taranis as Jupiter. This second group is somewhat corroborated by inscriptional evidence. We saw in the previous chapter that Teutates was given as an epithet of Mars at Magdalensberg in Carinthia, while there is some evidence for the association of Mercury with Esus.[286]

The link between Jupiter and Taranis, shown by inscriptions, is meagre and problematical. An inscribed altar from Chester dated to AD 154 bears a dedication to IOM Tanarus which could refer to Taranis, an error perhaps having been made in the transcription. Another, now missing, inscription from Dalmatia refers to Jupiter Taranucus and two more from Upper Germany to Deus Taranucnus. One in Greek letters from Orgon near Arles reads TAPANOOY. Gerhard Bauchhenss sees all these as deriving from the Celtic root *taran, to thunder, and thus to be identified with the Taranis of Lucan.[287] The difficulty lies in the fact that these inscriptions were not found in association with either mounted Jupiter figures or the wheel god, another unnamed Celtic deity who is represented as a Jupiter-like figure holding a wheel[288] but who may, indeed, be identical with the mounted Celtic Jupiter. However, the identification of a Celtic divine name which is etymologically thunderer with statues of a mounted god who looks like the Roman Jupiter wielding a thunderbolt is very attractive if far from proven.

The Siting of Columns

Some clue to the nature of the mounted Celtic Jupiter may be gained from looking at the types of sites on which devotees placed the monuments. Columns have been found in all the larger settlements of Upper Germany and eastern Gaul with the largest number coming from Mainz, perhaps a tenth of the column remains coming from this city.[289] They have also been found in the countryside indicating worship

by the indigenous rural population. They have been discovered inside and outside precincts, and inscriptions show that they were sometimes erected by landowners,[290] in some cases perhaps for private cult.[291]

Columns were raised in sacred precincts, often in the sanctuaries of other gods. The remains of at least three have been found in the peak sanctuary of Donon on the border between Gallia Belgica and Germania Superior. The majority of the dedications found on the site were addressed to Mercury and not Jupiter. Other likely peak sanctuaries show the same combination of Jupiter and Mercury worship. There is, for example, a sanctuary at Stuttgart-Bad Cannstatt where the remains of a giant column were found near an aedicula for Mercury. But in this case the sanctuary was located in the middle of the vicus. In Heidelberg-Neuenheim the remains of a Jupiter-giant column were found in a Mithraeum along with an altar dedicated to Jupiter Optimus Maximus.[292]

Some column remains have also been found in sanctuaries which are believed to have been dedicated to Jupiter. From the sanctuary at Grand-Falberg in the Vosges, the fragments of no less than six giant groups and an altar with a dedication to Jupiter have been recovered.[293]

The great variety of sites argues for a god of considerable importance and one whose powers were relevant to urban as well as to rural worshippers. The choice of Jupiter as the Roman equivalent of the mounted Celtic god suggests that the sky in one or more of its aspects was the latter's active domain, an idea perhaps reinforced by the placement of the figure on a high column and the prominence of the horse, an animal with considerable sky and solar connection in the Graeco-Roman world.[294]

But whatever their religious significance, the geographical distribution of the columns shows that they appeared mainly in regions which had been Romanized, however superficially. The observations that large numbers of columns were found in Romano-Celtic towns, that they were erected in sanctuaries which were dedicated, nominally at least, to Roman gods, and that they were raised on rural estates where the owners, if not the workers, would have absorbed the dominant Roman culture, are in keeping with the distinctly Mediterranean artistic vocabulary of the statuary.

The Question of Prototype

The problem which has faced all those who would study the origin of this rider composition is that no equestrian group has come down to us which can be identified as the likely model. Are the Jupiter-giant groups developments from an earlier giant and rider statue now lost or are they, as some scholars suggest, a variation, newly invented, on the Imperial cuirassed rider and fallen enemy, familiar from military tombstones, for example, but here with the enemy transformed into a snake-legged giant?

This second explanation of the Jupiter and giant group as a late hybrid — the union of a rider, perhaps Imperial, with a mythical figure, the two combined to suit Romanized Celtic patrons — is reasonable given the lack of any clear model. However, it is not necessarily the only possibility. While there is no way to prove any alternative hypothesis, there is, nevertheless, reason to believe that this argument *ex silentio* is not the best solution to the problem. For there is evidence to show that an image of a single mounted god engaged in battle with a snake-legged giant was known earlier and probably originated during the Hellenistic period. No statue survives even in Roman copy, but several minor works, some of Hellenistic date, are preserved which do prove that the subject itself — a mounted figure in combat with a snake-legged giant — did exist before the period of the Jupiter and giant columns.

Several examples of single rider and giant groups appear on intaglios.[295] A gem in the Hague has on it a version of the scene on the Jupiter-giant columns (Figure 31). The gem shows a horseman riding a galloping horse toward the right. He holds a spear in his raised right hand and appears to be riding down a snake-legged giant whose back is turned to the horse. The gem is dated by Marianne Maaskant-Kleibrink to sometime within the second half of the first century BC and the beginning of the first century AD.[296] If this date range is correct, it means that the combination of snake-legged giant with single rider could not have arisen first with the Romano-Celtic monuments. The gem is appreciably earlier than the Jupiter-giant columns which, as we have noted, tend to date from the second and third centuries AD. Nevertheless, the major elements of the column groups can be seen in the little engraving. Other rider and giant gems of different styles are preserved, but all agree in placing the giant with his back to the rider. This position is noteworthy because it is unusual.

Examination of rider and enemy groupings shows that an outward-facing foe standing, kneeling or lying extended (in the case of a fallen enemy or a giant) beyond the head of the horse is rare in rider and enemy encounters, with the exception of the figures on the Jupiter-giant columns. Horsemen are normally faced by their adversaries. Enemies in the prone position are relatively uncommon and tend to lie flat on the ground and slip beneath the body of the horse rather than kneel in front of it or raise themselves on their arms.[297] So it is worth remarking when this arrangement appears again in two terracotta figurines which come from Egypt (Figure 32). On each of these the horse is rearing so that its anterior hooves rest on the shoulders of the kneeling figure in front of it. The back of this figure is turned to the horse as he takes the animal's weight on his shoulders. Wilhelm Weber, who compiled a catalogue of Graeco-Egyptian terracottas, believed the groups to be genre figures, circus performers.[298] But it is also possible that they were modelled after a gigantomachy statue, perhaps from Alexandria, which has since disappeared.

Similar figurines have been found in Europe, as for example, one discovered at Voiron in France.[299] This terracotta is so remarkably like the Egyptian examples that they must have had the same source unless one is a copy of the other. All three are approximately 12 cm. tall. On each, the beardless rider turns his head to look over his right shoulder. His disproportionately large head makes him look very youthful, not at all like a typical Zeus. His right arm, held at his side, is set in a right angle bend at the elbow so

he must be grasping the reins of his horse. There is no sign that he has any aggressive intent, the absence of which is undoubtedly what suggested to Weber that this was a circus act. The enemy figure, if that is what he is, is kneeling. The bend of the knees is quite clear and there is no sign of thick, snaky legs trailing under the horse.

There are many questions to be asked about these little figures. No date was given in the published accounts of the examples cited above. They may, indeed, belong to the Roman period as the find at Voiron suggests, but their significance lies in the fact that, as we shall see below, there exist a number of columns on which the giant figures bear a very striking resemblance to the kneeling figures on the little terracottas. Yet it is unlikely that the figurines were the original models for the Jupiter and giant groups. Leaving aside the question of scale, the poses of the Celtic and Egyptian riders differ too much one from the other and only a minority of giants on the columns are in the kneeling position. Nevertheless, the comparison is intriguing. Where and when were these little statuettes made? Do they predate the Jupiter columns? If not, were the little figurines made in Egypt and brought to Gaul by returning Celtic soldiers because they looked like Jupiter and his giant? Or was the traffic the other way and the statuettes were made in Europe and taken as personal religious objects by Celts going east?

One Egyptian example was found in the Fayum, the other bought on the market in Cairo[300]. But no further light is shed on their origin. The fact that the riders are beardless and weaponless makes it less than likely that they were Celtic copies of Jupiter groups since they lack the essential characteristics which identify the mature god. The same argument, however, applies to any attempt to define their relationship to a Hellenistic mounted Zeus or Poseidon subduing a giant. So the little figures, although probably connected in some way with the Hellenistic gems and the Romano-Celtic columns, remain something of a mystery.

The concrete evidence, then, for an earlier rider and giant statue is slight. Only the gems show that the composition was certainly known in the last years BC but this does not necessarily mean that the engraving derived from a statue group. On the other hand, the representation in the minor arts of major statue groups reduced to miniature, two-dimensional form was common during the Hellenistic and Roman periods. In the case of the complex group representing the encounter of Odysseus and his crew with the monster Scylla, relief decorations incorporating the scene were known long before the group was actually found in 1957 at Sperlonga in Italy.[301] It is not impossible that the gems featuring the mounted gigantomachy are a parallel case for which the sculptural antecedent may yet be found.

The Possible Hellenistic Model

If we analyse the Romano-Celtic Jupiter groups themselves, the general character of the giant and rider composition as it appears on the columns also seems to argue for a Hellenistic origin. The way in which the horse and giant are conceived as an integrated group is strongly reminiscent of the advances in the organization of interdependent figures made during the middle Hellenistic period. This period saw an interest in falling figures, in the effect of the weight of one body on another and in the realistic movement of figures in three-dimensional space: bodies lean forward and twist and turn in new ways. Unfortunately, we can only examine these developments in the organization of *standing* figures as no equestrian groups of this type and period survive.

The Development of Interdependent Groups

Although the two statue groups analysed below contain neither horsemen nor their enemies, the techniques of representing physical interaction and the exploration of the falling body in space which the Hellenistic artists were discovering and developing, as exemplified by the Artemis and Iphigenia and the Menelaos and Patroclos groups, would have been applicable equally to horse and rider groups.

The statue group of Artemis and Iphigenia in Copenhagen (Figure 33) illustrates some of the new concern for representation of realistic physical interaction and movement in space.[302] It shows the two just at the moment when Iphigenia is rescued by the goddess and the stag substituted for her at the sacrificial altar. Artemis is standing in a nearly frontal position. Iphigenia leans forward, falling toward the viewer. The deity's restraining hand saves the girl from completing her fall by pulling her upward in a long sweeping arc. The girl's leg crosses behind that of the goddess. Although the group is probably meant to be seen with the body of the goddess viewed frontally, the falling girl breaks the frontal plane and draws the eye around the composition.

A similar and even more complex example is the group of Menelaos holding the corpse of Patroclos (Figures 34a, b). The statue has been restored by Bernhard Schweitzer from the so-called 'Pasquino' group and eight other fragments of copies of this same work.[303] The figure of Menelaos leans to the left, his legs wide apart as he supports the dead body of Patroclos which is slumped over his right arm. The dead youth is on his knees with his legs passing between the older man's feet; his torso forms a graceful arc as it twists, one shoulder coming forward, the other back, held by Menelaos's supporting arm. The intertwining of the two bodies and the stretching of the youth's torso by the force of its own weight against the restraining arm is similar to the stretching and arching of Iphigenia's body held in check by Artemis. It is similar also to the arched body of the giant on the Jupiter column whose torso likewise curves backward under the weight of the horse pressing against its shoulders. Thus the form which the body must take is determined directly by the actions of the figures associated with it. Prior to this, figures, both in the round and in relief, tended to be represented in a limited series of stock poses which could be fitted into any number of compositions by the varying of details or attributes. Groups were assembled by putting two or more of these figures together but not by relating their movements intimately one to the other. In the Menelaos group, we see something different. There is a clear causal relationship underlying the disposition of the bodies. Menelaos leans forward under the weight of Patroclos's dead body, but the body itself slumps as it does because of the position of Menelaos's encircling arm.

Like these standing groups, the relationship between the horse and giant on the Jupiter-giant column, although naturally limited by restrictions on the flexibility of horses, suggests derivation from a monument in which the artist attempted to explore realistically the effect that one body has upon another, in this case, the effect of pressure from the horse on the huge body of the giant. The way in which the giant is lying only partly beneath the body of the horse and struggling to rise again between its legs is just the reverse of the dead Patroclos slipping between the legs of Menelaos. But these opposing movements, one upward, one downward, both show the subject (Patroclos or the giant) being acted upon by a greater force (Menelaos or Jupiter's horse and, by extension, Jupiter himself). The paratactic has been replaced by true subordination.

Thus the giant, through his posture and, often too, his facial expression, is shown to be reacting to the weight of the horse. This is in strong contrast to that earlier instance of a horse being supported by a semi-human figure, the acroterion from Marasa (Locri) in Reggio Calabria dated between 440 and 420 BC (Figure 35).[304] There, a bearded Triton holds the front hooves of a horse from which a young man has just dismounted and is still in the act of jumping down. The slight bend of the Triton's arms gives no suggestion that he is troubled by the weight of the horse. Neither the horse nor the Triton has any real effect on the other's body. For it is only in the Hellenistic period that realistic interaction comes to be explored.

The Model for the Snake-legged Giants

Although the unified group of mounted god and supporting giant could have been created in the third century BC, the fact that the giant is represented as only part human makes it more likely that the original monument was the product of a slightly later period. Until the building of the Great Altar at Pergamon in the period between 180 and 160 BC,[305] the more usual form for representation of giants was as large and powerful humans.

Snake-legged giants appeared occasionally in the late fifth and early fourth centuries BC but were relatively rare.[306] Francis Vian dates the change from the fourth century.[307] His collection of Greek and Roman gigantomachies shows that in sculpture and vase painting from the Archaic period onward, giants were normally given human form. The exception was Typhon the monstrous son of Ge who was both snake-legged and winged.[308] A black-figure hydria in Munich shows Zeus aiming a thunderbolt at such a figure.[309] But the giants in battle with the gods on the east metopes of the Parthenon are, more typically, fully human.[310] The giant among the dead in the large group dedicated by Attalos I at Athens in the third century BC is still completely human in form.[311]

Although they did retain some giants in human form, the sculptors at Pergamon replaced many with monsters whose semi-human shape showed that giants were clearly a race apart. They were as easily identifiable as aliens as the Gauls were or the Persians.[312] Moreover, snake-legged giants are by the nature of their deformity always shorter than the gods — lower physically and symbolically.[313] The change also enhances the excitement of the battle in artistic terms as the snake-legs writhe with independent life while the giants fight and die.

Fragments of a relief including snake-legged giants carved under the influence of Pergamon are known from the temple of Athena at Priene of mid-second century BC date.[314] Again, the same monstrous figures are found on a frieze from the temple of Hecate at Lagina in Caria which was probably built in the last quarter of the second century BC.[315] Gigantomachies involving giants with snake legs are also known from the Roman period, for example, friezes from Corinth and Aphrodisias of Hadrianic date and from Lepcis Magna during the reign of Septimius Severus.[316] Thus, if the reliefs at Pergamon are truly responsible for the increased popularity of the semi-human giant in place of the human one, the Altar may be considered a *terminus a quo* for the production of our proposed Hellenistic prototype for the Romano-Celtic Jupiter and giant.

One type of figure that the sculptors at Pergamon used to great effect is the giant forced back on his knees or his snake legs by a goddess grasping his hair. His body arches as he tries to get away but he is held fast. The group of Athena holding Alcyoneus is perhaps the most familiar example (Figure 36). He is completely human except for a pair of wings. He has been brought to his knees and his face reflects the pain the goddess's grip on his hair has produced.[317] A similar group involves Doris, the wife of Nereus, who grasps the hair of a snake-legged figure and pulls his head sharply back.[318] Like Alcyoneus this giant's mouth is open and his eyes are wide as he tries to free himself from the painful grip.

This type of figure may have been the specific creation of the Pergamene artists or it may have come into being slightly earlier, during the third century, as a result of the interest in falling and bending bodies like the Iphigenia or Patroclos discussed above. Whichever is the case, a fragment of a fully-rounded arching male body, pinned down and with head (now missing) thrown back, was discovered at Sperlonga among the remains of the complex statue group representing Scylla preying on the shipmates of Odysseus (Figure 37a).[319]

The sailor to whom the backward-bending body belongs has been restored as lying prone on the ground, his legs flat behind him but his body raised from the hips partly by the pressure of his right hand on the ground and partly by the force of the dog-head of Scylla which bites at one shoulder and holds the other with a paw (Figure 37b). The sailor raises his left arm to push away the monstrous animal just as the giants at Pergamon try to resist their goddess adversaries. Even in its very poor state, the sailor's upper torso looks like a three-dimensional version of a Pergamon giant and, significantly, even more like some of the giants in the Jupiter-giant column groups.

Baldassare Conticello who has been reconstructing and studying the Sperlonga remains over a period of years is unwilling to come to any conclusions about their date. The complexity of the work suggests the middle Hellenistic period but whether the group is an original of that period, a copy or a truly Roman creation using Hellenistic forms,

Conticello is also unwilling to decide without further research.[320] But a recent study by Bernard Andreae has sought to prove that the Sperlonga Scylla group is a marble copy of a bronze original made between 188 and 168 BC and certainly no later than the middle of the second century because the composition is reproduced on a Rhodian relief vase of that date.[321]

Most likely also to be of Hellenistic date is a further example of a male figure with arching torso which was discovered in Egypt (Figure 38).[322] This figure is a Triton and he has been placed next to a standing figure of a nude Aphrodite. The group, which is in Dresden, is probably meant to represent Aphrodite rising from the sea. But as Achille Adriani points out, the two figures are completely different in the way they are conceived in space.[323] The Aphrodite is largely frontal, based perhaps on the Aphrodite of Cyrene[324] and ultimately on fourth century types. The Triton, however, reflects a later model. He leans forward arching his back and tilting his head rearward. Adriani considers that the inconsistency of conception is the product of late Hellenistic eclecticism in Alexandria which formed groups by combining earlier figures of differing styles and conceptions.[325]

The Triton is of interest because the sea creature shares with giants the half-human shape in which the lower limbs are replaced by animal elements. Unlike the giants, however, this form for Tritons was not a Hellenistic development. The Triton with its fishy tail is known from Archaic times, as for example the fragment of a limestone pediment from the Acropolis on which Herakles battles with a Triton whose long tail is still preserved.[326] The two-tailed Triton seems to have been adopted first in the fourth century, perhaps as an invention of Skopas.[327] In practice, although Tritons are sometimes represented with a single tail rather than two snake legs, there is very little difference in the handling of the torso between the Triton and the Hellenistic giant, so the Egyptian Triton in Dresden is also quite similar to the giants in the Romano-Celtic statue group, thus suggesting that this type of figure was something of a commonplace in at least several parts of the Empire during the Roman period.

Breaking the Spatial Barriers

Figures bending backwards like the giants, the Tritons and the falling and fallen humans appear to have exerted particular fascination on the artists of the Hellenistic period. They were an excellent vehicle for the further exploration of movement into three-dimensional space which seems to have begun in the late fourth century BC and is particularly evident in some of the works of Lysippos. Like the raised arms of the Apoxyomenos,[328] falling figures break the traditional spatial barrier of the picture plane. They advance toward the viewer in a movement perpendicular to the picture plane. An early example of the attempt to sculpt forward movement is the Tyche of Antioch by Eutychides of Sicyon.[329] The goddess sits in a complicated twisted position which invites the observer to look at her from more than one viewpoint. Beneath her feet, the personification of the River Orontes is shown swimming. The figure of Orontes is placed so that he appears to swim forward into the observer's space.

24

If we consider, as there is some reason to (see below p. 27), that the Jupiter-giant group was meant to be seen mainly from the front, then these attempts at breaking through the traditional barrier, disregarding the limits of the block and advancing toward the viewer, are characteristics which the column giants share with the Hellenistic works. To give one example, the impression of moving, almost flinging, themselves into space is unusually strong in the Jupiter-giant group from Tongres where two giants carry the weight of the horse.[330] They are set at angles over the front corners of the base. They appear to extend beyond the boundaries of the stone block from which the horse and rider were carved. This produces a strong sense of movement and also of tension. The effect of forward motion is undoubtedly enhanced, unintentionally so, by the loss of the horse's front legs so the giants seem to fall forward, hanging over the narrow base and looking extremely unstable. Instability, tension and figures suspended in space are also characteristics of the Scylla group at Sperlonga which, as we have seen, is Hellenistic or has Hellenistic antecedents.[331]

The Model for the Giant Facing the Rider

Although differing considerably one from another in style, a circumstance which implies largely local manufacture, the giants on the columns generally fall into three categories with regard to their posture. First, there are a few like those belonging to rider groups found at Butterstadt, Hommert (Figure 29) and Niederbronn,[332] in which the giant is seated on the ground facing the horse. He is not sitting upright but rather leaning backward with his upper body extending precariously beyond the base as if pushed downward by the weight and action of the horse. The giant in this position recalls the Celtic enemy who appears on the Roman tombstones produced in the Rhineland mainly in the first century. The tombstone of T. Flavius Bassus in Cologne,[333] for example, shows an enemy lying supine under the legs of the soldier's horse, the front hooves of which apparently rest on the Celt's shoulders. But the relationship between these figures and the giants is not especially close. It is unlikely that the strong outward thrust of the gigantic bodies on the columns, both in their prone and supine forms, can be derived from the tombstone reliefs where restrictions of space ensured that enemies were, in general, placed well beneath the body of the horse. Nor is there any sense on the tombstones of the horse and rider being carried or supported by the adversary below.

Two groups in the round, in the National Museum in Rome (Figure 39) and the Villa Borghese (Figure 40), give an indication of the way in which the rider and enemy of the tombstone reliefs could have been translated into three dimensions. They represent Amazons battling with naked male enemies.[334] The Amazons are, according to Bernhard Schweitzer, copies of late Hellenistic originals. The barbarians, on the other hand, are a later intrusion probably meant to give the figures a Roman allegorical interpretation, perhaps the triumph of Roman Virtue over the enemies of Rome.[335] The late Hellenistic period saw the return of interest in the single viewpoint in the orientation of sculpture. These compositions are meant to be seen in profile. The twist of the Amazons' bodies toward the side chosen for viewing and the strict profile of the horses make the observer less likely to want to walk around the group. If anything, the barbarians increase this effect. The fallen enemy in the National Museum group is seated on the ground, his torso sharply twisted at the waist so his upper body can be seen frontally. He turns his head in a second sharp movement to look up at the mounted Amazon. He has been placed so that he takes up nearly all the space under the rearing horse's belly and front legs and does not extend beyond them. In the Villa Borghese group, two barbarians are turned so that their bodies face the viewer. One kneels and the other has fallen. The kneeling figure, like his National Museum counterpart, turns his head to look up at his conqueror. Both these groups show how two unrelated elements could be brought together to form a unit.

The relationship between the Amazon and her enemy is artificial. There is no physical contact or true interaction. Contact is made only with the eyes. Eye-contact serves to unite the two elements and also to close the composition because the viewer's eye tends to follow the glance of the barbarian in toward the Amazon and the centre of the work. Although three-dimensional, the two groups have the same compactness and awareness of the frame that the tombstone reliefs have. Furthermore, the relationship between the rider and the barbarian is the same in both, clearly victor and vanquished, while on the Jupiter columns the relationship between the giant and the god appears more ambiguous.

Although both Amazonomachies include enemies facing the mounted figure, it is unlikely that this type of statue group was influential in the development of the form of Jupiter-giant composition in which the giant is supine and facing inward. In the group from Butterstadt, for instance, the giant is in a half-sitting position, almost reclining, with his upper torso poised well over the edge of the base. He is turned toward the horse. There is no torsion in his body. The impression given by the two Amazon compositions — that we are seeing not sculpture in the round, but very high relief — is nowhere evident in any of the Jupiter column figures. It is difficult, therefore, to suggest a derivation from existing monuments for the supine form of giant which, in any case, on current evidence, seems to have been relatively rare.[336]

Column Giants With Their Backs to Riders

The more frequent types of giant are those whose backs are toward the horse and rider. They fall into two groups and call to mind two figure-types which we have already discussed. One we may call the 'Sperlonga' type after the fragment of a sailor's torso found at Sperlonga (Figure 37a). In this the giant only raises the upper part of his body while his hips still remain on the ground. Like the Sperlonga sailor, he sometimes braces himself with his arm straight and his hand pressed against the ground. In a group from Altrip and now in the Speyer Museum, all the extraneous stone has been cut away from the giant's upper limbs and he is seen clearly to be balancing on his outstretched arms (Figure 28).[337] A fragment from Lichtenau, now in Carlsruhe, which preserves only the giant, shows him with his right arm pressed against the ground while the left is lifted (Figure 41).[338] Sometimes also the arm is straight but the hand does not press the ground. Instead it carries a club as on an example from Neunkirchen in the museum at Speyer.[339] On all these statues, the base ends where the giant's body touches the ground and he leans out over the edge into space.

The second variation in this outward-facing group of giants, which we may call the 'kneeling' type, is very like the small terracottas found in Egypt and France (Figure 32). This figure is not lying on his stomach but kneeling and taking the weight of the horse with his knees and back rather than his arms. This type of giant can be seen, for example, on a group from Pforzheim in the Carlsruhe Museum where the kneeling giant grasps a club in each of his hands which he presses against his sides (Figure 42).[340] The giant who supports Jupiter's horse on the monument from Steinsfort drops his head slightly forward and assumes much the same position as the kneeling figure in the statuette group from Egypt found in the Fayum.[341]

Another of these kneeling giants is part of a group now in the Stuttgart Museum, in which Jupiter drives a biga (Figure 43). The giant's snake legs bend at knee level and then curl behind him.[342] He supports the inner, front leg of each horse with his shoulders and the outer ones with his hands. In the finer examples like this one, the giant's body can be seen to be well muscled giving a strong sense of physical power.

One feature of this group of kneeling giants is that they do not lean forward quite so dramatically as the 'Sperlonga' type. Like the little terracottas, they bend forward slightly as a result of the weight they carry. But their upright position creates the impression of a more stable and compact composition than do either of the other two types of giant.

A giant who seems to incorporate something of both outward-facing types is part of a group from Grand.[343] This monster is kneeling but he is positioned so that he bends deeply at the hips, his body at right angles to his legs. He carries not only the horse's hooves on his shoulders, but also the animal's belly on his back. His head is missing but his upper torso extends well beyond the limits of the base — a characteristic of the 'Sperlonga' and not the kneeling type.

The relatively easy way in which the giants fall into several different compositional types suggests the possibility of more than one model, perhaps several variations on a Hellenistic rider and giant composition. However, here the lack of any proof for the existence of a Hellenistic group on this subject, and also of any clear indication of date and original provenance for the little terracottas, does not really allow too much room for useful speculation.

Facial Expressions

Another characteristic of the giants of the columns, which again seems to look back to Hellenistic types, is the representation of an animated, if not pained, expression on the faces. On the better preserved and better quality examples, the giant is usually clean-shaven but with a full head of wavy hair. His mouth is open and often, as, for example, the giant supporting the biga in Stuttgart or the group found at Ehrang (Figure 45), the open mouth reveals a full set of teeth.[344] The Stuttgart giant's head, moreover, is heavily lined from his exertion. The head of the fragment

from Lichtenau, even in its current poor condition, shows a fine rendering of the locks of hair and of the beardless face with deep-set eyes and open mouth (Figure 41). The head of Jupiter found with it confirms the impression of excellent workmanship.

The open-mouthed heads with their furrowed brows and bulging eyes recall the heads of giants from the Altar at Pergamon. We have already mentioned the giant Alcyoneus on the relief of the Great Altar whose hair is being pulled by Athena during the battle (Figure 44). He is clean-shaven. His mouth drops open as his head is jerked forcibly backward. His upper teeth are visible. Above his deeply set eyes, his brow is clearly furrowed. The realistic treatment of facial features under stress can be seen in other figures like the bearded Laocoön from the famous group in the Vatican,[345] the original of which Bernard Andreae believes to have been a later product of the Second Pergamene School.[346] Indeed, the posture of Laocoön as well as the emotional rendering of his head is strikingly close to that of the giant Alcyoneus.[347]

The rendering of emotion in heads by opening mouths, dilating nostrils or manipulating brow and forehead lines was not unknown to artist of the Classical period.[348] However, it is in the works of Skopas during the fourth century BC that we begin to see these devices used more freely. Eyes are particularly deep-set and upward-looking and mouths are slightly open.[349] Interest in the manipulation of facial features for expressive ends seems to have reached its peak in the early second century BC in works of the so-called Hellenistic Baroque, like the Great Altar at Pergamon. The heads of the Scylla group found at Sperlonga also betray the artist's interest in intense emotion — wide eyes, open mouth and emphasis on the lines and furrows of the forehead. This is exactly the type of head that one would expect to find on a Hellenistic model for the Romano-Celtic giant.

Not all giants at Pergamon are clean-shaven and the same is true of the giants on the columns. The head of a giant who is part of a group in Cologne is fully bearded, his hair and beard falling in thick locks.[350] The expression on his face appears to be less agitated than that of many of his fellows. Indeed, occasionally the facial expressions of the giants have appeared so benign that some scholars have doubted the interpretation of the Jupiter-giant group as a true gigantomachy.[351] The giant carrying the weight of the god's horse might be a helper like the Triton from Reggio Calabria (Figure 35) rather than an enemy. But as we have no information about the meaning of the Celtic rider and giant group, speculation on this point does not seem useful. It is worth mentioning, however, that a few giants deviate strongly from the Graeco-Roman tradition which suggests that some sculptors were working not only in a local style but with specifically Celtic images in mind.

One such example was discovered at Diedelkopf (Figure 46).[352] The horseman is only preserved from the waist downward. He appears to be of the expected form but the giant supporting him is extremely unusual. He is basically of the 'Sperlonga' type, stretched out under the horse. But his head is enormous. His features are very worn but his mouth seems to be open. He is lying on his stomach and leaning on his elbows with his hands above his head supporting the hooves of the horse. In contrast to the muscular bodies of so many of his fellow giants, he appears to be emaciated with his ribs protruding under the flesh. The proportions of the figure with its massive head bring to mind the heads which decorate the outer plates of the Gundestrup cauldron[353] and the little bronze god from Bouray in France whose body diminishes in size from his large head to his tiny feet.[354]

A similarly distorted giant belongs to a group from Neschers in the Auvergne.[355] Here the giant has been reduced to an enormous head. The style is relatively crude, probably the work of a local craftsman. The form suggested to Fernand Benoit the Celtic 'severed heads' which are known from southern France in particular.[356] However, rather than representing a trophy like a severed head, the giant from Neschers, like that from Diedelkopf, resembles the gods on the Gundestrup cauldron. On both the head has not been divided or severed from its body, but rather the whole has been reduced to its essential elements. For the Neschers giant, this means the head and also the arms to carry the horse. It might be said that here the Mediterranean image of the giant has, indeed, become completely transformed into a Celtic being.

Rider Statues on Columns

The raising of statues on columns was common both in Greece, and following the Greek example, in Rome. Although in Rome it was usual for the monuments to be placed in civic centres, in Greece they tended to be confined to sites of religious significance.[357] The equestrian statue of Aemilius Paullus at Delphi was mounted on a tall pillar usurped from an earlier statue of King Perseus of Macedonia whom Paullus defeated at Pydna.[358] Eumenes II of Pergamon also dedicated an equestrian statue of himself on a tall pillar at Delphi in the second century BC.[359] The pillars were as much as 10 m. high and oriented with the rider seen frontally as the main view.[360]

The Romano-Celtic mounted Jupiter too was probably meant to be seen from the front, the viewer coming face to face with the god. If this is so, it agrees with normal Greek practice, the Romans adopting both frontal and profile views for equestrian sculptures in the round. In his study of Hellenistic rider monuments, Heinrich Siedentopf has shown that, according to the evidence of their still-extant bases, the rider statues which lined the approaches to such temples as Olympia and Delos were meant to be viewed from the front. They were placed close to one another in straight rows so that the riders could 'watch' the people and processions as they came along. Moreover, in some cases they were placed so close together that it would have been difficult to get a satisfactory impression of the profile of the statue.[361]

An idea of what an observer coming toward the statues would have seen can be gained from a Pompeiian wall painting now in the Naples Museum which shows spectators approaching a group of three equestrian statues. The statues are mounted on bases which constitute approximately half the total height of each monument. The horses stand side by side facing the viewer. The riders' right

hands are raised and their hidden left hands probably hold the reins.[362]

Based on his examination of pedestals and statue fragments, Heinrich Siedentopf found that the two common types of horse, the standing or walking horse and the rearing animal, already discussed in Chapter Two in relation to the mounted Mars, were represented with almost equal frequency.[363] The former is known in sculpture in the round from the Classical period but the latter seems to have appeared first at the time of Alexander.[364] Horses in other postures were also produced, the kneeling horse of an Amazon in the Palazzo Patrizi, for example.[365] But such a pose was clearly not suitable as a vehicle for a hero or a triumphant god or emperor. The second and first centuries BC saw the return of interest in groups with only a single view point, the so-called 'one-sided' groups.[366] The Amazons of this type, copies of Hellenistic works, now in Italian collections (Figures 39 and 40) and studied by Bernhard Schweitzer, are again useful comparisons. For when they are compared to Jupiter of the columns or to the portrait statues, it is obvious that the point of view is different. As noted above, the Amazons are not looking straight ahead but turn to the side, their bodies twisted at the waist. This is not the case with the mounted Jupiter. He is seated facing front. Like the statues placed along the parade routes at Greek sanctuaries, he is in a position to 'watch' the activities of the worshippers.

The Jupiter Figure

Statue fragments from Greek sanctuaries show that the riders of both types of horse, standing and rearing, tended to be dressed in the uniform of high ranking military officers. The placement of the shoulders, as for example, on the rider torso found on Delos[367] suggests that the left arm was lowered with the hand grasping the reins while the right arm was raised either in a gesture of greeting or holding an object like a spear or emblem of power.[368]

The monuments studied by Siedentopf represent not gods but living and dead men who were honoured by cities or states with portrait statues of themselves as riders which were placed in major cult centres. Not all those honoured were military men but they were nevertheless represented as such.[369] We have already seen how the potent image of the rider as hero and possessor of power developed after Alexander and came to represent an acceptable vehicle for a god. Outside the Celtic lands, the example of the Egyptian god Horus represented as a rider in the Roman period comes to mind.[370] Horus in his long history had never been a rider but nevertheless became one, despite innate Egyptian conservatism, under this powerful influence, fighting his eternal battle with Set now from a horse. It is possible that under the same influence, either Zeus or Poseidon, as indicated by the evidence of the intaglios, also became a rider and fought giants from horseback rather than chariot sometime in the Hellenistic period. A statue group representing the mounted Zeus in conflict could be the prototype for the Romano-Celtic Jupiter. But less conjectural is the conclusion that the Hellenistic rider figure with his raised right arm provided the model for virtually all later riders including ultimately the mounted Jupiter of the columns whose horse is a descendant of the galloping or rearing type.

The uniformed Jupiter himself with his right arm raised to aim a weapon and his left holding the reins also conforms to the Hellenistic type but through the intermediary, no doubt, of a Roman, probably Imperial, monument or copy. Here we have the same process of transformation that, as we saw in Chapter Two, gave rise to the little rider figurines so relatively numerous among Romano-British finds.

A more traditional view of Zeus or Jupiter in battle with the giants is reflected in the group found at Weissenhof and now in the museum at Stuttgart. In this the god is represented wearing only a mantle. He stands in a biga pulled by two galloping horses both of which are being supported by a single kneeling giant (Figure 43).[371] The group was discovered at the end of the last century along with fragments of other statues — a torso of Hercules, a head of Mercury, a piece of a tombstone and two fragments of inscriptions.[372] In this case, the evidence from the coins of the Roman period show that the battle between the giant and god in his chariot was a popular motif. Coins of Antoninus Pius and Septimius Severus, for example, show a nude charioteer in battle with a snake-legged giant.[373] The figure in the chariot aims a thunderbolt at the monster. This identifies the charioteer as Zeus or Jupiter. The chariot on the coins is a quadriga but considerations of space may have made this vehicle an impractical choice for the sculptor of the Weissenhof group. Its height of 1.20 m. and its length of 1.05 m. make it quite feasible that it was placed atop a column like the horsemen. But for whatever reason, this interpretation of Jupiter in battle was not nearly so popular at the god on horseback.

To sum up then: like the idea of a statue on a column, the theme of the single rider and giant was familiar long before the development of the Jupiter-giant columns as we know from engraved gems. Moreover, the form which the composition atop the column takes looks, as we have seen, heavily influenced by Hellenistic ideas of space and realism. These two together suggest that the rider-giant theme may have been worked out at some point during the Hellenistic period as a sculpture in the round. This may have occurred after the appearance of the Great Altar at Pergamon which seems to have been influential in replacing the human giant with the snake-legged giant as the standard form of the creature.

The artisans who carved the sculptures for the columns seem to have had several different models corresponding to the different positions of the giants, but this need not necessarily imply that several different version of the Hellenistic gigantomachy existed. Although this is possible, it is also not impossible that once the plan of the composition was fixed, skilled artists, and some of the Romano-Celtic sculptors were very skilled indeed, could have substituted figures of similar type from other compositions. The Sperlonga sailor show that other compositions requiring figures lying prone and bending under the weight of an external force existed. Such a figure might have been successfully substituted for a giant who

was represented kneeling, for example, in the original sculpture.

The Sperlonga find proves that discoveries of large, complex and hitherto unknown groups may still be made and that it would be wrong to dismiss the idea of a Hellenistic rider group as a model for the Romano-Celtic group simply because it does not exist today.

Chapter 4

Epona

The development of Epona's imagery presents a different problem again from that of the two male deities. In the case of Mars, we appear to have a Celtic deity, or perhaps several, identified with the Roman Mars and represented in any of a number ways, the rider being one of them, a link perhaps between the standing Roman Mars and the theriomorphic Celtic representation as the horse itself. Jupiter fighting the giant, on the other hand, seems to be the result of a carefully worked out iconography which is consistent over a wide geographical area. But at the same time, again unlike Mars for whom many Celtic names are known, there is little indication of his Celtic identity beyond uncertain references to a Jupiter Taranis who may indeed be this god.

Very different is Epona who has no Roman identity and no Roman counterpart and whose Celtic identity is assured. Her relationship to horses is expressed clearly and consistently in her iconography and strengthened by the accepted etymology of her name as lady of the horses[374] as well as by references to her in ancient texts.[375] Since, therefore, there was no comparable Roman deity whose form Epona could take over, a new image had to be invented for her. What the models for this might have been present an interesting problem.

The Nature of Epona

Epona is often represented as mounted, but mounted side-saddle, on a mare which stands or walks slowly across the picture field (Figure 47). That her horse is a mare is clear from the fact that, in numerous examples, a foal is shown following its mother and sometimes nursing from her. In all but a few cases, Epona is dressed in a long flowing gown which reaches her feet. She is also sometimes veiled. Her attributes include the cornucopia, patera and basket of fruit. A small animal often rests on her lap. On those occasions when she is not shown mounted, she is either enthroned or, more rarely, standing with her horses gathered around her. A further small number of reliefs show Epona riding astride like a cavalier. But her horsemanship was of a different order to that of her fellow equestrian gods. Her side-saddle position and the tranquillity of her horse, particularly as it feeds its young, dissociate her from the hunting and fighting which play such an important part in the relationship between horses and the other horse-riding deities.

The attributes chosen for Epona are those concerned with fertility and nourishment, like fruit and the cornucopia. These bring to mind the numerous statues and figurines of Abundantia[376] and the seated mother goddesses.[377] Indeed, so similar is she to the iconographic type of the Celtic mother that Epona often looks like a mother goddess who has temporarily exchanged her throne for a horse. Assuming, therefore, that this identity of form implies some similarity of function, it is probably reasonable to say that Epona was a goddess of the 'mother' type charged with the protection of horses and, perhaps more importantly, with their fertility.

Epona may also have had other concerns but these are hard to recover. The stone statuettes, reliefs plaques and terracotta figurines, over three hundred objects,[378] which make up the known representations of Epona, use the common Graeco-Roman artistic vocabulary. Many of these objects were found long ago and clear contextual information was not provided by the discoverers and is not recoverable. Nevertheless, some hypotheses are possible based on circumstantial evidence. For example, the fact that a number of objects have come from areas in close proximity to water suggests a connection between Epona and water, probably in the form of sacred springs, streams or wells .[379]

The discovery of figurines of Epona in graves and the representation of Epona on tombstones — the series of stones from the big cemetery at La Horgne-au-Sablon near Metz is a particularly good example[380] — connect Epona with the dead, either as protector in a general sense, or as Fernand Benoit would prefer, as a psychopomp and symbol of victory over death.[381]

Dating and Geographical Distribution

Dating presents problems. There are a number of inscriptions mentioning Epona. René Magnen collected thirty-three. The oldest dates from the end of the first century AD or the beginning of the second and records the fulfilment of a vow to the goddess by Marcellus son of Maturus.[382] It was found at Entrains within the territory of the Aedui, an area in which a significantly large number of objects associated with Epona have been recovered. Other inscriptions extend the date-range into the third century, as for example, the inscription found at Thil-Châtel (Côte d'Or), dedicated by Sattonius Vitalis of the twenty-second legion, which can be dated precisely to AD 250–251.[383] Inscriptions from the German frontier, like that from Zugmantel,[384] are most likely to have as their upper limit a date of AD 260 when the *limes* was abandoned.

Some of the figures of Epona have been found in contexts which help to establish a date for them. A very fine bronze statuette of Epona seated side-saddle on a horse was found at Reims among coins of the second century (Figure 48). The horse walks to the right but the goddess turns her head slightly to look leftward. Her eyes are of silver. Her small size, 14.6 cm., and the fact that she was found with other bronzes including figures of Venus and Aesculapius, suggested to Salomon Reinach that the cache represented the contents of a *lararium* hidden in time of trouble.[385]

Recently, another bronze, mounted Epona, smaller (5.8 cm.) and of very much lower quality, was found at Poitiers in a context which seemed to date principally from the end of the first century (Figure 49). Epona is seated on her horse. She is wearing a long tunic with many pleats which fall obliquely across her legs. Around her head is what appears to be a twisted headband. Her right hand is missing but a handle over her arm may have been attached to a basket.[386] If the date of this figure is correct, it shows that, at the time the earliest known dedication were being written, a sculptural form of Epona already existed.

The distribution of finds of objects and inscriptions forms a distinctive pattern when plotted on a map (Map 2). Few figures have been found as far west in Gaul as Poitiers. The majority seem to be concentrated around Alise-Ste. Reine, the ancient *Alesia* and south along the Saône River. A lesser number are clustered around Autun — *Augustodunum* — to the west.[387] This region of high concentration was the tribal area of the Lingones and the Aedui[388] and it is possible that the cult had its origins here.[389] An inscription from Entrains, dated to the second century, mentions a temple of Epona,[390] and the early inscription of Marcellus, noted above, was found at Entrains within the ruins of a temple.[391] At Mellecey (Saône et Loire) in the ruins of what appears also to have been a temple was found a stele depicting the mounted Epona. This relief is noteworthy in that it measured 1.10 m. high by 63 cm. wide.[392] The relatively large size suggests that it was made for the temple in which it was found, perhaps as a cult relief.

A second area with a large number of finds relating to Epona runs along the banks of the Moselle River eastward in Gallia Belgica toward Germania Superior and the *limes*. It then fans out to take in the border lands, mainly between the Rhine and Main Rivers. Many representations of Epona have been found around the cities of Trier and Metz as well as among the border forts.[393]

Scholars studying the iconography of Epona have long been aware of a distinction between the image of the goddess favoured by the people of central Gaul and that preferred by the inhabitants of the eastern frontier.[394] In the case of the former, the overwhelming majority of figurines and reliefs are of the mounted Epona, riding side-saddle usually toward the right. The variation in which the mare is followed by her foal seems to be a product of the area around Autun and Alise-Ste. Reine.[395] Wilhelm Schleiermacher observed that the Eponas of the central western Gaulish regions tended to hold cornucopiae and paterae when they held anything at all, while those of the Rhenish areas are most often represented with baskets or dishes of fruit held in one hand.[396]

In the eastern area of concentration along the Moselle and Rhine, the mounted figure-type is supplemented by a standing or seated Epona accompanied by two or more horses (Figure 50). This group was given the name *Reichstypus* by Wilhelm Schleiermacher who saw in it the product of Imperial, not Celtic, thinking.[397] Representations of Epona discovered in areas outside the Celtic regions, in Rome or Bulgaria, for example, tend to be of this standing or seated type.[398]

The Graeco-Roman Models for Epona

In spite of the Celtic identity of the goddess, about which there appears to be no disagreement,[399] and the mainly Celtic distribution of her monuments, the models for the different iconographical types, whether 'Imperial' or Gaulish, come from the repertoire of Graeco-Roman art.

Although the regions in which most of the reliefs and statuettes were found have been characterised by Katheryn Linduff at the least Romanized areas of Gaul and the Germanies,[400] the towns, Autun, Alise-Ste. Reine, Metz and Trier, around which numbers of such objects have been discovered were Roman foundations. Thus Autun-*Augustodunum*, for example, was settled about 12 BC by Aeduans moving from their old stronghold of Bibracte.[401] At the end of Augustus's reign, a school was established at Autun for the sons of tribal nobility in order to teach them correct social and civic behaviour in a Romanized society.[402] Ultimately, Autun became the intellectual centre of Gaul. Its prosperity and *Romanitas* may be judged by the fact that it had the largest amphitheatre in Gaul, probably dating back to the first century AD.[403] But at the same time, its Gaulish heritage is underlined by the discovery of the remains of two round temples within the city near the crossing of the *cardo* and *decumanus*.[404]

Alise-Ste. Reine, the ancient *Alesia*, scene of the defeat of Vercingetorix, also took on the outward form of a prosperous Roman town. During the reign of Vespasian, a theatre was built there, larger than those at Arles and Orange. In the second century, a basilica and a forum were also constructed.[405]

The cities of Metz-*Divodorum* and Trier-*Augusta*, the capitals of the Mediomatrici and Treveri respectively, were also Augustan foundations. Trier was, by Claudius's reign, very likely the richest city in Belgica and it continued to expand under succeeding emperors.[406] The period between Claudius and the Antonines saw the building of public monuments of Mediterranean type in the cities of Belgica and these enhanced the impression of outward Romanization.[407] The development of such Romanized cities would, after the first generation, produce Gallic urban or perhaps semi-urban populations in nearby farmlands who considered Roman representational forms as the norm having known nothing else. They would have expected Epona, like their other deities, to have an identifiable physical form. Edith Wightman remarks: "Perhaps the most striking feature of the sculptured monuments is not that the elaborate ones are commissioned by the wealthy but that the custom spread well below the summit of the the social pyramid".[408] Material evidence for such usage is shown by the poor quality of some of the reliefs and the popularity of cheap, mass-produced, clay figurines.

The army too played a role in the spread of Epona's image in that the auxiliary soldiers of Celtic origin were the most likely bearers of the representations of Epona out of the Celtic heartland.[409] But the importance of their role is difficult to judge. In Britain, for example, images and inscriptions alluding to Epona are quite rare. One was found on Hadrian's Wall and another on the Antonine Wall.[410] These surely have a military origin. But other examples, at South Collingham, Alchester, Caerwent and Colchester, reveal less about their origins. For while the engraved cheek-piece with Epona standing near her horse and holding its bridle found at South Collingham may well have had military associations, there is no way to be sure that it was a soldier who owned or dedicated the pipe-clay fragment of Epona from Caerwent or the Epona found at the apsidal temple just outside of Colchester along with other religious objects.[411]

In the view of Wilhelm Schleiermacher, there is also uncertainty about the military connections of some of the reliefs found on the sites of *limes* camps. For example, he believes that the image found at Köngen belongs to the period after the departure of the troops.[412] Also, at Cannstatt, the majority of reliefs come from the civilian settlement.[413] So it may be that the spread of Epona's image depended not only on the military but also on civilian Celts who travelled on business or arrived as settlers or refugees. The small number of finds on military sites, however, may not be indicative of the level of importance the cult achieved in the encampments.[414]

Against this background of imposed Romanization, it is easy to see how the demand for a representational form of the hitherto aniconic (or possibly theriomorphic) goddess might arise. Espérandieu's survey of sculpture in Gaul and the Germanies shows that much of the work done in the western Empire was of high quality and this suggests the presence not only of Roman imports but also of artists who were trained in Rome or by Roman artists. There is, moreover, the possibility of itinerant craftsman moving from place to place and the existence of pattern books to explain some of the uniformity which is so noticeable in general throughout the Roman Empire. So it is quite reasonable to suggest that the first Epona images were produced in Gaul as adaptations of familiar Roman motifs already utilized within the province. As we shall see below, there is no lack of candidates for the role of model for either the mounted or seated Epona. Once the iconographic type was decided upon, the small size and portability of the images, some of which may have been made of wood like the mounted Epona from Saintes (Charente-Maritime),[415] made it possible, if not likely, that one relief served as a model for the production of others.

The army and military craftsmen, familiar with imagery from many popular cults, represent still another possible source for the development of the Epona image. This would have been particularly true for the 'Imperial' type.

The initial problem for the craftsman, perhaps in the first century AD, was to represent Epona visually for the first time. In order to do this, he would not have invented a new iconographical type based on his understanding of the Celtic deity's nature, but would have depended upon the Graeco-Roman imagery with which he was already familiar and fitted the goddess to the image rather than the other way around. The 'Procrustes-bed' character of this kind of operation means that some elements of importance which described the Celtic deity and her function may have had to be lost in the production of the icon. If, for example, the only images of Epona that had come down to us were of the Imperial type, her role as a rider or even her special relation to mares might not have been realised. It is possible, therefore, that other important clues to Epona's nature were lost in the accommodation to Roman prototypes.

The Side-Saddle Epona

Although there are many variations in detail among the Epona representations, there are five distinguishable major types which conform to different compositional models. The Epona mounted side-saddle is the most important, but there is also a group of figures mounted astride, a type standing near a horse and holding it by its bridle and the seated or standing figures accompanied by horses. Each of these requires a different model and each corresponds to a well-known Graeco-Roman compositional type.

Looking at the figure mounted side-saddle to begin with, a hypothetical first artist might have had difficulty in finding a female figure mounted on a horse to serve as his model. Apart from Epona herself, the type appears to have been uncommon. A gem from Naples, now in Munich, has a female figure represented on it who sits upon a mule which is walking toward the left (Figure 51). The lady turns to the right and lifts her left hand toward her face. In her other hand she carries a sceptre. She is fully dressed and wears a veil over her head. Her mule has a large bell around its neck. The date of this gem is second or first century BC. Elfriede Brandt suggests that this might be Epona.[416] However, the attributes and the early date make it unlikely. But if the lady could be truly identified as Epona the gem would certainly be the earliest example of the mounted Celtic goddess known, as there is little evidence for other Eponas before the first century AD.

Wilhelm Schleiermacher believed that the mounted Epona type derived from figures like that found painted at Pompeii at Regio IX, Ins. 2, nr. 24. The scene shows a goddess riding a donkey which is moving toward the left. She is seated side-saddle and carries a child. The painting is set in a niche in the wall. On the outer wall and facing inward are a pair of figures with paterae and cornucopiae. Below, at the base of the wall, is a snake.[417] The building itself appears to have had ramps for carts and animals which makes it probable that the owners would have especially venerated a goddess like Epona who protected animals.[418] Salomon Reinach, however, thought that the figure might be Isis with the child Horus.[419]

Whoever the goddess may be, the significance of the painting lies in its being an early Imperial representation of a woman riding side-saddle on an equine animal, and also in the possibility it opens up that figures of matronly deities on equines were not so uncommon in the everyday surroundings of the stable or the transport business.

Even if the Pompeiian goddess cannot be identified as Epona with certainty, Wilhelm Schleiermacher argued for a compositional connection between this lady and Epona, although in which direction the influence may have gone is not clear. There is good evidence for trade between Campania and Gaul in Samian ware which might have provided the opportunity either for a Roman compositional type to go west or a Celtic goddess to move east.[420] The mention by Apuleius's Lucius of a shrine to Epona in Thessaly demonstrates that the goddess certainly travelled outside of her Celtic homeland during the Roman period.[421]

But if the Pompeiian mounted goddess is really a prototype for the Celtic goddess (or shares one with her), hers is not the only image borrowed and adapted for the Epona figures. The Pompeiian painted goddess sits upright on her mount holding a child. Although the upright position is the most common posture for the mounted Epona, some Eponas lean toward the necks of their horses in a most pronounced way. It may not be impossible, but it seems very unlikely, that some variant of the mounted mother and child group could have had the mother reclining against the body of her horse, like the Epona from Allerey (Figure 52),[422] and still managing to hold her child securely. For the Allerey Epona is stretched almost full-length along the back of her horse. One hand touches the horse's head while the other, now broken, probably held a patera. She is nearly nude with drapery covering her hips. This figure is very far from the mother and child. She is believed by some to represent Epona carved in a nymph-like form to emphasize her connection with sacred water.[423]

The Reclining Side-Saddle Epona

Several other Eponas show a similar, if less pronounced, tendency to recline. A bronze statuette from Bâgé-la Ville (Ain) is a fully clad Epona leaning to the right along the neck of her horse. She holds the animal with her left hand and has a patera in her right.[424] The relief of Epona from Gannat (Allier) shows the goddess leaning slightly rightward with her head turned in profile to the right. She is haloed by a large scarf which billows out behind her. Like several other Eponas she carries a key as an attribute.[425]

These compositions show that some artists were adapting models that were quite different from the type associated with with the Pompeii painting. There is no evidence at present for an earlier side-saddle rider mounted on a horse in this reclining posture, but there are many examples of deities riding other animals which come very close to the compositional type.

There are four deities and mythological figures who regularly ride animals side-saddle and sometimes lean or recline on their mounts. All four of them have a long history in the Greek world and are often found as elements in Roman decoration or as objects of worship. The four are Dionysus who rides a tiger or a panther, Cybele on her lion, Europa mounted on a bull and the marine figures, mainly Nereids, who ride any number of fantasy sea creatures including hippocamps. If we look more closely at these four figures, we can see that they are all, to a greater or lesser extent, possible prototypes for the mounted Epona. And since several sit upright in addition to leaning, some are perhaps even stronger contenders than the Pompeiian goddess for the role of prototype for the commonest Epona.

Dionysus

The image of Dionysus on the panther has all the compositional elements of the leaning Epona. The theme of Dionysus on a great cat was particularly popular in mosaic and three examples will suffice to demonstrate the long history of the type. A mosaic from Pella depicts Dionysus nude and reclining on his panther which is moving to the

left.[426] He hold the animal around the neck like the Epona from Bâge-la-Ville. Another mosaic, a late Hellenistic example from the House of Masks on Delos, shows the god dressed in a long garment which reaches his feet. He is travelling right and raises both arms, holding a thyrsus and a tympanum. His panther turns its head to look back at the god.[427]

The importance of these two Greek mosaics in our context lies in the fact that a very similar mosaic was found in Roman London (Plate 3). Indeed, this one appears to be a conflation of the two variations just described. On it Dionysus is again nude and riding toward the left. He is very similar to the god on the Pella mosaic. However, his mount, a tiger, stands in an almost identical position to the panther from Delos.[428] There is no question of direct copying but rather the repetition of a popular motif associated with an important cult over a long period of time and distributed across a very large geographical area.

Cybele

The same may be the case with representations of the mounted Cybele. The figure of the goddess riding, and not simply accompanied by her lions, may go back to the fourth century BC. Pliny writes that Nicomachus the son and pupil of Aristides painted a Mother of the Gods seated on a lion.[429] The type was popular in the Hellenistic period particularly in Asia Minor.

In Rome one of the most important and famous figures of Cybele as lion-rider was that on the barrier in the Circus Maximus. This statue is not preserved but appears in representations of the Circus like that on the mosaic floor in the Piazza Amerina in Sicily.[430] The date of the raising of the statue is uncertain but it may have been put in place during the reign of Trajan.[431] Although, clearly, if this particular statue was erected by Trajan, it is too late to have been an original model for the Epona figures. But it could have influenced later craftsmen and patrons.

The lion-riding Cybele was already well-known in Rome and the provinces in pre-Trajanic times. It would undoubtedly have been one of the forms of icon familiar to worshippers as the Asiatic cult spread through the Empire after its introduction into Rome at the end of the third century BC.[432] A clay figurine, for example, found in a grave in Cologne and dated to the end of the first century or the beginning of the second shows the goddess seated on her lion travelling to the left (Figure 53).[433] She wears a high headdress and veil. The similarity between this figure and terracottas of Epona, particularly those whose heads are veiled or who wear high headdresses or hairstyles is evident.[434]

Europa

Europa too meets the requirements of a compositional prototype for Epona. In some ways she fulfils them better than the other candidates. She can sit upright on her mount, as on a bronze appliqué from Aquileia dated to the Imperial period,[435] or she can lean along its back as she does on a gem in The Hague (Figure 54).[436] This red cornelian of the first century AD shows Europa and the bull facing left. Europa stretches out on the bull's back in a pose reminiscent of the Epona of Allerey. Other Europas lean slightly toward their mounts as, for example, the Europa on the wall painting from Pompeii now in the Naples Museum (Figure 55).[437] Moreover, like Epona, but unlike Cybele, Europa can be represented either fully dressed,[438] draped around the hips as she is at Pompeii or, occasionally, completely naked,[439] or virtually so, as on the mosaic from Lullingstone Villa in Kent from the mid-fourth century AD.[440]

The iconographical type of Europa on the bull goes back even further than the lion-riding Cybele. Compositions with Europa mounted on the bull are known from Greece of the Archaic period. The relief from the Sicyonian Treasury at Delphi, which preserves only the lower half of the group, shows the heroine seated on the back of the bull with her knees turned rightward toward the animal's head.[441] She appears fully dressed just as she is in later fifth century representations.[442] By the fourth century BC, images of a nude Europa are known, like a relief lekythos from Athens in the British Museum where the heroine hangs on to the bull with her right arm while she lies diagonally across his body. Her only garment is her billowing scarf.[443]

That Europa might have been the model for Epona in some instances is suggested by Micheline Rouvier-Jeanlin's observation that terracotta figurines of Epona were moulded in sections, and in certain works, by inadvertence or inattention, the goddess has been put on a bull rather than a horse before firing.[444] A similar confusion may be the cause of the curious handling of the head of the horse on the Epona from Gilly-les Vougeot (Côte-d'Or) which appears more bovine than equine.[445] Moreover, these confusions suggest that both Europas and Eponas were being made at the same time and in the same workshops and, thus, we have the obvious opportunity for influence of one upon the other.

One final characteristic that the mounted Epona often shares with Europa is the scarf or mantle billowing around her head. It appeared on the Greek lekythos with the nude Europa mentioned above. It can be seen in the hands of a semi-nude Europa on a Roman decorated glass goblet now in the Musée Guimet.[446] On this, Europa holds her arms up to grasp the end of the scarf as it billows over her head. Epona, on a fine bronze from Loisia (Jura), holds her arms up in the same way.[447] Although she probably held a patera in her outstretched right hand, her posture and, indeed, her semi-nudity could easily have been adapted from a group of Europa and the bull.

Billowing scarves frame the heads of many Eponas, although this is incongruous where her horse appears to be standing still as at Brazey-en-Plaine (Côte-d'Or)[448] (unless we imagine a stiff breeze blowing). Interestingly, the scarf is found on the same central Gaulish reliefs that show a foal following the horse and rider.[449] Cybele, by comparison, does not appear to have been represented holding a billowing scarf. The reliefs of the goddess on her lion which are common on oil lamps,[450] for example, do not show the goddess framed by billowing fabric, so is it unlikely that the

lion-riding Cybele served as a model for this form of central Gaulish Epona.

Nereids

It is unfortunate for our attempt to discover the antecedents of Epona that the billowing scarf is not limited to Europa. Among figures who ride side-saddle, it is also common to Nereids mounted on sea creatures (Figure 56). No doubt its function is to represent in pictorial form the rush of wind created by the swift motion of the animal mount. Sea nymphs, like the other divine figures we have discussed, have a considerable history. The Nereid rider originated during the Classical period in Greece. She appeared initially in the first half of the fifth century BC in representations of the myth, inspired by Homer, describing the delivery of arms to Achilles.[451]

Nereids were often represented as part of a marine *thiasos,* a procession of sea creatures, humans and semi-humans which was particularly favoured as a decorative motif on mosaic pavings. A series of very fine black-and-white mosaic floors have been found at Ostia including many scenes of marine *thiasos.* In these, Nereids ride fantastic sea creatures like the sea cow, for example, ridden by the nymph in the Domus di Apuleio, room F at Ostia who leans against her mount, her right arm around his neck and her left arm clutching her drapery (Figure 57).[452] These black-and-white mosaic compositions began in the second century AD and remained popular until the second half of the third century. They were, therefore, contemporary with many mounted Eponas.[453]

That the rider in the sea was a popular motif before the advent of the mosaic *thiasos* can be seen from the number of gems engraved with this theme. The Kunsthistorisches Museum in Vienna has eight such gems, all dated to the first century BC. One, a cornelian, has a Nereid riding a hippocamp (Figure 56). The lady and her mount face left. Her scarf, held in her two hands, is billowing out behind her as she rides.[454] In Munich on a red jasper, a second century nymph rides a dolphin.[455] And on another cornelian from the third century, a Nereid rides a sea cow and carries a shield, obviously a reference to the story of the delivery of Achilles's weapons.[456]

We have already noted the suggestion that the Epona from Allerey represents the goddess in the guise of a water nymph, deity of a sacred spring. If this is correct, it is possible that, because of the association of ideas, the artist who produced this unusual Epona might have taken a figure like the Nereid on a hippocamp as his model. However, since sea goddesses as a rule do not wear long gowns and veils as so many Eponas do, it is unlikely that the basic Epona type was based on the mounted Nereid.

Other Side-Saddle Riders

For the sake of completeness we may mention one or two other figures who ride a beast side-saddle. One of these is Artemis who appears thus on a stag on a very fine silver dish in Berlin.[457] Another is the Maenad who is sometimes shown riding side-saddle.[458] Both of these seem to be uncommon compared to the four discussed in detail above, so probably can be discounted.

The discussion does show, however, that all the various elements which make up the mounted Epona do not point to any single model which can satisfactorily be traced. For it is also clear that the compositional type: human figure mounted side-saddle on a large animal, was an artistic commonplace dating back many centuries which had been transformed on numerous occasions before. Epona, then, becomes another of a long series of adaptations of this theme. The variations in her attributes, which seem to have a geographical root, may have been connected with different conceptions of the goddess within the distinct tribal areas. But, since all four of the possible models were still being reproduced regularly during the second and third centuries AD when most of the Eponas seem to have been made, the differences in formal composition, as opposed to iconography — the straight or reclining figure, the state of dress or fluttering scarf, are more likely to indicate different artistic models than cultual variations.

Epona Riding Astride

In 1953, Émile Thevenot and René Magnen listed 133 Eponas mounted side-saddle and only seventeen seated astride. Today, although more Eponas are known, the large discrepancy between the two categories of figures still exists. Furthermore, sixteen of the Eponas riding astride came from sites in ancient Belgica and Germania while only one, a fragment of a torso of a nude woman on a horse, was found in central Gaul. It was discovered at the edge of a brook at Saulon-la-Chapelle (Côte d'Or) and identified by Thevenot as Epona.[459] This identification would seem reasonable except for two difficulties: this Epona is unique in her total nudity, and Eponas riding astride (and fully clothed) cluster around the river Moselle, particularly around Trier and Metz. Here both manners of riding were represented as the remains from La Horgne-au-Sablon cemetery at Metz testify.

The stelae from this cemetery are often very worn but seem mainly to have had rounded tops with a border running around the entire monument. Espérandieu's catalogue number 4354 shows a side-saddle Epona on a well-proportioned horse,[460] while 4350 and 4351 (Figure 58), although very worn, are also representations of finely proportioned horses and riders.[461] On these latter, however, the horse is galloping and not walking and the rider is sitting astride. The stylistic similarity and high quality of these works suggest, if not the same sculptor, then the same workshop, probably an urban one, for most of the reliefs from La Horgne-au-Sablon, certainly E4350, 4351, 4352 and 4354.[462] The representation of a galloping horse in 4350 and 4351 puts these reliefs in the mainstream of horseman imagery and it seems likely that they were inspired by male riders although the usual posture of the horseman with right hand raised to throw his spear has been avoided.

That some of the artists at Metz based their reliefs of Epona on masculine groups seems particularly likely if we look at the stele E4356 also from the cemetery at La Horgne.[463] Unlike the others, this one is not apsidal in shape but has a pedimental top. The scene, set deeply in the niche, shows a female rider, probably side-saddle and probably Epona, but its poor preservation makes this uncertain, followed by an attendant. The follower also seems to be female if the broad and long garment she wears is an indication of gender. The servant and rider group appears to be unique for Epona but is, of course, common for human and divine males where the servant, sometimes as spear carrier, attends the hunting or fighting horseman.

E4352 shows a rider, probably female, astride a standing, right-facing horse. The relief is worn but the figure's right hand seems to be holding the rein. A similar relief, better preserved but of poorer quality, comes from Conteren (Luxembourg).[464] In this representation, Epona is on a left-facing horse and it is her left hand which holds the rein. Her right hand, incised on the background of the relief, is made into a fist which may indicate she was carrying something added later in paint.

A relief from Medingen (Luxembourg), also very fine, shows Epona astride with a small animal, perhaps a dog, on her lap.[465] There is no uncertainty about the identification here and it is probably reasonable to conclude that the craftsmen of the Moselle region created this form of Epona by adapting masculine rider compositions.

Epona Standing

Another rare form of Epona is that on the altar from Jabreilles (Haute Vienne).[466] This is a large relief (0.66 m. x 0.71 m.) on which Epona is standing in front of her horse and holding the bridle. She appears to hold a cornucopia in her other hand. Her posture is strongly reminiscent of the very common depiction of the Dioscuri standing in front of their horses, one of the compositions to be examined in Chapter Five.[467]

René Magnen lists five examples of Epona standing in front of her horse[468] to which can be added Miranda Green's example from South Collingham[469] and a recent find from Poitiers (Figure 59). This latter is a statuette, 30 cm. tall, in stone. Epona is standing frontally. She holds a patera in her right hand and a box-like object, perhaps a fragment of something larger, in her left. The horse is behind her in profile facing right. The horse's head and front legs are missing. The excavations revealed material that was probably laid down in the first three Christian centuries. The figure of Epona, unfortunately, does not seem to have been discovered in a dated context.[470]

Among René Magnen's examples of Epona standing in front of her horse, the figure from Néris in the Allier is unusual owing to the addition of a male child upon whom the horse leans its left front leg (Figure 60). Magnen considered him to be the personification of a spring.[471] The goddess herself is not standing frontally but turns toward the right, and one leg, now broken, is raised off the ground giving her the appearance of running.[472] Although several other monuments — a relief and a terracotta[473] — representing Epona have been found at Néris, which suggests she was well established there, it may be that the standing goddess does not represent Epona at all. A relief in the museum at Clermont[474] represents a woman accompanied by a child and standing in front of a horse. Although of somewhat uncertain origin according to Émile Espérandieu, this relief has been identified as Selene with Phosphorus (Figure 61).

The latter is represented as a small boy. The goddess stands in front of her rearing horse and grasps its bridle. Her head is framed by a billowing scarf and she carries a torch. The child, who has wings, stands beside her and looks back at her while leaning on his own torch. The child in the Néris statue group also looks back at the goddess, but the lady's arms and head are missing so that any clues to her identity in the attributes she might have carried have been lost. Nevertheless, the Selene and Phosphorus group remind us that not all goddesses accompanied by a horse in Gaul are necessarily Epona. In the case of Néris, the identification cannot be absolutely certain.

Reichstypus: Seated or Standing Epona and Horses

One class of Eponas which differs considerably from those above belongs to Schleiermacher's *Reichstypus*, so-called because these artefacts occur in Italy and in other areas of the Empire beyond central Gaul: North Africa, the lower Danube and on the upper German *limes* and in Belgica.[475] One example is also found in Britain but its exact provenance is uncertain.[476] In all, the composition is symmetrical. The goddess sits or stands between a pair of horses. A statue found in Rome shows the type (Figure 62).[477] The goddess is seated on a throne. The head of the statue is missing but the body is well preserved. Epona holds her hands out to caress two horses who are only tall enough to reach her lap. A second statue is also known in Rome.[478] The evidence of inscriptions reveals that Epona had devotees among the *equites singulares* recruited from the Rhine and Danube regions who were stationed in Rome.[479]

An altar found at Naix-aux-Forges (Meuse) shows the Imperial Epona standing rather than sitting.[480] A small horse stands on each side of her, one facing towards her gown, the skirts of which she seems to have gathered into a pouch to hold food (or it may be a basket that she holds). The other horse looks up toward her now missing head. On the side of the altar is an inscription[481] dedicated to Epona and the genius of the Leuci by a *beneficiarius* of the Twenty-Second Legion. Its date is AD 210-211. The altar shows two characteristics associated with the Imperial Epona: the balanced composition and the addition of an inscription. While it must be admitted that only a few Imperial Eponas are provided with an inscription, only a single example is known associated with a mounted Epona. Wilhelm Schleiermacher thought the reason was that the Imperial type had been the creation of soldiers and officials, groups of people likely to have been in the habit of augmenting their dedications with inscriptions; whereas many of the mounted Epona figures were found in the countryside where the local people, perhaps illiterate, would not have felt such an addition necessary.[482] The fact that so many inscribed dedications were made by military men supports this explanation.

Like the prototype of the mounted Epona, the compositional prototype for an Epona with a horse on each side is not difficult to find within Graeco-Roman art. The archetypal seated goddess accompanied by animals is Cybele, the Great Mother. The earliest known example of the goddess seated between two animals was found at Çatel Hüyük in Anatolia and has been dated to around 6000 BC.[483] This is the Great Mother's home territory and her history there appears to be impressively long.

In addition, the goddess flanked by animals is a well-known motif from the Bronze Age in Crete and the Near East and appeared also in Archaic Greece as, for example, at Sparta among the finds from the temple of Artemis Orthia.[484] But it is the adaptation of this theme in the Classical period which is most likely to be the true prototype of the Roman goddess enthroned between animals. A statue of Cybele was made in Athens around 430 BC. Later visitors described it as representing the goddess enthroned with a tambourine in her hand and with her lions beside her throne.[485] Although the original statue has never been found, the Athenian Agora has yielded many representations of this type.[486] Therefore, it seems reasonable to think that the very numerous figures of Cybele enthroned, found wherever the cult spread, reproduce this statue.

The other important goddess early represented seated in the Graeco-Roman world was Demeter, a mother goddess with many similarities to Cybele. The figure of Demeter perhaps best known to us is the one from the sanctuary of Demeter and Kore on the island of Cnidos. It was made around 330 BC.[487] The goddess is seated frontally. No identifying attributes have been preserved. However, although she bears a strong resemblance to Cybele, it is unlikely that representations of Demeter were instrumental in the development of the enthroned Epona figure. Demeter did not have the popularity in the Roman provinces that Cybele had.

Other goddesses were sometimes represented seated. Particularly in the form of small terracottas, personifications like Victory and Abundance seem to have been very popular. The same is true of small figures of the seated Athena.[488] Statues of seated goddesses holding cornucopiae identified as the personification Abundantia have been found in Gaul[489] although some of these may be Celtic mother goddesses wrongly identified. For these deities too are often shown seated according to the convention which prefers to seat 'mature' goddesses. Among the Oriental deities, Isis as well as Cybele was often seated.[490] But Cybele had animals flanking her throne.[491]

The evidence for the presence of Cybele and her cult in the western provinces, with the exception of Britain,[492] is abundant. Maarten Vermaseren observes that: "It may be safely said that wherever the Celts were under the Roman rule they adopted the Cybele worship. In early times it was…largely due to the Greeks and only at a later date to the Romans themselves for whom Cybele was a national goddess."[493]

It may be significant that at Pesch a relief of Cybele was found in the temple of the Matronae Vacalinehae. It has been suggested by Elmar Schwertheim that in Germania Inferior, Cybele's role as divine protector rather than as leader of an orgiastic cult was dominant and she was associated with the local mother goddesses and worshipped along side them.[494] Schwertheim, however, detects no evidence for a fusion of the two cults.[495]

The monuments of the Great Mother in Germany have been collected by Elmar Schwertheim. The cult, he believes, was brought by Oriental soldiers originally, but it quickly spread to the Celto-Germanic people.[496] Interestingly, the only temple to Cybele to be preserved in Germany is on the site of the Roman fort at the Saalburg. The Metroön is a small building of which only the foundations remain. It lies outside the fort just beyond the civilian settlement. It is also very close to a Mithraeum.[497] The Metroön was built in the middle of the second century by a centurion of the Twenty-Second Legion stationed at Mainz.[498] Half a century later, members of this legion were making dedications to Epona.[499] That Cybele like Epona has followers along the frontier is further confirmed by the discovery of four inscriptions to the Great Mother from Mainz-Kastell near Wiesbaden.[500] A relief of the mounted Epona was also found there.

The overlap between Epona and the Great Mother may have no significance in cult terms. There is no evidence that the two were worshipped together although they are both linked by a similarity of functions to the Celtic cult of the Mothers. However, with respect to the question of prototype for the seated Epona, the proximity of Cybele as a model may be relevant. It is possible that the *Reichstypus* was first developed in Rome because, as we have seen, the Roman Epona is a seated figure flanked by her horses. But the popularity of Cybele on the German frontier and the familiarity of Gaulish and Germanic soldiers with her cult, make it just as likely that the new type originated from the *limes* itself or the major cities nearby like Mainz or Trier.

Just how close the figure of Epona can be to Cybele may be seen in the little bronze Epona in the British Museum (Plate 4).[501] Epona is in a seated position although there is no chair or throne beneath her. She is flanked by two very small horses, a male and female. Each has ears of corn in its mouth. On the patera which she holds in her right hand, and also on her lap, are more ears of corn. On her left arm she holds an object which has been identified by Catherine Johns as a yoke.[502] The curved base of the statuette and the rivet holes where the seat should be suggest that this figure was a decorative fitting on a cart or chariot.[503]

The seated position of the goddess is obviously reminiscent of Cybele. Even the fact that her hair is allowed to fall in two tresses on her shoulders[504] seems to be an echo of the Great Mother since the hair on most figures of Epona is dressed differently. But the most striking similarity is in the two animals flanking the goddess. Although the small size of Epona's horses has been considered a puzzling feature,[505] the diminutive stature of the horses would be explained if the artist were using the enthroned Cybele flanked by her lions as the model for the seated Epona. The lions which accompany Cybele are normally much smaller in relation to her size than they would be if we could imagine such a tableau in real life. This is probably not such much because they are mortal and, therefore, must be smaller than the deity, as has been suggested,[506] but because they serve as attributes for the identification of the goddess. Cybele has a number of special attributes such as the tympanum or the high polos or mural crown. But several of these she shares with other deities. Only the lions are special to the enthroned Cybele and it makes no difference how large they

are. A small statue in Rome shows the enthroned goddess flanked by seated lions whose heads reach her knees.[507] A series of relief terracottas show the Great Mother seated on a ship with her lions facing toward her (Figure 63). Each lion stands on a small pedestal and, relative to the goddess, is the size of a miniature lapdog.[508] Sometimes, as on a relief from Constanţa-*Tomis* showing Cybele in association with the Thracian Rider (Figure 80), her lions, presented frontally and reaching only to her knees, appear like nothing more than elegantly carved armrests for her throne.[509] It is their presence itself that is significant.

Artistic considerations would also suggest that the composition is more compact and focuses more directly on the goddess, if large and powerful animals are reduced in size. A relief of Epona from Köngen, whose talented sculptor seems to have preferred as literal a representation as possible, includes two very large horses facing away from the goddess (Figure 64).[510] They are placed behind the seated figure and they stand one behind the other, one facing left, the other right. The goddess is no longer the highest point or the main focus in a triangular composition. The horses, because they are so large, are unable to eat out of Epona's lap or be caressed by her and there is no contact between the animals and the deity. They turn away from her, presumably, so that the artist can fit the two horses into as small a space as possible. For if the horses were to turn facing the goddess, one on each side of her, the relief would have to be widened by the length of an equine body on each side. We may wonder why the horses are not shown frontally as they are on the standing Epona from Naix-aux-Forges[511] since the creator of the Köngen relief was a sculptor of some skill.

A number of reliefs of the seated Epona show the horses facing her. In most cases the horses are small enough to allow them to eat out of her lap. This type seems to be the most widely dispersed. Examples are known from Rome, a statue;[512] from Aptaat in Bulgaria, a relief[513] and from Algeria at the ancient *Portus Magnus*, another relief.[514] On a relief from Worms, two small horses are both facing right and the one on the far right turns his head around to eat from Epona's lap on which a basket of fruit is resting.[515]

A large and complex relief from Beihingen enlarges on the theme by multiplying the number of horses: three on the left and four on the right. These fill the upper register of the relief while below is a scene which involves a vehicle drawn by three horses on the left side and the sacrifice of a pig on the right.[516] This latter brings to mind the inscribed bronze relief from Alise-Ste. Reine dedicated to Epona.[517] It shows a man driving a cart which is pulled by a mare. The significance of these two representations is not obvious, but the Beihingen example may show some activities of Epona's cult. The organization of the relief with the cult figure in the top register and cult scenes below is similar to the organization of the Dacian Rider plaques but on a larger scale (0.60 m. high x 1 m. wide). The Alise-Ste. Reine bronze may also show a cult scene or it may be simply a votive offering from a cart owner or driver.

The most uncommon of the 'Imperial' representations of Epona is the standing goddess flanked by her animals. The same is true of representations of Cybele. A standing Cybele between her lions does not seem to have been popular as a votive offering or personal icon and is therefore rare. So if we assume that, as it appears from the discussion above, models for Epona were adapted generally from the commonest iconographical types, a relationship between standing figures of Cybele and Epona is unlikely.

But many other female deities contemporary with Epona were represented standing frontally. This is the case for many of the Celtic goddesses who stand paired with a male deity: Nantosuelta,[518] for example, or Rosmerta.[519] The same is true for more exotic deities like the consort of Jupiter Dolichenus.[520] So it may be that the standing Epona was adapted from a goddess who was not normally associated with a pair of animals. The Epona from Seegraben, for instance, stands frontally surrounded by five horses.[521] One of them is placed directly in front of her. Another is behind her while the rest, in this badly worn relief, seem to float about her head. This composition owes nothing to the balanced Classical Cybele.

A few of the Eponas mounted side-saddle may reflect the influence from the 'Imperial' group in the addition of horses on each side of the goddess and her mount. A mounted Epona from Bregenz in Austria shows the goddess seated on her mare going toward the right.[522] She holds a patera or a dish in her right hand from which a small horse, a foal perhaps, is feeding. Behind the foal is another larger horse facing left. In front of Epona's mare are two more horses facing left who lift their heads to Epona's mount.

The mould for a similar relief was recently found in southern France at Lectoure-*Lactora*.[523] The mounted goddess, in the same pose as the Bregenz relief, has now only one horse on the left, facing left and eating from her patera, while a second horse walks to the right slightly in front of Epona's mount. Coins and pottery found on the site suggest a date range from the late first century to some time in the second.[524]

All the evidence available affirms that the cult relief and votive image of Epona and all its forms belong to the first few Christian centuries. The earliest examples may come from the end of the first century and this corresponds with the date of the earliest inscriptions.[525] But the majority that can be dated come from the second and third centuries.[526] Although only a fraction of the hundreds of Epona figures are datable, the dates correspond to the period during which small portable cult reliefs flourished in many parts of the Roman Empire and it may have been under the impetus of the increasing popularity of this kind of offering and imagery that pressure grew for a hitherto aniconic Epona to take on a Roman pictorial form. The form which Epona took when she appeared depended not on the development of a new artistic vocabulary but on the adaptation of a very old one.

Chapter 5

The Dioscuri

The Dioscuri or Castores were the only mounted gods in the western Roman Empire whose rider imagery can be traced back beyond the Hellenistic period. This fact introduces a new problem to consider in trying to understand the relationship between Graeco-Roman deities and gods of adjacent cultures. Unlike Mars and Jupiter, the identification or conflation of the mounted Graeco-Roman twins with mounted Celtic gods would not have necessitated any drastic adjustment to standard Roman iconographical forms. For this reason, again in contrast to Jupiter and Mars, identification of any given monument as representing a 'Celtic' rather than 'Roman' Dioscurus becomes extremely problematical. There is often no discernible difference, except perhaps in archaeological context, to help us to place the image in its correct cultural niche.

The Nature of the Dioscuri

The Dioscuri were young adventurers closely associated with horses. They were worshipped in the Roman Empire particularly in their Roman character as the Castores whose exploits as heroic riders were part of Roman historical myth. The Greeks knew the Dioscuri as the youths of Zeus, the *Dios Kouroi*, the god's sons by Leda wife of Tyndareos.[527] Homer called them "Castor, breaker of horses" and "the strong boxer Polydeukes".[528]

In some stories they were born from an egg, the result of Zeus's meeting with their mother when the god took the form of a swan. Their sister Helen was born at the same time, as was their other sibling Clytemnestra. Among the four, Polydeukes and Helen were immortal and Castor and Clytemnestra were mortal. Clytemnestra became the wife of Agamemnon and Helen married Menelaos.[529] But Helen also had a considerably longer history as a goddess and she was often worshipped together with her brothers, represented in art as a group of three with the goddess in the centre.

The twins were associated with death owing to the mortality of one of them. The desire of the brothers never to be separated was tested when the moral Castor fell in battle. The resulting compromise, in which both brothers spend one day in the upper world and the next in the lower one, had an important influence on the metaphysical speculations of the Hellenistic and Roman periods. And we shall see, in this connection, that the Dioscuri are often represented on sarcophagi.

But the brothers were most often seen as saviours both in military situations — coming to the aid of armies in battle — and as rescuers of individuals in distress particularly at sea.[530] They were, therefore, attractive to young men as youthful and heroic riders, perhaps to be emulated, and to other elements in society as *soteres*, saviour gods to be called upon in times of need. Moreover, they were probably seen as more approachable than some of their seniors.

The legend that grew up in Rome of their appearance at the battle of Lake Regillus in 496 BC gives an example of the type of behaviour attributed to them. The dictator A. Postumius Albus, so Livy tells, vowed a temple to Castor if the Romans won the battle.[531] R. M. Ogilvie suggests that, in fact, this was in the nature of an *exortatio*, an attempt to turn a deity who was patron of the enemy over to the petitioner. In the case of the Dioscuri, the brothers seem to have heeded the call and came to the aid of the Romans in the form of two youthful horsemen. The temple was dedicated in 484 BC and the cult of the Dioscuri was established in Rome. The twins remained patrons of cavalry.[532]

The Development of the Dioscuri Image

Among the earliest surviving statues of a pair of brothers are two figures found at Delphi and generally known as Cleobis and Biton, remembered for their extraordinary devotion to their mother, a priestess of Hera. Their act of filial piety in yoking themselves to their mother's cart in order to give her the means to visit the temple of Hera at Argos won for them the goddess's greatest gift; they were allowed to die in their sleep. However, in the opinion of Paul Faure, this identification is incorrect, the result of an erroneous restoration of the accompanying inscription.[533] These well-known figures, a pair of early *kouroi*, dated about 580 BC, according to Faure, are actually the Dioscuri and not Cleobis and Biton. The statues represent the brothers standing, not mounted.[534] Like so many of these early male figures, there are no attributes or symbols evident and only the inscription reveals their identity.

It has also been suggested that the archaic horseman from the Acropolis whose body fits the 'Rampin Head' in the Louvre may be an early example of a mounted Dioscurus. The fragments suggest that there was a pair of these horsemen and Antoine Hermary believes that they may have been part of an attempt by Pisistratus to associate his sons Hippias and Hipparchus with the Dioscuri.[535] John Boardman, however, is doubtful: if they do date from the suggested 550 BC, they may be slightly too early for the return of the tyrant. Moreover, it is questionable whether the statues would have survived the fall of Pisistratus if they were so closely associated with the family.[536] This does not, however, mean that the statues could not represent the Dioscuri, but devoid of that particular political connection. Indeed, it is difficult to imagine whom they represent if it is not Zeus's sons. But whether the mounted pair are the Dioscuri or not, they are proof that monumental rider statues were created during the sixth century BC in Greece.

No cult statues of the Dioscuri are known from the Classical period.[537] A stamnos in Oxford by Polygnotos, dated 450-440 BC, shows the Classical conception of the twins. Their names are written on the vase so the identification is certain.

The brothers are dressed alike. Each wears only a chlamys which covers his body. Both wear boots and each has a petasos, a broad-brimmed hat, hanging at his back secured by white strings around his neck. Both carry spears.[538] They are riding over the sea which is indicated by the dolphins and curved lines playing around their horses' hooves. The significance of the sea-ride lies in the role played by the Dioscuri as saviours of sailors and those in difficulty at sea.[539]

Artists of the Classical period represented the brothers both mounted and on foot. According to Antoine Hermary, about forty percent of the depictions show the Dioscuri mounted and sixty percent show them on foot. They wear a chlamys in three-fifths of representations but a chiton in only one-fifth. In half the representations both hold spears.[540] All these elements are still found in Imperial imagery. The only change was the replacement, beginning in the last centuries BC, of the petasos by the pilos, the round or bullet-shaped, brimless hat which then became the characteristic headgear of the Dioscuri.

This substitution of one type of headgear by another was possibly the result of the identification of the Dioscuri with other pairs of gods such as the Great Gods of Samothrace or the Cabiri.[541] The representations, now largely disappeared, of these latter gods are considered by some scholars to have influenced the choice of attributes which were acquired by the Dioscuri during the Hellenistic period.[542] During the Hellenistic period also, the stars which identified the Dioscuri as astral gods came to be placed on their piloi. In time, the star and the pilos, which probably began as identifying attributes, became symbols which were used to replace the human form of the gods, particularly on coins in the eastern part of the Roman Empire.[543]

The Greek Dioscuri had a rich mythology and this was often represented in vase painting of the Classical period: the rape of the Leucippides, the Calydonian boar hunt, the expedition of the Argonauts as well as the adventures involving their sister Helen. However, none of these stories appears to have had any important influence on the representations of the Roman period; for the popularity of narrative scenes began to decline during the Hellenistic era.[544]

New formulae for representing the twins seem to have emerged during the Hellenistic period. One was the horseman, the type descended from the riders of the Classical period and related particularly to the hunting and fighting horsemen of friezes and funerary reliefs. That the Dioscuri were revered as fighters can be seen from the number of legends in which the two divine figures are described as fighting at the head of an soon-to-be-victorious army. The Roman story of their appearance at Lake Regillus is one such legend and may have been responsible for the use of the motif of the mounted brothers charging an enemy with tilted lances on Roman coins of the Republican period.[545]

The Dioscuri in Rome

The Dioscuri came early to Rome. If such twin hero-gods were an original Indo-European phenomenon, common to all Indo-European religions, cognate, for example, with the Asvins of India, the presumed Roman manifestation must have been lost altogether or evolved far enough away from the original so as not to be immediately recognizable as related (like Romulus and Remus perhaps). Thus, the Dioscuri were welcomed not as a pair to be identified with indigenous gods, but as newcomers to be adopted by Rome.[546]

The earliest inscription found in Italy relating to the Dioscuri dates from around 500 BC and comes from Lavinium on the Latian coast. This inscription mentions both brothers by name. But the archaic text, on a bronze plaque, is a mixture of Greek and Latin with an Latin enclitic *que* after the name of Pollux but an identification of the pair as 'youths' QUROIS in Greek. Despite the Greek word and names, the use of the Latin conjunction, as well as the archaic Latin characters in which it is written, indicates a Latin speaker.[547] The brothers seem to have come from the Greek settlements of Magna Graecia, perhaps by way of Lavinium, to Rome.[548] They came to Rome as rider-heros who saved the city in her time of need. But their characters were to be adapted somewhat to suit Roman tastes. In Rome the mortal Castor became the dominant brother while the immortal Pollux took second place. The pair were called by the name of the dominant brother — 'Castores'.[549] In spite of the fact that the brothers were thought of as riders who fought side by side with the cavalry, they were rarely represented on horseback. Coins of the Republican period show them riding together but this type did not become popular in larger art forms.

The temple to Castor, the fulfilment of Postumius's vow, was dedicated on the Forum in 484 BC, but no pictorial evidence remains for the shape of the sculptural monuments. The most ancient representation known seems to be a coin of 275-70 BC with the head of a male figure wearing a pilos who must be identified with Castor, the dominant brother. On later Republican coins, Pollux was restored to his brother's side and the two are seen as riders galloping with lances tilted toward an enemy on the right.[550]

Imperial coinage continued the rider motif. It was not uncommon for boys born into the reigning family to be identified with the divine twins as, for example, Nero Caesar and Drusus Caesar, sons of Germanicus and the elder Agrippina. Although they were not twins, just brothers, the two were represented on coins struck in AD 37 and 40 as young riders closely resembling the Dioscuri.[551]

On the vast majority of monuments in Rome and in the western part of the Empire, however, the rider image was rejected in favour of the standing hero and his horse.

The Standing Dioscurus

The origin of the Dioscurus standing with his mount probably lies with a major work of the Classical period.[552] The fact that the gods are not mounted suggests an origin in the period prior to the Hellenistic, before the horse and rider has become a composition of sufficient dignity to represent a god. That the Dioscuri were not more often represented mounted after the Hellenistic period was most likely the result of the force of tradition which in later times resisted fundamental changes in the manner in which the gods were depicted.[553]

Several examples may be sufficient to show that the horse and standing hero motif was well known in the Classical period. Harald von Roques de Maumont illustrates the tentative reconstruction of a monument deduced from the remains of its base (Figure 65). The base comes from Athens and held a work by the sculptor Lykios made just before the middle of the fifth century BC. The depressions in the base suggest that it held a figure of a horse and a standing man who was turned toward the animal.[554] The reconstruction takes the liberty of showing the man holding the reins of the horse.

One of the metopes of the Temple of Zeus at Olympia of approximately the same period as the statue base shows Herakles with one of the horses of Diomedes. The fragments which remain can be reconstructed as a standing figure holding the reins of a horse rearing behind him. He holds the reins in his left hand while he raises a club with his right.[555] The group does not differ significantly from the Dioscurus standing by his horse. The same can be said for the dismounted rider near his horse on the west frieze of the Parthenon.[556] Similar groups appear on Hellenistic votive and funerary reliefs (Figure 66).[557]

In Rome the popularity of the standing Dioscurus motif seems to have begun around the first century AD.[558] The brothers were often represented without their horses and leaning on their spears. This type may be connected with the Alexander of Lysippus who stood holding a vertical lance and who was also perhaps identified with one of the Dioscuri (Plate 1).[559] The variation on the standing type in which the twins are accompanied by a horse protome is most probably the creation of Roman art of the end of the first or beginning of the second century.[560]

Among the most famous of the statues of the Dioscuri still extant are the two pairs in Rome. The two brothers on the Piazza del Quirinale are probably from the second century BC. They are standing next to their rearing horses and they each raise one arm as if to grasp the reins of their agitated animals. So impressed with the pair were the Romans that later generations gave them a remarkable pedigree. A post-Constantinian inscription nearby reads *Opus Phidiae e Opus Praxitelis*.[561] The second pair, rather less dramatic and also of Hellenistic date, stand at the entrance to the Piazza del Campidoglio. The brothers wear only mantles and their characteristic piloi. Their horses stand beside them resting on three legs with the fourth, the outer foreleg, raised. Each Dioscurus turns slightly inward so that the pair are mirror images.[562]

The Dioscuri in the Western Provinces

The monuments of the Castores in the western provinces, nearly always of this standing type, can be divided into four groups:

(1) monuments on which the twins are worshipped straightforwardly as gods of Greece and Rome;

(2) monuments, particularly in Gaul and Germany, on which the Castores are commemorated or worshipped, such as altars or Jupiter columns, but which, inscriptional or iconographical evidence suggests, may actually be dedicated to local deities in the guise of the Graeco-Roman gods and therefore not always easy to tell from (1);

(3) monuments, like sarcophagi, on which the brothers appear outside a cult context and may be interpreted according to the astrological and philosophical speculations current in the Hellenistic period and the early Empire;

(4) monuments which are associated with gods of the mystery religions like Jupiter Dolichenus or Mithras and on which the Castores appear as accompanying deities whose functions and interpretation are related to the cult myth but also to speculations of type (3) which became incorporated into cult teachings.

Thus, compared with the deities we have looked at already, the artistic origins of the Dioscuri may be relatively easy to trace. But at the same time the added dimension of symbolic and mystery interpretations make the true nature of the various manifestations of these gods even more difficult to ascertain.

It is perhaps striking that the physical form which the Dioscuri-Castores take in all these different categories is the same. The representation which dominates all others during the Imperial period is of the young, generally nude, hero standing with his horse. When he is clothed, it is often in a cloak and a pilos. He may be leaning on his spear. The horse is seen in profile standing behind the god who holds the reins. Sometimes the whole horse can be seen,[563] but sometimes the artist shows only the front half.[564] The type is also not uncommon on eastern reliefs and Fernand Chapouthier illustrates a number among his triad groups.[565]

The Dioscuri among the Celts

In Celtic lands, one of the earliest known examples of the standing twins can be found on the blocks from the pillar of the *nautae* discovered in Paris. This monument dates from the reign of Tiberius.[566] One block preserves the upper halves of four figures and the name of Castor can still be read. The brothers are clean-shaven, holding spears and their horses' reins, and they are also wearing body armour. Of particular interest is the fact that on the other two faces of the block are deities who are not Roman but Celtic. Their inscribed names can be read as [C]ernunnos and Smert[..os].[567] The presence of the Dioscuri on this monument with its mixed representation of Roman and Celtic deities raises the question as to whether here the Dioscuri-Castores were worshipped as Roman deities or were identified with similar Celtic gods.

The Greek historian Timaeus is reported to have written that the Celts of the coastal regions worshipped the Dioscuri above all other gods: for according to their tradition from ancient times, the gods came to them from the ocean.[568]

Emil Krüger attempted to locate these Dioscuri-worshippers in Gallia Belgica particularly among the Ambiani[569] but not all scholars would agree with his conclusions[570] since the literary evidence is second-hand and imprecise and the archaeological evidence is capable of other interpretations. The representations of the Dioscuri which Krüger collected are mainly of the dismounted rider type which show clear Roman influence and, therefore, cannot be used alone as evidence for pre-Roman worship of the twins.[571]

The other horse and rider figures collected by Krüger, chiefly figurines and coins, cannot be identified with certainty as the Dioscuri and thus may be riders other than the divine twins. We have already looked at other Celtic gods who were mounted. The evidence, therefore, is inclusive but does not rule out a pair of Celtic twins. Among the Vedic Indians we have already mentioned the Asvins, a pair of twins strikingly similar to the Dioscuri. And speaking of the Germans, Tacitus says that they worshipped twin gods called the Alci. They were worshipped in a grove and attended by a priest dressed as a woman. There were no images.[572] So it is quite possible, as indeed some scholars believe, that twin hero-gods are part of the Indo-European heritage common to Celts as well as to Greeks and Indians and probably Germans.

Inscriptional evidence shows that under the Empire the Dioscuri were identified with Celtic deities. Both Castor and Pollux appear on inscriptions in Gaul and Germany and among the Celts of Spain. Pollux in particular was identified with the Celtic god Vintius. At Seyssel near Annecy (Haute Savoie) two inscriptions were found: *Vintio Au[g] Polluci* and *Deo Vintio Polluci*.[573] Dedications also exist to Pollux alone just as they do to Castor alone.[574] The equating of Pollux with Vintius is complicated by the fact that from Vence comes an inscription on which Vintius is identified with Mars not Pollux.[575] Emil Krüger believes that this indicates that the Dioscuri were invoked by the Celts as both the Castores (*Castoribus* at Beaucaire)[576] and the Martes (*Martibus* at Illasi near Verona in northern Italy),[577] the double Mars. The Martes are named as Divanno and Dinomogetimaros on an inscription from St. Pons in Narbonensis (*Divannoni Dinomogetimaro Martibus*).[578] The inference, then, for Krüger is that the Martes, Castores, Divanno and Dinomogetimaros are all to be identified with the Celtic Dioscuri.[579]

Not all scholars accept this equation. Paul-Marie Duval does not believe the case to be proven.[580] Nevertheless, the altar found at La Graufesenque seems to be pictorial conformation of the links between Celtic twin gods on the one hand and the Graeco-Roman Dioscuri and Mars on the other (Figure 67).[581] The altar has figures on three of its four faces. In the centre is a goddess in a long garment but with no identifying attributes. On each lateral face of the altar is a god dressed in military costume and carrying a spear. The placement of the figures strongly recalls the Dioscuric triads of the eastern Empire and also the groups often carved on the lower sections of Jupiter columns. The military dress of the male figures suggests Mars, although during the Imperial period it was not unknown for the Dioscuri too to be dressed in military attire. We have already seen this on the Parisian *nautae* monument. In general though, groups with the Dioscuri in body armour usually occur in places like Egypt

where there is little likelihood of confusion with Mars.[582] Moreover, on these Egyptian works, the identification of the god is made absolutely clear by the inclusion of symbols specific to the Dioscuri.

In the case of the Gaulish altar there are no special symbols preserved, no stars and, indeed, no horses. The pose of the two gods with the right arm raised and leaning on a spear is common to both Mars and the Dioscuri. However, the Martes of the altar are helmeted which is not usually the case with the Dioscuri. Finally the fact that the site of La Graufesenque is only 75 km. from St. Pons de Thomières were the inscription naming the Martes was found[583] is a strong indication that it is they who are represented here and that elements of the iconography of the Dioscuri have been borrowed for their representation. The relationship between the Martes and the Dioscuri is unclear. The lack of an inscription directly naming the Dioscuri as Divanno and Dinomogetimaros or, indeed, the Martes as Castor and Pollux allows some doubt about the identification.

The Dioscuri on Jupiter Columns

Standing Dioscuri have also been identified on the blocks forming the base of Jupiter columns. The group of three — a Dioscurus standing on each side of a central, usually female, figure — so common in other part of the Empire, has been used here but split into its component parts with a separately framed relief for each figure. An example from Nehweiler in Alsace consists of three separate reliefs on three sides of the block. One of the Dioscuri stands on each lateral face with a figure of Fortune on the centre front.[584] The block is certainly part of a Jupiter column.[585] A similar stone comes from Pforzheim but here the figure in the centre is Victoria rather than Fortuna.[586]

The immediate artistic predecessor of these blocks is most likely to have been the Great Mainz column erected during the reign of Nero. One of the rectangular blocks of the column base has an inscription on the front face while a Dioscurus is represented on each side face. On the back is a figure of Apollo.[587] The presence of the Dioscuri may be explained by their position as progenitors of the Domiti Ahenobarbi family, of which Nero was a descendant,[588] as well as their familial associations as sons of Jupiter and half-brothers of Apollo.

Looking at the Jupiter columns, we may ask whether here too, despite any association of the Great Mainz column with Nero, the Dioscuri on the blocks of the base, like Jupiter himself at the summit, may be Celtic deities in Graeco-Roman form.[589] The Dioscuri do not, as a rule, appear on the so-called 'four-god' stones which form part of the high pedestal base and are elements in the iconographical programme for the Jupiter columns. Only a very few, such as the stone from Dielkirchen, include them (Figure 68).[590] The Dielkirchen stone is unusual not only because one of the Dioscuri is represented but because he occupies only half the field on one side of the stone. Above him, with just its lowest quarter remaining, is a vehicle pulled by a horse. Only the wheels and the horse's legs can be made out. The three deities on the other sides: Mars, Jupiter and Victoria, fill the whole picture field on their respective sides. The figure of the Dioscurus is of the common type — nude, standing youth grasping the reins of a horse which faces right.[591] Krüger wished to associate the wagon with the Matres and particularly with Epona so that both lower and upper sections of the relief could be construed as representing horse deities.[592] However, while, as we have seen, several of Epona's monuments do include horse-drawn wagons, there is too little of the Dielkirchen vehicle to ascertain whether a satisfactory connection could be made between it and Epona.[593]

The block on the Jupiter columns which normally stands above the four-god stone most often carries images of the gods of the days of the week on it. But a small series, mainly from the area east of the Rhine and south of Speyer, carries reliefs of the Dioscuri.[594] These may well be the result of the influence from the Great Mainz column. Indeed, Gerhard Bauchhenss suggests that because of their closeness to the Great Mainz column, the columns with the Dioscuri blocks are earlier than those columns on which the gods of the days of the week are carved,[595] suggesting perhaps an early stage of development before the complete iconographical programme for the columns had been worked out. This, however, remains conjecture.

If we attempt to look for a specific relation between the representation of the horse-riding Dioscuri and the mounted Jupiter atop the column, we also draw a blank. Unfortunately, except for the stone from Benningen, none of the Dioscuri stones has been found near a Jupiter and giant group.[596] Furthermore, the Jupiter group from Benningen like the group from Weissenhof consisted of a Jupiter driving a chariot over the giant rather than riding a horse.[597] We may speculate that the lost fragment of the Dielkirchen stone should be restored as a driving Jupiter and reflects some special connection between the Dioscuri and Jupiter as charioteer.

The narrow geographical distribution of the Dioscuri motif on Jupiter columns, perhaps as a result of the fusion of the Dioscuri with a pair of very localized gods, and the curious Dielkirchen block with its unusual iconography make a further case for a Celtic interpretation of the Dioscuri existing side by side with the Roman one in the western provinces.

The Dioscuri and the Afterlife

The interpretation of images within categories (1) and (2): straightforward dedications to gods Roman or Celtic, can be linked to those of category (3): symbolic or metaphysical significance, in works like the relief on the funerary stele from S.-Julien-les-Martigues. It shows a Gallo-Roman family from the end of the Republican period. They are framed by the Dioscuri who are symmetrically placed. The brother on the right wears a shirt, perhaps of mail, and a mantle while his twin on the left wears a draped garment. Only the front half of the horse is represented.[598] The early date of this monument makes it particularly interesting. The compositional type in which the Dioscuri frame the deceased is familiar from sarcophagi, mainly of the second and third centuries AD and the symbolic meaning of the twins on the S.-Julien relief is probably similar to these. However, since

this particular work is rather early for such ideas to have come from Rome, the influence here may be Greek.[599]

Even in the earliest Greek poetry, the Dioscuri were celebrated as saviour gods. They exercised this role in regard mainly to armies but also to sailors and other seafarers. As gods who protected travellers against the hazards of the sea, it was not surprising that they also became protectors of the dead who make the journey over the sea to the next world.[600] In addition, the unique situation of the Dioscuri living one day in the Underworld and the next in the light helped them to become identified with the possibility of life after death. Thus they are, at one level, protective deities and at another, symbols of the hope for eternal life.

On the relief from S.-Julien-les-Martigues, J.-J. Hatt thinks that some kind of fusion between the Hellenistic Dioscuri as symbols of immortality and Gaulish belief in the afterlife may have been achieved.[601] For the Gauls too believed in a life beyond death. The blending is perhaps indicated by the unusual dress of the two gods framing the family group. Although what the significance of the two costumes is, we cannot tell. It may be that we have a Celtic interpretation of the Dioscuri as guardians of the dead or the two costumes may even symbolize the two worlds, earthly and heavenly, that the Dioscuri occupy alternately, an interpretation possibly owing more to Hellenistic speculation than to Celtic myth. In any case, for Hatt, this work marks the beginning of Roman provincial art in Gaul.[602] Whether we accept this synthesis or not for the end of the Republic, the blending of Graeco-Roman form with Celtic content is certainly clear in the following centuries under the Empire.

A funerary relief, already considered in relation to Mars, from La Horgne-au-Sablon near Metz, illustrates the hybrid nature of the Roman-Celtic Dioscuri and their association with the afterlife (Figure 7).[603] The Dioscuri are shown nude but with shield, spear and a helmet. They stand together, both holding the spear in the right hand and leaning on the shield on the left. Above them on a ground line of her own is a figure of Minerva drawn to a scale about half that of the twins. She too has a spear and shield. Also the stone itself is unusual in that it appears to be conical.[604] In this relief we seem to have combination of the Dioscuri with Mars. The inclusion of Minerva emphasizes the military motif. We know nothing about the Celtic twins, if these be they, but the representation of the Dioscuri in the guise of Mars on a funerary relief may be meant to emphasize their role not as psychopomps or symbols of eternal life but as guardians of the dead. The conical stele bears a, probably fortuitous, resemblance to the pilos worn by the Dioscuri.

It is a fact that the number of funerary monuments in the western Empire on which the Dioscuri appear is relatively small, which may call into question the importance of the role of the divine twins in beliefs about the afterlife in the Romano-Celtic world. Although we have just seen that some link does exist, the great sarcophagi found in significant numbers in Italy, which were often made in the Near East,[605] appear not to have been favoured or copied in Gaul or Germany to any great extent nor were their Dioscuric motifs transferred to other media. The few examples known from the western Empire come from the south of France which suggests Greek rather than Roman influence. It is difficult to see Celtic ideas in any of them although they are not necessarily easy to interpret. One from Aix shows Leda reclining while three babies surrounded by egg shells sit on the floor before her.[606] Another has a scene of the death of Hippolytus. The Dioscuri are represented and one of the brothers leans on his spear in a manner reminiscent of the twins on the stele from La Horgne.[607]

In the eastern parts of the Roman Empire the Dioscuri often appear on sarcophagi of the kind which use columns as a device for separating and framing individuals and groups along its long side. A sarcophagus related to these was found at Arles.[608] It dates from the third century AD.[609] The long side of the sarcophagus consists of four arched spaces divided by columns. Under the two centre arches are two married couples with right hands linked. Occupying the two outer spaces are the Dioscuri (Figure 69). Both twins are standing so that their bodies are frontal but their heads are turned inward toward the central scenes. They hold the reins of their horses which face outward. Only the front halves of the horses are represented. The treatment of the figures is somewhat clumsy. They are squat and poorly proportioned. The one striking feature is that the right-hand twin is bearded while the left one is not.

The Dioscuri are often represented on sarcophagi where they frame loving spouses. The fraternal love and loyalty of the brothers came to symbolize a wider love.[610] But at the same time, the love of the brothers can be seen in a cosmic context. According to Franz Cumont, the inseparable Dioscuri representing the two halves of the sky are emblems of universal harmony, while the love and fidelity of the husband and wife can be seen as the spirit which assures the perpetuation of the universe and the universal harmony.[611]

But the Dioscuri are also heroes who achieved divine life after an earthly death. Their lives were characteristic of heroes. They took part in adventurous quests with other heroes and it was upon the death of the mortal twin that they gained full apotheosis. Their history is close to that of the archetypal hero Herakles who is also often represented on funerary monuments. Like the Dioscuri, Herakles was taken to heaven at death and, according to Cumont, the appearance of these heroes on funerary monuments represents the hope of the dead that they too will obtain the same favour.[612] On the Arles sarcophagus, the two Dioscuri are distinguished by an apparent difference in age signalled by the beard of the right-hand figure. Émile Espérandieu has suggested that these represent the deceased during his life — the left hand figure, and the deceased in death on the right,[613] although why the dead man should be bearded is unclear unless the left hand figure represents his youth and the right his mature appearance at death.

The Dioscuri as representatives of the afterlife in the western empire is not nearly as common as we might expect, perhaps this role was taken by the Martes — Mars identified with Celtic twin deities. A far more common image of the divine sons of Zeus is as associates of the gods of the mystery religions who made their westward away across the Empire in the wake of soldiers and traders.

The Images of the Dioscuri in the Mystery Cults

Representations of the Dioscuri became known in the western Empire through the spread of these Oriental religions. This was particularly true of the cult of the Dolichene Jupiter where the Dioscuri-Castores appeared frequently as companions of Jupiter and his consort.

The Dolichene cult originated in the town of Doliche in ancient Commagene between the Taurus Mountains and the Euphrates River. It is most likely that Doliche's Jupiter was an ancient deity whose history stretched back to Hittite times as a storm god[614] and a god of the mountains.[615] Images of the Imperial Jupiter Dolichenus show him as a bearded god in Roman military dress standing on the back of a bull. He usually holds a lightning bolt and sometimes a double axe. His cult was extremely popular among Roman soldiers although it was not limited to soldiers as Michael Speidel's study of the army's relation to the cult has shown.[616] The earliest cult document from outside the god's home region comes from Lambaesis in Africa. It was dedicated by a commander of the legion there in AD 125/126.[617] The cult declined quickly after the destruction of its main sanctuary at Doliche by Shapur I of Persia in AD 253 or 256.[618] During its period of popularity, it spread through the Empire particularly along the military frontiers, like the Danube and Rhine, and into Britain. However, finds have also been made in areas well behind the frontier like Italy, Dalmatia and Thrace and in civilian areas in Noricum, Pannonia and Dacia.[619]

The Dolichene Castores

Along with Jupiter and his consort, known as the Dolichene Juno, two male figures appear as companions or guardians. In many of the extant pictorial representations, these are in the guise of the Graeco-Roman Dioscuri-Castores. Inscriptions refer to these figures as *Castores* alone or as *Castores Conservatores* and a number of the dedicants are themselves called either Castor or Polyduces.[620] However, it is certain that the Greek twins were not the original pair who supported the Commagenean god. For although many of the votive monuments to the god include Dioscuri of the familiar type, for example, a bronze votive tablet from Mauer an der Url,[621] some present the pair in quite a different form.

The alternate form which the Castores can take, as for example on another bronze votive plaque this time from Heddernheim,[622] is quite different from the canonical representation of the Dioscuri (Figure 70). The two figures are older, bearded and dressed in Roman cuirasses. Like Jupiter they may hold lightning bolts, but their most striking characteristic is that their bodies end at the hems of their military kilts. Below these there may be stylized rocks as at Heddernheim or two truncated pyramids as on the relief, now lost, from Iason in Moesia Superior.[623] On this latter relief the two figures clearly also wear Phrygian caps. Pierre Merlat believes this pair to be rock geniuses in origin, mountain spirits who as acolytes accompany and support the god of mountains and storms.[624]

In addition, according to Merlat, this idea of support is represented in western imagery by the Graeco-Roman Dioscuri being supported from below by a pair of giants. The fragments of an altar found at Mainz and dedicated to Dolichenus by one C. Iulius Maternus, a merchant, has such a scene carved on its side (Figure 71). On each side of the altar stands a nude Dioscurus armed with a lance and holding his horse by its reins. Below each figure is an anguipede giant who supports the ground line of the upper group with his upraised arms like an atlantid. The symbolism of this pair of reliefs goes back, in Pierre Merlat's opinion, to the originally chthonic nature of the Dolichene acolytes.[625] The giants, then, represent the earth, perhaps even the mountain, like the rocks of the Heddernheim relief which support the apode Castores, symbols also of stability.[626]

The difference between the two sets of twin figures is probably the difference between an Oriental representation and an Occidental one.[627] That is, the bearded pair without legs were the original figures as they arrived from the East. The substitution of the Greek Dioscuri represents an attempt to revise the image of the Dolichene companions to make them more comprehensible to the Occidental believer. If this is so, it means that representations of the Graeco-Roman Dioscuri ought to be later than the Oriental Castores whom they replace[628] although the conservatism of religious imagery suggests that both were probably in use at the same time.

Dolichene Monuments in Britain

Although many monuments to Jupiter Dolichenus have been found in the western Empire, particularly on the *limes*, the region which has produced some of the most interesting sculpture incorporating the Dolichene Dioscuri is Britain. The site which has been most rewarding in this respect is Corbridge, the legionary supply base south of Hadrian's Wall. The temple on the site has yielded a frieze of which slightly less than two meters still exists. Its date is third century and it shows the sun-god Sol on the left riding toward the right on a winged horse. Next to him is a Dioscurus standing at the entrance to a building (Figure 72). On the far right is a tree and another nude figure.[629] The relief was recognised as representing the Dolichene gods by I. A. Richmond and among the figures missing from the frieze, another twin has been assumed.[630] The work itself is provincial. The figure of the extant twin is interesting because it represents a variation on the normal type. As is usual for the standing Dioscuri, this young man wears a mantle, holds a spear in his right hand and the reins of his horse in his left. However, his horse has been placed beside him rather than behind him and is presented on a slightly smaller scale than he is. This disposition of the figures is not found in any other examples of the standing Dioscuri and probably reflects the sculptor's desire to fill as much of the space beneath the roof of his building as possible.

A second relief from the same site and of the same subject is on a square panel on which the partially preserved form of one of the twins stands in the usual position in front of his horse (Figure 73).[631] The execution of this group is quite different from that of the long frieze. The carving here is deep and the folds of the mantle worn by the youth are indicated by deeply cut parallel lines. The impression is

again one of a local artist but one quite different from the sculptor of the long frieze. The relief must have been paired with a second very similar group. Between these was placed a panel bearing a radiate bust of Sol which has also been preserved.[632] These panels may have been shown on the exterior of the shrine.[633]

Some Mithraic Dioscuri

Jupiter Dolichenus was not the only god to incorporate the Dioscuri into the pantheon surrounding him. Evidence that the Dioscuri sometimes appeared on Mithraic monuments comes from a relief plaque from Vienne on which the lion-headed god stands in the centre, his body encircled by a snake. At the left, on a much smaller scale, is a figure of a Dioscurus standing in front of his horse. He holds the reins in his left hand while his right is raised. He and the horse turn toward the right. So it is likely that a companion figure stood on the now missing right side.[634]

A relief of one of the Dioscuri was found in a context which suggested it might have come from the Walbrook Mithraeum in London or from a nearby temple.[635] Again, the compositional type is the familiar one.

The employment of this same composition almost without exception makes it virtually impossible to distinguish the religious situation into which the representation is meant to fit without contextual clues. Thus, for example, a Dioscurus from Leicester may be related to a mystery cult[636] or may represent a Romano-Celtic god. The repoussé decoration of a bronze cheek piece from Brough with one the twins in the usual standing pose suggests a straightforward representation of one of the Castores[637] and is reminiscent of a cheek piece from South Collingham on which Epona is shown in a very similar posture. But it is not possible to be sure which aspect of the Dioscuri the owner of the horse understood by this image.

Unusual Variant Types

A few other types of image were used to represent the Dioscuri but these occur very infrequently. Small bronze figurines are known particularly from Gaul. In one example, a youth stands holding a lance in his right hand while his left rests on his hip.[638] He is without a horse, even as a protome, but his pilos has stars attached to it to ensure correct identification as one of the twins. This must also be the identity of a small statuette of a nude male found at Wroxeter. The little figure carries nothing but he wears a Dioscuric pilos. It has been suggested that this is a Greek work, perhaps from Magna Graecia and of Hellenistic date. The ring which passes through the pilos may mean that the figure was used as a pendant, as an amulet, perhaps, passed down from previous generations to finally rest at Wroxeter.[639]

A similar but less accomplished figure was found at Canterbury in 1986. This Dioscurus carries what appears to be a torch in his upraised right hand, although it may possibly be part of a larger object. The same or similar article may once have been in the hand of the Wroxeter figure. The Canterbury Dioscurus is of somewhat lower quality than the Wroxeter twin and may possibly be later in date or manufactured in a non-Greek area of Italy.[640] The carrying of figurines, presumably as amulets, is documented by Pliny who refers to Nero as always carrying a statuette of an Amazon and Gaius Cestius being so unwilling to part with his that he carried even onto the battle field.[641] This latter certainly suggests the figurine was carried as an amulet or good luck token. The fact that the owner of the Wroxeter statuette was a soldier is therefore significant. The Canterbury Dioscurus may also have come with the Imperial Army.[642] Because of their role as saviours of armies in battle, the protection of the Dioscuri must have been actively sought by soldiers through protective devices like amulets in the form of statuettes, gems or images on armour like the cheekpiece decorated with a Dioscurus found at Brough.[643]

The fraternal bond between the twins is emphasized in another uncommon composition where each twin is shown with an arm around his brother's shoulders. A glass intaglio at Gottingen University shows the brothers in this way.[644] It may be this pose too which is represented on a block in Bonn (Figure 74). On one of the sides of the block is a figure of Juno; on another, the remains of a head. But on the third side is a strange and, unfortunately, poorly preserved group which looks like two heads emerging from a large body mass and supported by four legs. On each side of this creature is a tall staff which looks like a thyrsus.[645] Emil Krüger is sure that this is a Dioscuri group and introduces Spanish amulets of pairs of embracing twins for comparison.[646] However, the details of the Bonn relief are so difficult to make out, for example, one pair of legs seems to have very rounded calves, the other pair is extremely thin, that it is hard to know exactly what is being represented. If this group is the Dioscuri, it has no known antecedents among the major and minor monuments of the western Empire and, indeed, looks like nothing familiar.

The Dioscuri in the East

The image of the standing Dioscurus accompanied by his horse was, as we have seen, the form most commonly used in the western Empire. The East favoured a different formula: a triadic group with a pair of gods flanking a goddess, the gods sometimes mounted. This preference is probably related to the long history of this type of group in the East and the important role of the goddess, by whatever name she is identified, in the eastern parts of the Roman Empire. Only very few monument that we have looked at in the western Empire show an association of a goddess with the twin gods. Moreover, the representations of mounted Dioscuri which appear relatively often in the East are correspondingly rare in the West.

Tracing the range of the goddess and twin god representations across the eastern Empire is beyond the scope of this study, but they need to be discussed in some detail nevertheless, because of the influence of the triadic group and the mounted Dioscurus on two cults which do lie within the western part — albeit the most easterly edge — of the Roman Empire. The artists who created the imagery for the Thracian Rider cult and, more particularly, the Danubian Rider cult with its twin riders looked for inspiration to the mounted form of the Dioscuri developed during the Hellenistic period.

The Three-Figure Group

In Greece one of the favoured compositional forms for the Dioscuri from the Hellenistic period onward was the three-figure group which was studied in detail by Fernand Chapouthier. The typical three-figure group has a goddess in the centre with a Dioscurus on each side (Figure 75). Chapouthier believed the goddess to be Helen, the sister of Castor and Pollux.[647] The Dioscuri were closely associated with their sister who was worshipped at Sparta possibly from Mycenaean times.[648] Helen is perhaps to be identified with the goddess on monuments of Hellenistic date found at Sparta on which the brothers flank a female figure in the form of a *xoanon* (Figures 75, 76).[649]

Such three-figure groups were common over a long period at Sparta. They may have been related originally to the *Potnia Theron* figure, the mistress of the animals who stands with an animal or bird on each side of her or held in her outstretched hand. It is, indeed, a type familiar in Roman times, as we have seen, used for Cybele and her lions or Epona. And since this arrangement can easily be imagined developing into groups of three humans, it has also been suggested that the goddess who accompanies the Dioscuri on the Hellenistic Spartan reliefs is not Helen but the *Potnia Theron* herself, the Spartan goddess Artemis Orthia.[650] So the three may stand at the end of a long tradition. Ivories discovered during the excavations of the temple of Artemis Orthia and dated to the seventh century BC included several of the *potnia* type as well as a group of slightly more advanced style representing a man standing between two women, the same composition as the Dioscuri groups but with a reversal of gender.[651]

Fernand Chapouthier took the problem further and traced the history of the three-figure group back to Bronze Age models. He investigated connections with Asia Minor where this type of composition was also very widespread.[652] Indeed, it may have been eastern influences coming to Greece during the Orientalizing period which account for its popularity at Sparta although some continuity with Bronze Age models cannot be ruled out.

On Hellenistic and Imperial reliefs of the Dioscuri and Helen, the goddess faces front and the brothers, although frontal, lean toward her and turn their heads in her direction. The posture of the goddess shows little variation from work to work, but the brothers' pose may vary. They are sometimes mounted, sometimes standing without horses or holding the reins of horses that wait behind them. When the twins are riding, they ride toward the goddess. In some representations, the goddess is identified only by her symbol, usually a crescent moon. In these cases the brothers stand side by side or face each other on horseback.[653]

Although the three-figure composition itself appears to be very old, Fernand Chapouthier found no evidence for the distinctive Dioscuri and goddess group being older than the Hellenistic era. The earliest examples are symbolic triads found on coins like those issued probably by Berenice Syra, wife of Antiochus II Theos in the third century BC. These show piloi or stars on either side of a horn of plenty.⁶⁵⁴ However, Chapouthier did not find any evidence for the full-figured image prior to the end of the second century BC.⁶⁵⁵ The Spartan examples referred to date from the first century BC.⁶⁵⁶

According to Chapouthier, the three-figure group was a particularly Aegean motif.⁶⁵⁷ It is certainly found mainly in the eastern part of the Roman Empire. We have seen very little evidence for it in the Roman West. Moreover, the Dioscuri represented as riders are also found predominantly in the eastern part of the Empire, usually, in fact, as part of the three-figure reliefs. In his catalogue of 105 of these triadic representations, Chapouthier lists only eighteen examples of mounted twins. However, many of the entries in the catalogue are coins, gems and symbolic representations and few of these show mounted figures.

The triad groups in which the Dioscuri are mounted are mainly reliefs. When these reliefs with standing figures of the twins are counted, we find that the two groups exist in virtually equal numbers. New finds of similar mounted groups in Asia Minor have been published recently by Louis Robert who suggested that the popularity of these may derive from the fact that they actually represent not the Greek Dioscuri but local gods accompanying a local goddess in the guise of and identified with the Hellenic deities,⁶⁵⁸ a circumstance similar to the identification in the West of the Dioscuri with local Celtic gods.

The Dioscuri and the Thracian Rider

A comparable kind of identification, this time of the dead with the Dioscuri, may be the meaning of a relief from Macedonia (Figure 77). It dates from Imperial times.⁶⁵⁹ The relief shows a group of three riders, two facing right and one left, riding toward a statue inscribed *Chaire*. It comes from Kerdylion in the Strymon Valley in modern northern Greece and it appears to be a funerary monument for three brothers, represented here as Dioscuri. One is named Dioscorides, which perhaps suggested the subject of the monument to his heirs, but the other two have Thracian names.⁶⁶⁰

Indeed, the galloping riders with their flying capes are strongly reminiscent of the figures on Thracian Rider reliefs which form the subject of Chapter Six. The similarity between the tombstone and the Thracian Riders could be intentional. Chapouthier illustrates another funerary monument clearly representing a Thracian Rider and his double facing a tree with a snake twined around its trunk. The name of the father of the two deceased is Dioscorides which suggests, as on the relief above, that here we have a representation of the dead as Dioscuri-Thracian Riders.⁶⁶¹ Alexandra Cermanović-Kuzmanović has pointed out that in Macedonia the monuments of the Thracian Rider are, for the most part, funerary in character and there is indeed some suggestion of an identification on these tombstones of the dead with the god.⁶⁶² In addition, Gawril Kazarow records one example of a Thracian Rider plaque from Bulgaria on which the god is addressed in the plural as *Theois Dioskorois*, the Thracian Rider worshipped as the Dioscuri.⁶⁶³ Unfortunately despite the plural form of the dedication, nothing about this plaque distinguished it from other single-figure Thracian Rider reliefs.

The Macedonian relief of Dioscorides and his brothers, on the other hand, is unusual and may incorporate elements from several sources. In addition to the use of a composition commonly employed for the Dioscuri and the representation of horsemen resembling the Thracian Rider, Chapouthier sees in this relief the influence of the Cabiri who in Macedonia were worshipped as three male figures rather than the more usual two.⁶⁶⁴ The identification of both the Macedonian triple Cabiri and the three dead, heroized brothers with the divine twins may have prompted the increase in number of the Dioscuri, assuming always that the horsemen were really meant as Dioscuri in the first place.

A relief from Skopje in southern Yugoslavia shows the more typical form of the mounted Dioscuri attendant on the goddess. The quality of the relief is poor but the horsemen appear to approach the goddess at a gallop, their mantles flying. They wear tunics and pointed piloi. The female figure in the centre, although indistinct, seems to be crowned or nimbed and may be carrying a torch or sceptre.⁶⁶⁵

A poorly preserved Hellenistic relief of the Dioscuri discovered at Istros, the ancient *Histria* (Map 3), shows the brothers galloping toward the right where two figures stand raising their right arms in adoration (Figure 78). The twins wear short tunics.⁶⁶⁶ Although both figures are facing in the same direction, the representation of the Dioscuri is very similar to the Skopje relief. It may be that works of the Histrian type were the ancestors of the riders of the Skopje relief and also of the Thracian Riders of type B where the horseman is galloping toward the right and the tree and the snake are sometimes replaced by figures of one or more women.

The *Histria* relief is particularly important as direct evidence for mounted Dioscuri groups in the geographical area in which the Thracian Rider of the Imperial period developed. Unfortunately, in spite of the work done by Ernest Will,⁶⁶⁷ it is not possible to be too specific about the antecedents of the Thracian Rider. The Rider with his female companion or adorant may have been derived from any of a number of sources of which the representation of the Dioscuri is one.

For the group of deities on the so-called Danubian Rider plaques, however, the derivation seems to be more clearly apparent. As we shall see in Chapter Seven, although compositionally their debt to the Dioscuri is obvious, the Danubian gods differ from the twins and their goddess in numerous details and are not normally confused with them. Indeed, it is evident that the image of paired riders never became completely identified with the Dioscuri alone. So the creators of the Danubian Rider compositions could borrow the twin horseman, without subsuming the identity of their gods into that of the Dioscuri.

The overwhelming impression gained from studying the monuments of the Dioscuri-Castores in the western Roman Empire and, to a lesser extent, in the East, is one of compositional and iconographical uniformity despite a variety of powers and functions attributed to them and of any number of different contexts in which they might be represented. As seems to have been true of so many of the popular gods of the Roman period, one form in particular became the established icon which was then copied with little or no variation each time the deity was required, whatever the context. In the case of the Dioscuri, the mere representation of a nude young man standing in front of a horse was enough to make the identification unambiguous without recourse to further symbols or attributes.[668] Moreover, as we shall see below, the mounted Dioscuri are a possible, if not likely, prototype for several different divine riders, but the Dioscuri standing with their horses lent their form only to Epona who, on rare occasions, was represented in this way.

Chapter 6

The Thracian Rider

The Thracian Rider and also the Danubian Riders of Chapter Seven introduce different problems again from those already considered. First, they represent the easterly portions of the Western Empire and they look mainly to Greece not to Rome for their inspiration. Secondly, for the Celtic deities discussed above, the form of cult was likely to be the kind of tribal or public religion open to all that we know from the public cults of Greece and Rome. But in the case of the Danubian Riders certainly, and the Thracian Rider possibly, we are looking at forms of worship which were closer to the eastern mysteries with their initiations, sacred meals and promises for the afterlife. It is, of course, possible that some of the Celtic gods were worshipped in this manner, but the iconographic evidence for mystery-type worship, which we see full-blown in the Danubian Rider cult, is absent from any of the Celtic material. The evidence for the Thracian Rider is ambiguous on this point, although some scholars believe the rider was worshipped with mystery rites.

Finally, the artistic antecedents of the Thracian Rider and the Danubian Riders are similar. They both rely heavily on well established and easily identifiable Graeco-Roman types coming ultimately from the mounted Greek hero whose evolution was traced in the first chapter. The two cults share this derivation with the mounted Dioscuri.

The prototype, therefore, for the horseman imagery of these two cults is well known in general terms. For this reason, the next two chapters, while still examining the question of prototype, concentrate on looking at the range of cult representations and how they developed and indeed, what the image can tell about the cult itself.

The Evidence

The so-called Thracian Rider is one of the most enigmatic of the rider deities. He is known primarily from the large number of small votive plaques which have been found in those modern countries whose territories includes the ancient homeland of the Thracian people. Most of these reliefs come from Bulgaria where over 2000 of them have been found.[669] A smaller number have been discovered in Romania and the former Yugoslavia and the northern parts of Greece and European Turkey.

Virtually all that is known about this deity is the information that can be gleaned from the iconography of the plaques themselves and their often brief inscriptions. Many of the dedications, both in Latin and in Greek, refer to the god as *Heros* or *Heron* and the name is often accompanied by one of a number of epithets many of which, in spite of intensive study on the part of Eastern European scholars, have not yet yielded their meanings. Others, however, clearly refer to deities of the Graeco-Roman pantheon and this allows us to infer something about the nature of the Thracian god and his cult.

With regard to the cult of the Thracian Rider, ancient authors are virtually silent except for a brief notice by the Alexandrian poet Callimachos stating that the deity was indeed named Heros.[670] References to Thrace and the Thracian religion make no mention of the cult of Heros. Nevertheless, these notices too have been carefully studied to see if they might contain clues, however cryptic, to the beliefs and workings of the cult.

The earliest mention of the Thracian people comes from Homer where they were already famed for their horses: "here are the Thracians, new come, separate, beyond all others in place, and among them Rhesos their king... And his are the finest horses I ever saw, and the biggest".[671] Although this chapter of the *Iliad* is considered by many to be a later interpolation of perhaps the sixth century,[672] the story of Rhesus could well have been a recasting of old, familiar material.[673]

That a horseman was associated with Thracian royalty can be seen from the coin issues of the Odrysian kings.[674] The earliest known examples of the use of Greek coin types by Thracians are those of Sparadokos, brother of the king Sitalkes. The coins date to the mid fifth century BC.[675] The obverse shows a rider advancing left and wearing a short chlamys and a small hat. He holds two spears horizontally across the picture field at waist level. On the reverse is an eagle.[676] Later rulers used similar images. Coins of Seuthes III, for example, depict a rider on a galloping or rearing horse. Beneath horse and rider there appears to be a wreath.[677]

It has been suggested that the horseman deity began as a dynastic god. If so, it could be he who is depicted on royal coinage. Some of the epithets of the Thracian hero indicate a role for him as leader of his people and founder of the various tribes:[678] *archagetas, genikos, patroos, patrios*.[679] We may perhaps see here a parallel with the Celts, also famed as horsemen. As we have seen, their tribal gods and divine progenitors were represented as mounted even when assuming the identity of non-riding Graeco-Roman gods like Mars or Jupiter. We shall see later that the Thracian Rider also appears to have been identified with a Greek god who is not usually a rider — Apollo.

Forms of Representation

The most common type of evidence for the worship of Heros is the votive plaque. It is normally made from marble or limestone. A measurement of 24 cm. x 21 cm. x 9 cm., as in the case of an example from Constanţa in Romania, ancient *Tomis*,[680] is not unusual, although much larger examples do exist. The shape of the plaque is generally rectangular with a rounded or straight top, the former being more common in Bulgaria[681] and the latter in Romania.[682] The relief carving is low, often summary, with details probably painted in.[683]

Typically the rider is represented as a young man riding a horse toward the right (Figure 79). He may be nude but often he wears a chlamys which flutters behind him and sometimes a chiton. On the most common type of relief, the rider's right arm is raised. In his right hand, he holds a spear which he is poised to throw. He is a hunter not a warrior. Sometimes the target animal is not shown within the relief field but is probably to be imagined beyond it. This is only one of several compositional variations. Similar figures are also to be found on funerary monuments within the Thracian cultural area.

One of the first scholars to attempt a comprehensive study of these monuments was the Bulgarian Gawril Kazarow who, in his study of 1938, collected and classified the known Bulgarian specimens.[684] His classifications became the standard forms of description for Thracian Rider typology. His categories are still being extended to include new variations as they are discovered.[685]

Kazarow observed that the plaques could be divided into three main iconographical and compositional groups. These he labelled A, B and C.[686] Each group was then seen to have subtypes which differed one from the other by the number and type of additional iconographical details. Briefly, the system is as follows:

Type A (Figure 80, left-hand side). The rider advancing toward the right or standing still and holding a dish or only the reins in his outstretched right hand. Sometimes the right hand of the rider is resting on the rear flank of his horse. This type is often provided with supplementary figures who also appear in both other groups.

Kazarow breaks down the groupings with supplementary figures and objects as follows:

• a tree stands in front of the rider and, in some examples, a snake coils around the trunk;

• in front of the rider is an altar, often with a flame burning on it;

• the rider, altar, tree and snake all appear together;

• before the rider is a tree and behind the horse is a servant who holds the horse's tail;

• before the rider stands a female figure rendered frontally and dressed in a long chiton and mantle who sometimes raises her right hand or holds a dish;

• beneath the horse is a hound who often follows a boar running to the right but sometimes the boar is alone.[687]

Several other, more uncommon, variants are also to be observed. In one the usually standing type A horse is represented galloping. In another the rider has a shield slung over his left arm, and in a third the male servant holding the horse's tail is replaced by a female figure.[688]

Type B (Figure 79) To this group belong the reliefs which show the rider at the hunt, galloping to the right with his right arm — often decorated with an armband — holding a hunting spear or swinging a lance. Several new compositional elements are present:

• the rider has an altar before him on which the horse sets his right foreleg;

• in front of the rider are two frontal female figures, sometimes with an altar also, while behind is the horse-tail-holding servant.[689]

Another characteristic of type B is the group of animals which appears beneath the horse's belly. These are sometimes seen in type A but form a more logical part of a scene depicting the hunt rather than that showing the weaponless rider. The animals include a hound and often a boar who is either running from or being bitten by the dog. A lion, who may be shown leaping upon a bull, also appears on a few examples. Other animals which appear as quarry are the deer or stag and the hare.[690]

One of the more interesting variations on the type B rider is the composition in which the rider's raised right hand does not hold a spear or other implement but is formed into the gesture called the *benedictio latina* where three fingers of the hand are outstretched and the rest pressed into the palm (Figure 81). It is fairly infrequent: Kazarow lists 21 examples out of his nearly 1200 monuments.[691] A cultic significance has been suggested for it[692] which will be discussed below.

Type C (Figure 82) The third group embraces the reliefs which show the rider returning from the hunt. With his raised right arm, he holds a fawn by the hind legs behind him. Its head and forequarters are being bitten by a dog or two dogs. Often on the ground is what appears to be an overturned vase from which a liquid gushes. The supplementary figures and objects familiar from types A and B — an altar, a male servant and female attendants, a tree and snake — also appear in type C. On a few reliefs, the game animal, deer or hare, is held high by the rider as if to provoke the dogs into snapping at the prize.[693]

The three types, which surely represent the periods before, during and after the hunt,[694] seem to indicate the normal limits of the iconographical variety of the Thracian Rider. Other variants are exceedingly rare. A fragment of a marble relief from the Roman city of Teurnia in Noricum may represent a Thracian Rider standing near his horse. The relief shows the dismounted rider between his horse and a tree with a snake.[695] This type does not seem to be represented among the discoveries from Thracian lands. It is possible that the model for this standing horseman was the common image of the Dioscuri who, as we saw in Chapter Five, appear at times to have been identified with the Thracian Rider.

One or two other unusual variations are worth mentioning. These include a limited number of reliefs of types B and C where two riders are shown, one larger and moving right and the second smaller facing left. This latter is usually placed in the upper left hand corner of the relief field. Occasionally, also, the normally clean-shaven figure is shown bearded and even more rarely, he is represented with multiple heads. Kazarow lists three reliefs on which the single rider appears with three heads on his shoulders. One relief is known where the rider is given two heads. In all cases, the polycephalic figures are bearded.[696] Finally, we may note that some riders, of types B and C as well as type A, carry shields on their left arms.

History of the Rider Image

The majority of the Thracian Rider monuments date within the second and third centuries AD, but several earlier examples exist which make it evident that the iconography of the rider-hunter had been worked out by the Hellenistic period. Two fragments of terracotta reliefs of type A riders were found during excavations at *Histria*-Istria, one of the ancient Greek cities of the Black Sea coast in present-day Romania (Map 3). Both fragments preserve the bodies of rider and horse and one also retains the rider's head wearing a petasos. The two riders are dressed in chiton and chlamys and both appear to be holding an object, probably a patera.[697] The pieces were dated by stratigraphic evidence to the third century or possibly the beginning of the second century BC.[698]

The discoveries stimulated the researchers to re-examine objects from earlier excavations on the same site and another similar terracotta plaque was then found. This one was even more fragmentary than the two other finds. All that remained were one of the forelegs of the horse, the upper part of an altar and the major part of a female figure on the far right. The figure, possibly standing on a pedestal, was wearing a long chiton and a himation wrapped around her. The altar was decorated and the flame could be seen.[699] Although there is no way of being certain that these figures represent the Thracian Rider, all the iconographical elements are typical of the rider monuments of the Roman period. Thirty-one rider monuments have been found at *Histria*[700] of which these are the earliest, but no temple or sanctuary dedicated to Heros is known from any part of Romania.[701]

In Bulgaria, by contrast, the earliest Hellenistic examples of the Thracian Rider have come from a site known to have been a sanctuary of this god. The site is at Galata south of the ancient coastal town of *Odessos*, now Varna. Two reliefs believed to be of the third century BC were built into the walls of the early Christian church erected after the demolition of the rider's sanctuary.[702]

The first of these, though badly worn, shows three trees, a fleeing deer and part of a horse and rider of type B. The second, also type B, shows a rider in a pointed cap. To the right of the horse is an altar behind which stands a tree with traces of a female figure beyond. Both reliefs are dated by the excavator on stylistic grounds to the third century BC.[703]

None of these earliest examples is inscribed, but another relief found at *Odessos* is dated to the second or first century BC and includes an inscription to Heros Karabasmos.[704] This is a type A relief set in a gabled stone. Another type A relief with an inscription was found at Patrabana. It probably dates from the first century BC or first century AD. The relief shows the horseman before an altar to the right of

which are a female figure and a tree with a snake coiled around it. The inscription tells us that the god is Heros Perkon (or Perkos).[705] It appears then, that although the proof is limited to only a small number of reliefs, the iconography of the cult of Heros the Thracian Rider and compositional types A and B were developed in all their essentials during the Hellenistic period.

The compositions of types A and B can, as we have seen, be traced to the Hellenistic period in Thrace and Dacia (Romania) but type C, the return from the hunt carrying the booty, appears to have been a product of the Roman era. The rider carrying game is first found during the period from the end of the second to the beginning of the third century AD. It seems to be a secondary development from relief type B.[706]

The Letnitsa Treasure

It is possible that some even earlier works are related to the development of the horseman type, although this is considerably more conjectural. It happens that a series of 'treasures' has been discovered in burial mounds in Bulgaria including items on which horsemen figure prominently. One of the most interesting of these treasures comes from Letnitsa and has been dated to perhaps the first half of the fourth century BC. The pieces, which show little influence from contemporary Greek art, are ornamental horse trappings, silver-gilt plaques to decorate the harness of a horse.[707]

Of the twenty-three extant pieces, eight represent horsemen.[708] Among these eight, there are a number of iconographic similarities with the later images of the Thracian Rider. Five of the Letnitsa plaques show riders wielding a spear like the type B of Kazarow's classification. One shows a rider holding a bowl in front of him, similar to type A but facing left (Figure 83). Three of the riders are beardless; five are bearded. A bear and a boar are represented in one hunt scene.[709]

To be sure, there are many other and enigmatic elements in these scenes which cannot be associated with the Thracian Rider in his Graeco-Roman form. Nevertheless, the finding of such a series, which was produced within a century or so of the earliest known examples of the familiar Thracian Rider, suggests the possibility of some sort of already existing schema based on myth or legend. Petre Alexandrescu has suggested that, although an iconographic continuity between the representations of the North Balkan treasure of the fourth century BC and the Roman monuments cannot be shown, the ideas which motivated both sets of representations could have been the same, or similar, Thracian myths and gods.[710]

The Search for Possible Prototypes

The works of art or compositional types which furnished the models for the Graeco-Roman Thracian Rider have been investigated in detail by Ernest Will.[711] To begin with, Will has rejected any attempt to find a direct line from the rider compositions to the major monuments of the Greek world. However, it may be asked whether there is an relationship between the youthful image of the mounted Thracian Rider and the mounted Dioscuri. As we have already noted, from the fifth century BC the two brothers were represented as riders either nude or dressed in a chiton like the Thracian Rider. Although it is not possible to point to specific prototypes for the Thracian Rider among the representations of the Dioscuri, there was a tendency, already observed in the examination of other new divine images, for artists to look for models among existing representations of other gods. The Dioscuri, being horsemen and heros as well as gods, could easily have provided the general model on which the Thracian Rider was based in that earliest form which appeared in the Hellenistic period.[712] This would be particularly true for the type A rider who, like the Dioscuri, is not holding a weapon in an attack position.

The unusual dismounted rider on a relief found in Noricum,[713] mentioned above, looks very much like an adaptation of the other composition associated with the Dioscuri, the dismounted rider leading his horse. This type was favoured in Gaul and the German provinces. The artist has identified the rider as Heros rather than Castor or Pollux by adding the tree and snake. The use of the adaptation suggests that some similarity between the gods, if not the cults, brought this composition to the mind of the craftsman.

The Thracian Rider composition, for Will, represents only a late variant on the vast series derived from images of Greek mounted heros. This view can even be stretched to include prototypes for the various additional figures and attributes associated with the Thracian Rider. All of these can be found in Greek examples.[714] Thus the artists, faced with providing an acceptable image for the Thracian god, drew upon the already established forms of the Greek hero with whom the Thracian god shared some characteristics, particularly of a chthonic nature.[715]

The most probable place for this development to have taken place would have been the Greek cities bordering on the Black Sea.[716] We have already seen that some of the earliest examples of the Thracian Rider composition and iconography come from *Odessos* and *Histria*, both cities of the Greek Pontic coast.

One of the most interesting observations made by Will concerning the Thracian Rider prototypes refers to the characteristic style of gallop found on the reliefs. Scholars had long since noticed a difference between the placement of the horse's legs representing a gallop in Greece, especially in Attica, and in the Orient. In the art of the former, the rear legs of the horse are flexed so that they bend inward toward the horse's body and the hooves are shown below the hind quarters (Figure 39, for example). By contrast, the latter represents the horse's hind legs as stretching out beyond the rear of the body so that the hooves are shown below the tail (Figure 81).

The Oriental gallop has a long history in the ancient world. Egypt of the New Kingdom, the Mycenaean civilization and Syrian sites like Ras Shamra all provide examples of horses pulling chariots in which the horses' legs are represented in a manner so widely splayed that this form has been given the name of 'flying gallop'.[717] On the ridden horses of the

first millenium BC, the extreme splay of the horses' legs is somewhat modified as, for example, on the reliefs of Assurbanipal.[718] This same form in which the horse's legs and body describe an arc can be seen on a horseman relief from Cavus-Köy dated to the 4th century BC.[719] This relief is of particular interest because it is of mixed Oriental and Greek influence and shows a mounted hunter attacking a boar which is also being bitten by his dogs. Behind the boar is a tree and behind the horseman is a retainer. The horse and rider are clearly in the Oriental tradition. Like the riders of the Assyrian Palace reliefs, this horseman sits straight on his mount with his knees barely flexed. The galloping horse bends his head low and a broad 'V' shaped space between the horse and rider is created.

In the Greek conception, the gallop is less a forward motion than an action of rearing as before an obstacle.[720] The body of the horse forms a greater angle with the ground line, and the upright horseman, a smaller angle, with the horse's neck and head. The 'V' shaped space very often disappears. The combination of these two modes of representation into a single new type is identified by Will in the stele of a horseman from Abdera dated to the third century BC. Here the elongated gallop where the horse's back legs are stretched out behind his body is combined with the emphatic diagonal of the rearing horse. The horse's forelegs are flexed as are the knees of the rider.[721]

During the Hellenistic period this form of representation increased in frequency until it became the main way of representing riders. It is the normal form for the Roman period and for the Thracian Rider whose artistic prototypes must, therefore, have been mainly Hellenistic rather than Classical.[722] It is interesting to note that among the earliest of the known Thracian Rider reliefs, one from the sanctuary at Galata shows horses in the Classical Greek form of gallop with flexed hind legs,[723] to be dated just before the transition.

Stylistic Development and Chronology

Most scholarly interest has been focused on the iconography and interpretation of the cult of Heros, but some work has been done on the stylistic development and chronology of the reliefs themselves.[724] Manfred Oppermann has examined a series of reliefs found in the northwestern part of Bulgaria mainly at Glava Panega near Lukovit and Batkun near Pazardzik, with examples also from the surrounding area. The relief plaques show sufficient similarities in style and iconography to be considered as a single group, most likely products of local workshops based around the two sanctuaries at Batkun and Glava Panega. The group takes its name from these cult places, the Batkun-Glava Panega group.

The reliefs of the Batkun-Glava Panega group are of Kazarow's type B. The rider is shown in three-quarter view dressed, unusually, only in a chlamys. The workmanship is generally careful and the upper edge of the plaque is rounded to form a deep arch under which the figures are set. Additional details may include a youth holding the horse's tail and also a small horseman riding toward the left who sometimes appears in the upper left hand corner of the relief. The reliefs appear to date over the period from the last quarter of the second century to the first decades of the third century AD.[725]

Close study of the reliefs of the Batkun-Glava Panega group, together with plaques of a slightly different, but clearly related style, has allowed Manfred Oppermann to draw conclusions about iconographical and stylistic development of the Thracian Rider image in western Bulgaria. It appears, for instance, that it was these masters who introduced the miniature rider into the iconography at the end of the second century and they may also have been responsible for the creation of type C, the rider returning from the hunt.[726]

Another variation which is significant for dating the reliefs is the change in the rendering of the forelegs of the horse. In the reliefs of the earlier Batkun-Glava Panega group, the forelegs are extended well forward of the animal's body and widely separated. This type appears to last into the early decades of the third century. However, toward the end of the first half of the century a new type emerges where the legs are more strongly curved and placed close together and nearly parallel to one another. Now the front hooves of the horse rest on the altar block, sometimes appearing to fuse with it.[727]

Similar information can be gleaned from groups of reliefs from other centres. Oppermann has also shown that a relationship exists between the products of the southern group of Pontic cities in present day Bulgaria and the northern group in Romania, a relationship which is closer than that of either group to its hinterland areas. Because of this, he has been able to discuss and date Romanian examples with greater precision than had been done previously.[728]

The Cult and its God

Range of the Cult

Only in Bulgaria, the ancient Thrace proper, have sanctuaries of the Thracian Rider been found. It is a curious and interesting fact that no sanctuaries of the Thracian Rider have been discovered in Romania so far. Nor have the finds from sanctuaries of other gods in that country included votive offerings to Heros.[729] Nubar Hampartumian has listed 195 examples of Thracian Rider artefacts which cover the Roman provinces of Dacia and Moesia Inferior within Romanian territory. Of the find-sites in Dacia, six out of fourteen were *municipia* and *coloniae*; in Moesia Inferior, only five of the 31 settlements were urban centres,[730] although the greatest number of finds came from the Graeco-Roman coastal cities of *Tomis* (Constanţa), *Histria* (Istria) and *Callatis* (Mangalia) (Map 3).[731]

The reason for the concentration of horseman reliefs in the coastal area and not inland in Dacia is suggested by Radu Vulpe who points to the historical connection between this part of Moesia Inferior (or Scythia Minor) and the province of Thrace, namely that both made up the territory of the Odrysian empire which united Thrace in the fifth century BC.[732] The kingdom, which only excluded certain groups of

autonomous mountaineers within the Thracian territory, appears to have been founded sometime after 480. By the time of its second king, Sitalkes, it had an area under its control with the Danube as its northern frontier, the Aegean as its southern and the Black Sea as its eastern frontier.[733] The legacy of the union between Scythia Minor and Thrace was perhaps the introduction of the Thracian Rider to the Black Sea coast.

Although the cult may have been implanted in Scythia Minor by the influence of the Odrysian kings, its form in this area appears to have differed from that in the Thracian homeland. Vulpe sees this as the result of the different nature of the population, the people of Scythia Minor being predominantly Getic mixed with enclaves of Scythians.[734] Although the Getes and the Dacians are of Thracian stock[735] and Herodotus called the Getae the noblest and most just of the Thracian tribes,[736] their language and some, at least, of their customs seem to have differed from those of the Thracians proper. The small number of Thracian horseman plaques found outside the Pontic cities of Moesia Inferior — only 33 in Dacia[737] — the lack of temple buildings and the lack of local epithets, such as we shall find in Thrace,[738] all support the probability of a somewhat different form of worship for the Thracian Rider outside Thrace proper.

Thracian Rider Sanctuaries

Numerous temple sites are known where hundreds of reliefs with inscriptions have been found in Bulgaria. Only a small amount of information about these sanctuaries has appeared in western European languages, but enough to give an idea of the type of building in which the rider would have been worshipped.

A sanctuary of the rider was discovered in 1971–72 in the village of Daskalovo in the Pernik district. It was sited approximately 120 metres north of a mineral water spring.[739] The form of the temenos was nearly rectangular and divided into a courtyard and a temple building. The complex was oriented east–west on its long axis. The temple itself was in the western part and connected to the enclosure wall.[740] It was rectangular, 7.5 x 6.8 m., and consisted of two rooms: the cella and an antechamber. A series of sandstone bases oriented north–south in front of the temple are most likely the remains of a colonnade. However, no traces of the columns were found, which suggests that they were made of wood. The sanctuary entrance was found on the east with its threshold preserved *in situ*.[741]

In the centre of the sanctuary was a structure made out of two rows of dressed sandstone lying one over the other. The excavators believe this to be the remains of a large altar placed out of doors in front of the entrance to the temple. Not far away there were traces of a channel running from northeast to southwest which probably conducted liquids away from the altar.[742]

From inscribed objects and votive reliefs, it was evident that the sanctuary had been devoted to the Thracian horseman worshipped under the name of *Asklepios Keiladen*, an epithet which appears to be local. Among the 1430 or so votive tablets found, representations of the Thracian Rider predominate in Kazarow's types B and C. Reliefs representing Asklepios, Hygieia and Telesphores were also present, so the excavators believe that the sanctuary was most likely a healing shrine dedicated to the Thracian Rider who appears to have had healing aspects and was, thus, identified with the Greek healer Asklepios.[743]

Dates for the sanctuary have been established by epigraphic and stylistic evidence. A pair of inscribed statue bases were found which can be confidently dated to the years AD 231 and 241 on the grounds of the consuls named and palaeographical characteristics.[744] A number of the reliefs of the Thracian Rider found at the sanctuary belong to the Batkun-Glava Panega group and can thus be dated to the end of the second century and the first decades of the third.[745]

Using similar comparisons and epigraphical evidence, another stylistic group from the site can be placed later in the first half of the third century AD, further corroborating the suggested date. Moreover, the very abundance of Kazarow's type C argues for a date in the first half of the third century. It is also possible that some reliefs belong to the end of the third and the beginning of the fourth, but the dating criteria are not sufficiently precise to be certain. Coin finds suggest dates between the reigns of Septimius Severus and Julian, that is, between the end of the second and the middle of the fourth century AD.[746]

Sanctuaries established in the Hellenistic period are also known. Galata in the region of *Odessos* shows evidence of having had a temple to the Thracian Rider which dated back to the third century BC. We have already seen that some of the earliest examples of rider reliefs come from this site, although the greatest number of monuments found there belong to Imperial times. Some of the structure of the temple remains. It appears to have been a rectangular building divided into two unequal rooms. The architectural elements found during the excavation suggest that the cult building was rebuilt during the Roman period. The god was here worshipped under the name of *Heros Karabasmos*.[747]

A site in the interior of Thrace at Draganovec was described by Gončeva and Oppermann as a rectangular building divided unequally into two rooms. There were traces of a tiled roof and additional buildings on the site. The finds included plaques of the Thracian Rider, the inscriptions on which made it clear that the god of this sanctuary was the rider under the guise of Apollo.[748]

Inscriptions

Although these brief notices give us very little idea of the nature of Thracian Rider sanctuaries beyond the barest outline, it is evident that the rider was not always worshipped under his own name and appears to have fused with several Graeco-Roman deities. At Daskalovo, the inscriptions showed the rider worshipped as Asklepios; at Draganovec, he was Apollo. At Galata, he was addressed as *Heros* with the surname *Karabasmos*, one of a series of epithets, some of them, at present, untranslatable.

The importance of the inscriptions is unquestionable as they represent a major source of clues to the meaning of the cult.

The majority of votive plaques, however, are not inscribed. But from those that are, we can learn much. The inscriptions confirm that the god was normally addressed as 'Heros'. The epithets that attach to the name are of several different types. Some of these identify Heros with a well-known deity as, for instance, an example from Kicevo in the province of Varna where on a relief with a type A rider the inscription reads *Hero Asklepio* …to Heros Asklepios.[749]

Other inscriptions on rider plaques addressed to Graeco-Roman deities, however, do not call upon them as Heros. Often dedications in a form like *Theoi Apolloni* are found on votive plaques bearing one of the standard images of the horseman. Thus, reliefs from several sites in the province of Varna have type B horsemen above a dedication to the god Apollo.[750] One example, for which only the inscription remains, shows a dedication of a combined type: *Theo Hero Apolloni*.[751] On occasion the word *kyrios* is substituted for *theos*.[752]

But the most interesting series of epithets is that in which Heros is called by names of local or ethnic origin. They seem to be most common in, if not exclusive to, Thrace. In the Scythia Minor area of Romania, for example, such epithets are apparently not found except as imports. Thus, a stela and altar of *Heros Manimazos* found at *Tomis* may represent the spread of the cult into the north Pontic city from its likely seat at *Odessos*.[753] The reliefs dedicated to Manimazos from both *Tomis* and *Odessos* show the type A rider.

The marble stela from *Tomis*, however, has a second representational field beneath the rider group and clearly illustrates the problem of ambiguity in the reliefs. In the upper zone the rider is shown facing a veiled woman standing with a patera in her hand. The altar, snake and tree are also present. On the register below is a masted ship in which two figures are standing with arms raised. Some scholars have connected this pair with the Dioscuri who were protectors of sea-farers. Others suggest that the figures in the boat have nothing to do with the twins but may represent the last voyage of the dead; Heros often appears on grave monuments and so, clearly, was associated with death and the afterlife. It is also possible that the ship and sailors indicate that Heros Manimazos himself was a protector of sea-farers without further associations and syncretism.[754] However, as Hampartumian observes, the fact that the donor was named Dioskourides could tip the balance in favour of an identification of the two figures in the ship as the divine twins.[755]

The Rider as Apollo and Asklepios

A similar deity to Manimazos is the god called *Heros Karabasmos*. He too appears to have had his origins in Pontic Thrace. He had a sanctuary, discussed above, at Galata. Here again there are problems of interpretation. An inscription from *Odessos* is known with the dedication *Hero Apolloni Karabasmo*,[756] but the epigraphic remains from the sanctuary at Galata to the south of *Odessos* have produced no similar example nor evidence of an identification between Apollo and Karabasmos.[757]

An epithet which is clearly identified with Heros as Apollo is *Aularkenos*. The main spread of this epithet is in eastern Bulgaria. Several artefacts inscribed with this epithet are known from the sanctuary at Draganovec.[758] One of these, a type B relief, is dedicated to Apollo as *Aulousadenos*, a form related to Aularkenos. It shows the rider holding a lyre in his left hand which is raised high behind the head of the horse.[759] A second relief from the same site shows a type C rider also holding a lyre in his left hand; the relief is inscribed *[A]polloni Aulousasa*.[760] A third relief with the same inscription as this latter shows a type B figure with no lyre but a shield over his left arm.[761]

The first two of these reliefs show a welcome association of inscription with iconography. The plaque dedicated to Apollo clearly illustrates the identification of the Thracian Rider with Apollo by means of his attribute, the lyre. The fusion of the two deities is unambiguous. The third plaque shows the rider without specifically Apolline attributes. Without the enlightening inscription it would have been impossible to know to which god or to which aspect of the rider it was dedicated. Conversely, anepigraphic examples have been found which show the rider holding a lyre and these must clearly refer to Apollo. We have seen this problem often enough in considering the identification of Celtic deities with Roman ones on the far western edges of the Empire. Here we see it again within a more Hellenic ambience.

A second Greek deity with whom the Thracian Rider seems to have been fully identified is Asklepios. Inscriptions address him as *Hero Asklepio*,[762] *[Ask]lepio Kempeno*[763] and *Kyrio Asklepio*.[764] The Thracian Rider as Asklepios appears in all three of Kazarow's iconographic schemes. There is nothing on the inscribed reliefs to differentiate them from the majority of Thracian Rider images. However, what may set apart the dedications to Asklepios is the fact that, as at Daskalovo, the representations found along with the rider plaques included those of Hygieia and Telesphores.[765] As with Apollo's lyre, we find imagery familiar from Graeco-Roman cult present when the Thracian Rider is worshipped as Asklepios.

The *Benedictio Latina*

One iconographical form which is common to Heros as Apollo and Asklepios is the figure of the rider with his hand raised in the so-called *benedictio latina* (Figure 81). Several examples with inscribed dedications to Apollo carry this gesture: a plaque from Cerkovna in the Varna district [766] and another from the central Targoviste area.[767] Similar examples can be found of dedications to Asklepios: one from Gorica in the south-eastern Burgas area[768] and a second, again from the Targoviste area, from Medovina. Here the relief is badly worn but the gesture seems to be that of the *benedictio latina*. Medovina may be the site of a temple as yet unexcavated.[769]

The gesture of the *benedictio latina* is closely associated with the cult of Sabazios, especially in the form of a free-standing hand making the gesture. A particularly interesting example comes from Krassen in the Tolbukhin district of Bulgaria. This is an ivory hand and arm up to the elbow. The hand holds a pine cone with an open-work

representation of a horseman. He is in the type B position but the animal he hunts is a bear.[770] For Margarita Tacheva-Hitova, the gesture on the part of the Thracian Rider signifies his syncretism with Apollo. As Sabazios is also identified with Apollo, the transference is reasonable.[771] But Asklepios also uses the gesture. Perhaps here also it emphasises the link with Apollo, but its actual significance is not known. One suggestion is that the *benedictio latina* gesture may be connected with the mysteries of the Thracian Rider, a mystical sign understood by the faithful.[772] But this does not explain its use by Sabazios or the other gods with whom it is associated unless the mysteries are seen as involving several of these deities.

The Nimbus

An attribute which may be relevant to the identification of Heros with Apollo is the nimbus which is found very occasionally carved behind the head of the rider, mainly, but not exclusively, on tablets originating in the former Yugoslavia.[773] In all, five such monuments have been found along with one from Batkun in Bulgaria where a shell replaces the nimbus. Although few figures have a nimbus represented plastically, there is no way of knowing how many were produced with the nimbus painted on.[774] The presence of the painted nimbus may have identified the deity as Apollo where no lyre was represented. The commoner rayed crown of the sun god is very rare on rider reliefs. Kazarow knew only one.[775]

The relationship between Apollo and Asklepios, on the one hand, and the Thracian Rider, on the other, appears to be one of total identification so that the two Greek gods, who were not normally mounted, now became riders. As with the Celtic examples, the identifying characteristic of the local god — his nature as a rider — is the basic form onto which the foreign characteristics are grafted. Neither Apollo nor Mars was conceived as a rider by the Greeks and Romans but syncretism blended their attributes with those of the local god, just as it added their names to the invocations made to him. A relief showing two riders, both of type A, and both facing an altar and a snake-entwined tree in the centre of the composition, is clearly inscribed with a dedication *Apolloni kai Asklepio Berakelenois*. This last being a local epithet apparently given to the pair of deities. The relief was found at Krupac in the northeast of Yugoslavia close to the border with Bulgaria. The area has a warm spring nearby and it is not impossible that there was a temple on the site.[776]

The Thracian Rider as Dioscurus

There is some limited evidence for the Dioscuri being equated with the Thracian Rider rendered in duplicate. The identification of rider god with rider god seems natural. A plaque from the sanctuary at Ljublen shows two riders both facing right. The left hand figure is of type B and the right, type A. They face a standing female figure.[777] Oppermann believes that the evidence is good for an identification of Heros with the Dioscuri in the south central part of Bulgaria. This area, the Rhodope Mountain range bordering on modern Greece, was the home of the Bessi tribe and it has produced a relatively large accumulation of monuments dedicated to the twins. One relief in Kazarow's collection has a dedication to the Dioscuri.[778] It comes from this area and is a conventional representation of the single Thracian Rider. The evidence of the dedication combined with the strong representation of the Dioscuri in Bessi territory suggests an earlier Thracian cult which came to be identified with the horseman twins through Greek or possibly Roman influence.[779]

It is by no means obvious, however, that every pair of riders is meant to be the Dioscuri. The two riders from Ljublen may represent a duplication of the rider in order to show him undertaking his two major acts. A pair of opposed horseman placed in a pedimental top of a stela from *Sucidava* (Celeiu-Corabia) in Romania could also be the Dioscuri but may again only represent a duplicated form of the Thracian hero.[780]

The Thracian Rider and Other Gods

The relationship of the rider to other deities appears to be rather different from his relation to Apollo, Asklepios or the Dioscuri. He is represented, on occasion, with Dionysus, Cybele, Hermes and other members of the Graeco-Roman pantheon. He appears, thus, as a companion to his fellow deities. The three named deities are given their familiar attributes but identification of other figures in the Graeco-Roman pantheon associated with the Thracian Rider is often tentative.

Dionysus

One of the commoner gods associated with the rider is Dionysus. The reliefs show Dionysus as a separate figure accompanying, but not identified with, the rider. The majority of reliefs with an identifiable figure of Dionysus seem to come from the Romanian Pontic coast. A particularly complex example is a relief clearly dedicated to Dionysus and not to the rider. The inscription is *Dionyso Kathegemonei*. Dionysus stands in the centre of the relief wearing a wreath around his head, long chiton and high boots. He is holding a thyrsus in his left hand and a kantheros in his right. On the left is a statue of Priapus on a round base with a panther to the right. In the upper left hand corner, a bearded satyr with goat's legs gathers grapes. Silenus (or perhaps Pan) stands on the lower right of the relief holding a staff in his right hand and balancing a tray of fruit. In the upper right hand corner is a figure of a Thracian Rider facing right. In front of him are an altar and a snake-entwined tree.[781] The rider, thus, is only one of a group of deities who frame the main focus of the composition and, no doubt, of worship — Dionysus.

If, on this relief, the rider appears to be of secondary importance, equated with Silenus or Priapus, on other monuments the Thracian Rider and Dionysus confront each other as equals. Another relief, from *Tomis* like the last, shows a type A horseman holding the reins in his right hand and facing a frontal figure of Dionysus, easily identified by the thyrsus and kantheros he is holding. His panther rests at his feet.[782]

On a relief from *Callatis*, another type A rider, but this time carrying a patera and wearing a helmet, rides toward two other deities. On the left, immediately in front of Heros, is Hermes, identified by his large caduceus and the purse he holds in his right hand. Next to Hermes, on the right, is Dionysus again, dressed in a fawn skin and with attributes we have already seen: thyrsus, kantheros and panther. All three deities are equal in size but only Heros rides.[783]

Jupiter

We have, from Moesia Inferior, some interesting cases of what appears to be the identification of the Thracian Rider with Jupiter: two reliefs, one from *Axiopolis* (Cernavoda) and another of unknown province, on which the rider appears to be carrying a sceptre.[784] As evidence for an identification between Heros and Jupiter, these reliefs seem very weak, if not unacceptable, but two Latin inscriptions — to *IOM Heroi* and *IOM Heroni* — are known which show that such a syncretism did take place if only rarely.[785]

Cybele

Among the other deities often associated with the Thracian Rider is Cybele. Here again the figure most commonly appears on reliefs from the Black Sea Coast. One of the finest examples is a marble relief from *Tomis* on which a type A rider holding a patera rides toward an altar, tree and snake beyond which is a seated frontal female figure (Figure 80). The figure wears a veil and a polos on her head and is seated on a throne flanked by two lions. She holds a patera in her right hand and a tympanum in her left. The attributes identify the woman as the Great Mother.[786] Constantin Scorpan has pointed out that Cybele is the only one of the Oriental deities to be associated with the Thracian Rider.[787] No examples of demonstrable syncretism or even partnership with deities like Mithras have come to light, although subtle influence cannot be ruled out.[788] As Scorpan has suggested, perhaps the reason Cybele's inclusion was acceptable is that, although she was worshipped by the Romans as the Great Mother with an eastern-type cult, she had long since been assimilated in Greece and was, therefore, thought of as a legitimate member of the Graeco-Roman pantheon.[789]

The Iconography of the Thracian Rider

For Constantin Scorpan, the representation of the tree and, especially, the snake show that the Thracian hero was a god of vegetation, fertility, nature and life, consequently also of the afterlife and immortality.[790] Related to the question of Heros as fertility god are the reliefs which depict a bearded rider who raises, instead of a spear, a cornucopia, an obvious symbol of fertility.[791] Kazarow associated these bearded figures with a bearded man holding a cornucopia who appeared on Odessan coinage and was addressed as *Theos Megas*. In the earliest representations, he was depicted standing, holding a cornucopia and patera, sometimes with ivy or vine-leaves around his head.[792] On the coins of *Odessos* of around 200 BC, he began to appear mounted. This deity, called Derzis, Derzalas or Darzalas, was at some point fused with the Thracian Rider who took over some of his characteristics and this appears to be what we see on the rider plaques with the bearded horseman.[793]

The rider reliefs often include the figures of one or more women standing on the right in front of the rider. On occasion the figure is seated. We have already seen that sometimes the woman can be identified as Cybele. Other examples on which attributes exist or are clear enough to make a firm identification are rare, and most scholarly suggestions are very tentative. Writers are content to call these female figures simply adorants. However, the gesture observed in some of these women, with one hand grasping the reins of the horse, does not suggest a worshipper.[794] A seated female figure can also be seen making the same gesture on another relief.[795] She has none of the special attributes of Cybele. On some examples, the woman merely stands frontally. Aleksandrina Cermanović-Kuzmanović has suggested that this figure is a goddess and the consort of the rider.[796] There is no way to prove this, but the suggestion invites a possible parallel with one of the Letnitsa plaques.

As noted above, some of these Letnitsa pieces prefigure, accidentally perhaps, the types A and B of the Thracian Rider reliefs of the Roman period. Another one of these silver gilt plaques may be the precursor of the group depicting the rider with the standing woman. This plaque shows a man and a woman in the act of sexual intercourse.[797] The woman is sitting with her arms around the man and a second female figure looks on. This latter carries a twig in her right hand and a long narrow vessel in her left. If the figures are, in fact, deities, it is most likely that the scene represents a sacred marriage. The appearance of a second figure suggests that the episode is connected with some myth or legend rather than just a ritual mating. The Roman period plaques do not, of course, show anything so crude as the representation on the Letnitsa relief, but the presence of the female figure may in itself be enough to signify the sacred marriage of the two deities. The second female figure in the Thracian Rider reliefs would then be the counterpart of the second woman on the Letnitsa plaque. Such a hypothesis would also support the idea of Heros as a fertility deity.

The Thracian Rider on Tombstones

The figure of the rider appears very often on tombstones. Of the sixty inscribed monuments found in the Romanian part of Moesia Inferior and Dacia, thirty-nine were votive and the rest funerary. So similar are these two groups in composition that without inscriptional clues, it becomes very difficult to differentiate between the two types. Interestingly too, in Romania the majority of inscriptions engraved on votive monuments are in Greek, while those on funerary monuments are mainly in Latin.[798]

The problem with respect to the funerary monuments is to distinguish Heros the god from the dead man as rider-hero. That the two are conceived of as separate at least some of the time is confirmed by funerary monuments from the former Yugoslavia on which a rider appears in the gable of the stela and again in the lower register.[799] It would seem reasonable to see the figure in the gable as the rider god and the figure below him as the heroized dead man.

The tombstones with representations of the Thracian Rider often have two registers of carved images. An example from *Tropaeum Traiani* (Adamclisi) shows the type.[800] In the upper register is a horseman riding to the right who holds a wreath in his right hand. Under the horse is a hound attacking a hare. A veiled woman, rendered frontally, stands at the far right. In the relief field below the horseman, a funerary feast is represented. A bearded man and two children recline before a three-legged table. Again on the right is a veiled woman but this time she appears seated on a throne. The image of the horseman on this relief does not differ substantially from those on votive plaques except in the detail of the annular object in the horseman's hand. Hampartumian's identification of it as a wreath makes sense especially as another tombstone from Adamclisi has only a single wreath on it.[801] The condition of the relief makes it difficult to tell whether the rider's hand makes the *benedictio latina* gesture, but it is possible.

It may not be unreasonable to suggest that the wreath in particular, and possibly the gesture also, represent the belief of the deceased and his family in the victory over death through the Thracian Rider. This happy result may have been brought about by the deceased's participation in the mysteries of the rider, as Aleksandrina Cermanović-Kuzmanović suggests,[802] if worship of the rider took that form, or perhaps the promise of immortality required faith alone without formal initiation. The names of the deceased on both tombstones — Scoris and Daizus — are Thracian.[803]

An inscription on a Thracian Rider plaque from *Odessos: Agathenor Apatouriou Neos Heros* has been interpreted by Georges Seure as indicating a belief that at death, the deceased became an incarnation of his god Heros; in his turn he became the new Heros.[804] If this is true, then it is probable that the rider figures on the tombstones who exhibit attributes of the Thracian Rider are in fact the heroized dead assimilated to the god.

If we look at what is plainly a Roman military tombstone with a horseman relief found in Romania, we can see how it differs from the Thracian Rider tombstones. The stela belonging to T. Claudius Maximus was found at Philippi and dates from the second century AD.[805] The relief shows the deceased himself in military dress, sword drawn, riding to attack a seated figure in the lower right hand corner. The seated figure is dressed like the Dacians on Trajan's column and the inscription lists the *Bellum Dacicum* among the dead man's exploits. The figure under attack has been identified as Decebalus. The relief shows none of the attributes which would associate it with the Thracian Rider cult. There is no wreath, altar, or snake. The horseman makes no special gestures. He confronts a man not an animal. The tombstone belongs to the mainstream of Roman military rider stelae.

Seeing that there are clear differences between the Thracian Rider tombstones and the standard Roman military monument, we may ask whether the tombstones of Thracian soldiers outside of Thrace betray any mark of the Thracian Rider cult. Quite a number of the military tombstones with reliefs of riders and adversaries belong to Thracians. Most date from the first century AD during a time when the ethnic regiments still retained their cultural identity.[806] So we should expect that men serving with Thracian regiments were, in fact, Thracians. Sometimes this assumption can be substantiated by information from the inscriptions, as when Longinus whose tombstone is at Colchester tells us that he comes from *Serdica* (Sophia).

An examination of these reliefs with respect to elements which might specifically connect their owners with the cult of the Thracian Rider reveals nothing. Even the relief of Dolanus Bessus with his typically Thracian name[807] exhibits no notably Thracian elements. All the horsemen are dressed in military costume. Their adversaries are clearly identifiable as Celts, their contemporary enemies, and there are no hints of the attributes of the Thracian horseman. This does not rule out the possibility that the cult had adherents among the Thracian elements of the Roman army. The problem may be one of date. Most of the tombstones date to the first century, whereas most of the rider monuments belong to the second and third centuries. The Thracian Rider tombstones may represent a later development.

The Thracian Rider is a god who still eludes clear definition. He seems mainly to have been identified with Apollo and Asklepios but there are also identifications with other deities and companionship with still others. His iconography drew on Greek rider imagery of a very common type which would have been easily accessible to artists throughout the Graeco-Roman world; so it is impossible to pin down his artistic antecedents with any precision, just as it is difficult to pin down his functions. In these he can be compared perhaps to the gods of the Celtic world whose powers encompassed a far wider range than those of the Greek and Roman gods who were their iconographical models. However, in artistic terms, unlike the Celtic gods, the artistic type of the Thracian Rider appears to go back at least to the Hellenistic period and possibly, in native Thracian form — if the identification of the figures from the Letnitsa treasure are correct — to an even earlier period than that.

Chapter 7

The Danubian Rider Cult

The Danubian Rider cult, so-called from the single rider or pair of horsemen who appear on the cult reliefs, is one of the most problematic of ancient religions. The cult deities and rituals are preserved for us pictorially on small plaques which are our only evidence for the cult's existence (Figure 84, for example); nearly all finds have been anepigraphic and even the names of the presiding deities are not known.[808] Although thirteen engraved gems, some of which are inscribed, have also been associated with the cult on account of their imagery, most of the words inscribed on them are incomprehensible or of little help in identifying the gods of the cult or its participants.[809] Thus all the information we possess about the cult and its spread have had to be deduced from careful reading of the archaeological evidence and from interpretation of the images on the plaques.

The complexity of the iconographical programme, which is evident from the large number of objects and figures on even the earliest of the Danubian Rider relief series, has led scholars to the conclusion that we are dealing here with a mystery cult characterized by initiation, the imparting of secret knowledge to members and the ranking of initiates into grades. The Danubian Riders appear to have been worshipped by a closed membership, as Mithras was, rather than publicly like most ancient deities. The objects and animals depicted on the reliefs must represent symbols associated with worship or with the cult myth.

Unfortunately, the vast majority of these stone and lead tablets were not found in archaeological excavations but were either chance or surface finds or bought on the antiquities market. Of the 232 items catalogued by the Romanian scholar Dumitru Tudor in his *Corpus Monumentorum Religionis Equitum Danuuinorum*, only 31 have some indication of an archaeological context[810] and few of these are precise enough to be useful in dating. Nevertheless, enough is known about the general provenance of the finds to give a good idea of the spread of the cult. The greatest number — one hundred and ninety — catalogued by Dumitru Tudor were found in the Danubian provinces of Upper and Lower Moesia, Upper and Lower Pannonia and Upper and Lower Dacia.[811] An additional six, mainly from *Carnuntum* and *Viminacium* in Pannonia, have been published by Kurt Gschwantler.[812] Twelve were found in Dalmatia, and only one from the most westerly Danubian province of Noricum was known to Tudor,[813] although a second has recently been found.[814] Thrace has only produced two reliefs and Italy, six.[815] Three of the Italian examples come from *Aquileia*. This last is not very surprising since *Aquileia* on the Adriatic was a major trading depot for the exchange of goods between Italy and the Danube regions.[816] Even after the opening up of other routes into the interior took some of the importance from this centre,[817] the population must have remained mixed, with many traders from the Danubian provinces, particularly nearby Pannonia.

Only two relics of the Danubian Rider cult have been discovered in the provinces further west. One in Gaul and the second in Britain. The former was found at *Portus Abucinus* (Magny-le-Port) in the remains of a Roman villa. It is now lost but seems to have been a lead plaque similar to many found in the Pannonian provinces in particular.[818] The latter is a small stone roundel found in London which will be discussed in more detail below.

The Earliest Cult Images

The cult seems to have had its beginning in the province of Dacia. This is suggested by the fact that, although the largest numbers of rider plaques are found in Pannonia, those reckoned to be the earliest come from Dacia. It appears that the original form of the cult scene was a single rider facing a goddess. A relief from the city of *Apulum* in Dacia Superior[819] is probably one of the earliest (Figure 84).[820] On a plaque of white marble, measuring 37.5 cm. x 30 cm. x 5 cm., with a rounded top, a single horseman is represented. He is bearded and dressed in Oriental costume including Phrygian cap. He holds an elongated object which might be a double axe. Beneath his horse is a naked human figure lying prone. To the right of the horseman are two women standing on a pedestal. The left hand figure wears a veil over her hair and the right hand figure brings her hand up to her mouth and inclines her head. Above the women is a tree round which a snake is winding itself, while next to the tree and above the horse's head is a male bust. Behind the horseman, in a damaged area on the far left, a pair of feet show that an attendant once stood there.

There is a series of cult symbols in a register beneath the rider's feet. They include a lion, a ram, a three-legged table with a fish on it, a krater with two drinking horns above it, a cock, a spiral column and a last object which looks like a Phrygian cap. This relief also has an upper border in which a pair of snakes is rearing up and facing toward the centre.[821]

Based on his study of extant Danubian Rider reliefs, Dumitru Tudor came to the conclusion that these single rider plaques were the earliest of the series, with the paired riders developing later. However, since the rider cult left no epigraphic evidence, there was no way to check this conclusion independently when Tudor was writing. Fortunately, the situation has changed recently. Manfred Oppermann, who has studied the stylistic development and iconography of the Thracian Rider, has been able to connect many of the stone Danubian Rider plaques with the Thracian Rider series on stylistic grounds. These latter can be dated by their inscriptions, as can similarly related Mithraic material. For it seems likely that all were made in the same workshops. Thus the *Apulum* relief can be associated stylistically with a particular group of Thracian Rider reliefs which spread over the north and south of the Balkans and which can be dated somewhere between the end of the second century and the beginning of the third century AD.[822] This is a slightly later date than that suggested by Tudor who believed the earliest plaques to have developed in the first half of the second century[823] although, of course, it is not certain whether *Apulum* represents the very earliest iconographical type. Earlier examples may come to light, but it appears at present that this cult belongs mainly to the last century of the pagan Roman Empire.

It has thus become clear that Tudor was right about the single rider reliefs, his class A, being the earliest. The archaeological evidence, moreover, on which Tudor based his claim of primacy for Dacia shows that the majority of these class A reliefs come from Dacian territory: seventeen as opposed to eight from Moesia, four from Dalmatia and none at all from Pannonia.

Origins of the Cult

Since we know none of the names of the deities and the cult is not mentioned in any written sources, discovering anything about its origins is extremely difficult. Evidence for Dacian religious practices from any period is limited. Herodotus has supplied some names and cult associations for the Dacians before the Roman conquest[824] and these have been much studied. Hadrian Diacoviciu summarizes the known pantheon this way: Zamolxis, a chthonian deity; Gebeleizis, a sky god; a female deity corresponding to Hestia/Vesta; a warrior resembling Ares/Mars and also the goddess Bendis corresponding to Artemis and Diana.[825]

Unfortunately archaeology has not been able to confirm the literary notices. The Dacians seem to have been mainly aniconic although a few images have been discovered like the bronze bust of a female (Bendis?) from Piatra Roșie.[826] The excavations at the ancient capital of Sarmizegetusa have yielded interesting results in the form of a series of circular alignments of columns probably made of wood with limestone bases. Other remains are rectangular and appear also to be composed of rows of columns of wood or stone. These are considered likely to be temples: similar buildings have been discovered at other Dacian settlements.[827] No figural art seemed to accompany these remains nor could it be quite certain how these buildings were used; although if they were open to the sky this could suggest a celestial deity.

At Piatra Roșie, a miniature vehicle was discovered which may represent a sun chariot or wagon.[828] If this is the correct interpretation, it could mean some role for the horse as celestial draught animal. The horse seems to figure only rarely in Dacian archaeological finds, as, for example, the figurine discovered at Ocnița among objects which date from Augustan times. This is a human figure with a horse's head. It must have some cultic or magical significance, but more than that is difficult to say.[829] What relationship these few finds have to the horses ridden by the Danubian horsemen is impossible to determine, but they do at least suggest that the horse may have played a part in Dacian worship before the development of the later Danubian Rider cult. The archaeological remains in Dacia, then, give away few secrets. It may be that the Danubian Rider cult developed against a background of sky and sun worship, perhaps reflected in the fact that, of all the religions studied by Ernest Will in his monograph on cultic reliefs, next to the Mithraic cult, the cult of the Danubian Riders made the most consistent use of the Sol and Luna busts.[830] Moreover, celestial imagery played an important part in the symbolism of the cult at all times although the influence may have come as much from other religions as from earlier Dacian beliefs. One of the characteristics of the Danubian Rider cult is its apparent openness to imagery, symbols and ritual from other religious sources.

The Danubian Horseman

There are many examples of the cult's willingness to borrow from other religions. At the representational level it is evident in the cult's pictorial development. Most scholars agree that the single rider type of composition was borrowed from the image of the Thracian Rider (Figures 79, 80).[831] In both we have the horseman facing right and raising his right arm. Female figures on the right hand side of the plaque are also common to both, as are attendants walking behind the horse. However, the Danubian horseman tramples a figure, human or animal, under foot which the Thracian Rider never does. This suggest a fundamental difference between the divine natures of the Thracian and Danubian Riders, the hunter and the warrior.

The close ethnic and geographical relationship between the Thracians and the Dacians makes it not unreasonable to suggest that a mounted god like the Thracian Rider also existed among the Dacians. The rider reliefs from the Letnitsa treasure discussed in Chapter Six, confirm the existence of a mounted god or hero from perhaps the end of the fifth century BC in Thrace. Although there is no comparable evidence from Dacia, a similar entity there could have been the origin of the single Dacian Rider. The geographical area of the two cults, although overlapping somewhat, is not the same. The Thracian Rider had his centre between the lower Danube and the north coast of the Aegean while the Danubian Rider cult stems from the Roman provinces of Dacia, Moesia and Pannonia. The two overlap directly, for the most part, only in Lower Moesia.[832]

Many of the Danubian plaques have a large variety of symbols either in separate registers or surrounding the main figures. These are absent in Thracian Rider imagery. Oppermann's observations on the stylistic relationship between the stone cult reliefs of the two cults, however, suggest that it was in the Dacian workshops that the iconography of the Danubian Riders was worked out, at least for the early single figure plaques. It must have been on the basis of the obvious similarities in subject matter that the Thracian model was employed.

The Figure Beneath the Horse

Despite the similarity in appearance between the Thracian Rider and the Danubian Riders, the figure of the dead man found beneath the hooves of the Danubian horse, shows clearly that the Thracian and Dacian gods were not alike in function. The Thracian Rider is a hunter who raises his spear against game animals. The Danubian Rider is a warrior whose enemy lies beneath his feet. In most cases the dead man lies prone and is very small in size in comparison to the main figures (Figure 85).[833] Even where the riders are not raising their spears but grasping their horses' bridles, they stand on stiff, prone human figures as, for example, on a relief from Lower Moesia in the Sofia Museum.[834] It is probably not worthwhile to look for a model for this small prone figure. For it seems unlikely that such crude figures required a model. Indeed, the stiffness of these figures, particularly in less able works, suggests that craftsmen merely carved a small standing figure but rotated through 90 degrees so that it lay on its side. Thus on the few examples where the enemy figures can be seen to be clothed, no attempt is made to alter the folds of the garment to represent the drapery of a fallen foe.[835]

Some of the dead are carved with more care. A plaque from Paracin in the former Yugoslavia shows the trampled figure as a body lying prone with arms bent so the hands lie close to the face. The silhouette of the body is well drawn, curving clearly at the shoulders, buttocks and calves.[836] The figure is also in scale with the rest of the figures on the plaque. Parallels with this composition which come to mind are the figures of the dead who lie under the horses of the Sassanian kings in triumph and investiture scenes, particularly the investiture of the first Sassanian king Ardashir (AD 224–241) at Naqsh-i Rustam.[837] Here too the figures lie prone and are dead or, at least, unresisting. However, the similarity is most probably due to the similarity of subject matter or symbolism — the dead enemy as proof of the triumphant strength of the conquering warrior — rather than copying one from the other or from the same model.

On the other hand, a small number of Danubian horsemen are trampling enemies who are not dead and whose form may owe something to the Roman trampling rider motif. In particular a relief in Czechoslovakia, but perhaps originally from Transylvania, shows a horseman riding a rearing or galloping horse (Figure 86).[838] The rider raises his spear to strike a figure below him who is trying to rise using his arms to brace himself. He appears to be rising from a prone position, the worn state of the relief makes his exact posture difficult to determine. A curving line below the armpit may indicate the pectoral muscle which suggests that his body is slightly turned toward the viewer. The figure calls to mind a number of parallels. An Etruscan funerary urn at Cortona has a similar figure raising himself up as a mounted warrior comes from behind, spear raised for the kill.[839] Turning to sculpture in the round, the figure recalls the giants under the horses in the Celtic Jupiter and giant groups who may, as we have seen, have a Hellenistic prototype. Neither of these comparisons is meant to offer a model for the Danubian Rider group, but rather to suggest that this particular artist was drawing his ideas from standard types, perhaps military pattern books, rather than improvising his own enemy figures.

In a few other cases, like the plaque from Dacia Superior inscribed with the name of *Germanos*, the enemy lying supine with his arms raised may also refer back to tombstone types. The Celtic enemy lying on his back and reaching up to stab at the horse above him was a common figure and could possibly be the ultimate source for the Dacian enemy particularly where he is lying with his knees bent.[840] The close association of the cult with the military[841] makes it likely that such imagery was familiar even though the majority of the tombstone reliefs were produced in the Rhineland and Britain during the first century AD.[842] It is not unreasonable to think that many of these tombstones were still standing in the second and third centuries and were familiar to soldiers and craftsmen who travelled across Europe at that time.

The Two-Rider Image

It has been assumed that the beginning of the Danubian cult imagery occurred sometime after the end of Trajan's Dacian wars (AD 106) and the establishment of Dacia as a Roman province.[843] The war would have opened up the area to new influences and begun the transformation of a native cult into an Oriental-style mystery. For this was what the Danubian Rider cult seems to have been. The plaques with the single rider would have begun to be produced some time in the second century although the large number of cult objects which surround the central scene suggest that the religion was already of the mystery type when the reliefs were produced.

By the first quarter of the third century, paired-rider plaques were being made together with the earlier single-rider type.[844] The two-rider plaques form Tudor's class B and they are by far the most common class of monument (Figure 87). Only thirty-one out of the total reliefs currently known are class A monuments.[845] Dumitru Tudor believed that the change took place at the latest by the second half of the second century[846] but Manfred Oppermann's stylistic-epigraphic study indicates the early third century.

The one British find, a small marble roundel now in the Museum of London,[847] is a simple version of the double rider composition and can serve as an example of the typical class B relief (Plate 5). The relief is damaged in the upper right-hand corner but its diameter has been measured at 11.5 cm. It is divided into a main scene and a smaller, lower register. The main scene consists of a pair of opposed horsemen both of whom are facing a female figure wearing a long girded tunic. She is standing between the two riders. In front of the woman is a three-legged table on which lies a fish. The left hand horseman wears a short tunic and Phrygian cap and raises his right hand (but no spear can be seen) apparently to strike a man lying prostrate beneath his horse's hooves. Part of a bust is visible above the horse's head and an attendant stands behind the horse. The image of the right-hand horseman, which should be similar to the one on the left, has broken away with only another prostrate man and the foreleg of a horse remaining to make the identification of this relief as a Danubian Rider plaque quite certain.

The new composition with its focus on two opposed horsemen facing a central female figure is based on the representation of the Dioscuri. As we saw in Chapter Five, there are two compositional types used most commonly to depict the Dioscuri and their horses. In the composition apparently favoured in the most westerly provinces — Germania, Gaul and Britain — the twins are dismounted and stand by their horses. In the composition more usually found in the eastern part of the Empire, the Dioscuri are mounted and they and their mounts face toward the goddess between them. The Danubian Riders appear not to have been represented in the first form but always in the second. However, they differ from the mounted Dioscuri, just as they do from the Thracian Rider, by the addition of a prostrate figure, human or occasionally animal, beneath the horse. Moreover, unlike the Dioscuri, the Danubian Riders sometimes hold raised spears or double axes as if about the strike. The mounted Dioscuri in the triad compositions are often represented unarmed, and when they are armed, their weapons are held in a resting position, not poised for a strike.[848] So it is interesting to note that armed Danubian Riders (Figures 84–86), based mainly on the hunting Thracian Rider, make up a large proportion of Tudor's class A figures; while in class B, the two rider composition derived from the resting Dioscuri, the proportion of armed figures is smaller (Figures 87, Plate 5). In part, the change to a less aggressive posture for the pair of horsemen may be the result of the change of pictorial model. The commonest form of the Thracian Rider found is Kazarow's type B hunter with raised spear. This was the model for the single Danubian Rider plaque. When the model was changed to the Dioscuri, the more peaceful form of the rider came into being following this model. However, this new arrangement may also be the result of a changed relationship between the horsemen and the goddess whom they now more often salute. The new composition moves the pictorial emphasis from the centrally placed rider facing the standing female on the right, to the now-central female figure flanked by two riders who seem to be subservient to her. Their salute to the lady, who appears more clearly than ever to be a goddess, looks like adoration.[849]

The Divine Banquet Plaques

A tiny group of four plaques exists which Tudor calls class C. They show only a divine banquet of a kind which was occasionally depicted on the more complex representations of class B. They have all been found in Moesia Inferior.[850]

The Imagery of the Cult

In spite of the lack of written records, through patient study of the plaques, scholars have begun to build up a coherent picture as to the nature of the cult. A series of plaques made during the third century, mainly out of lead, are pictorial encyclopedias of cultic practice and symbolism (Figure 88). These plaques all have several registers, sometimes as many as four or five, on which not only cult symbols and cult deities are represented, but also what appear to be the rituals of the cult itself. This type of plaque, when it is of Dacian or Moesian origin, is often made of stone; but the majority of those from Pannonia are of lead.[851] The lead plaques were cast in numbers from the same moulds so that often several copies of the same composition are extant. The centres of manufacture of lead reliefs were most likely cities like *Sirmium* in Pannonia from which they might be carried to other areas. Edward Ochsenschlager, who excavated at *Sirmium* (where eight plaques have come to light), observed that of the fifteen known examples of one single compositional type, eleven were found in Pannonia, two in Moesia Superior, one in Gaul and one is of unknown provenance.[852] There also seems to have been an area of

manufacture in Dacia in the region including the cities of *Romula, Sucidava* and *Orlea*.[853]

The lead reliefs vary in detail, but, for the most part, they include more symbols and activities than do the stone plaques, although some of these elements, especially the symbols, may have been painted on the stone. The division into registers already apparent in the earliest stone plaques is carried much further on the metal reliefs so that many have four registers and follow a clear iconographical programme.

The Lead Relief Plaques

A recently published lead plaque from Pannonia shows many of the characteristic elements and the enormous complexity of the symbolism (Figure 88).[854] It comes from the Pannonian city of *Viminacium* and measures 10.9–10.3 cm. in height and 8.7–8.5 cm. in width. The picture field is divided into four zones which are separated one from the other by horizontal lines. In the uppermost register, under the central arch is the sun god Sol driving a quadriga. The horses are only shown as protomes, but it can be seen that the inner pair have their heads turned inwards while the outer pair are turned outward and upward. Sol is standing in his chariot. He wears a rayed crown on which the rays are shown cleft at the ends. He wears a tunic and chlamys and his right hand is outstretched in greeting. In his left hand he holds a globe and a whip. In the background, to the right, is a star. Under the left hand arch, which curves behind the main arch framing Sol, is a bust which is also Sol, possibly with a star on his head (the relief is somewhat worn). In the corresponding place on the right is a bust of Luna on whose shoulders the points of the crescent moon are visible. Both hold a torch in front of their left shoulder.

In the second register is the central scene of horsemen and female figure — the goddess. This register is no longer the largest and takes up only approximately one quarter of the available space. The goddess stands in the middle of the composition. She wears a girded chiton and is holding a cloth in both hands in front of her body. On each side of her head, there is a star. The riders face inward and both hold up their right hand in greeting. Their dress is difficult to distinguish but they certainly wear mantles which flutter behind them. Above the mantle of each rider is a lamp. Under the hooves of the left-hand horse is a fish; under the right is a man lying on his back. Behind the left rider is a figure of an armed warrior (Mars) who wears boots and a high crested helmet. He is armed with a spear and shield. Behind the right rider is a woman dressed in a chiton and himation who is holding her right hand before her face.

The third level shows scenes which appear to be the actual rituals of the cult. In the middle of the register and taking up the most space are three figures standing around a table. The middle figure, to judge from the hairstyle, is a woman. She holds a beaker in front of her breast and has her right arm raised to her head. The other two figures who seem to be wearing long garments are certainly men. They reach toward a semicircular object (bread?) of which there are three on the table. In the middle of the table is an oval platter with a fish on it. The scene on the right side of the register must be connected with this meal because the three naked men, who are standing there, are looking, and probably coming, toward the table. They hold each other by the hand or shoulder.

On the left side of this third register is a completely different scene. It shows a tree with a branch projecting to the left. An animal's decapitated body can be seen hanging from the branch. A man in a short tunic is skinning it. Behind him stands another man in a short tunic who is wearing a ram's head as a mask.

The last and fourth register presents a series of cult symbols, from left to right: a branch with leaves and a cock below it, a coiled snake, a small table or candelabra, a kantheros with curved handles, an unidentified heart-shaped object, a lion seated with his tail raised behind him, a three-legged table on which lies an indistinct object that may be a fish.

Compared to these intricate lead reliefs, even the most complex stone reliefs have less information. They rarely have more than three registers, although Tudor publishes one where the Sol and Luna register is surmounted by another on which stand the fragmentary remains of hooves belonging to a bull or a ram. This relief is unusual too in having an inscription which reads *Germanos epoiesen*[855] which may indicate an individual preference in the choice of scenes, perhaps a piece specially commissioned from Germanos by a patron. On the whole, however, the lead reliefs give a fuller account of the cult practice and symbols.

Gems with Cult Associations

The gems, of which thirteen have been associated with this cult, show as much variety as the plaques. No provenance is known for any of the gems, unfortunately. One is now in the British Museum (Figure 89).[856] It has the familiar scene of opposed riders facing a woman who holds out her hands beneath the muzzles of the two horses. The horsemen trample on naked men lying prone. The reverse has an unintelligible inscription in Greek letters ΘΟΥ, ΡΙΚΗΛ. In Vienna, a cornelian is carved with a three register representation like a stone plaque in miniature.[857] On it the goddess and riders inhabit the first level with the busts of Sol and Luna missing. The second level is given over to the celebration of the cult banquet. The third register also seems to involve elements of cultic ritual. What may be a grate, associated with the bull or ram sacrifice, especially in the form of the taurobolium or criobolium practiced mainly by the cult of the goddess Cybele,[858] is represented as well as a male figure wearing a ram's head and a female who raises her hand to her mouth.

The Cult Goddess

According to Dumitru Tudor, the primary deity of the cult is the goddess who stands between the horsemen, not the horsemen themselves. She always appears on the reliefs although on the single rider reliefs her position at the side makes her seem to be of less consequence than the rider who, with his horse, takes up all of the central picture space. Moreover, the goddess seems to lack any specific attributes, although the fish is most likely associated with her. But her position may be compared with Helen on monuments of the Dioscuri. Here too the central female

figure is given no personal attributes. In his 1935 study of the Dioscuri, Fernand Chapouthier suggested that in such a case, if the goddess is not characterized by any emblem of her own, then her association with her companions is sufficient to identify her: the sister is identified by her relationship to her brothers.[859] Similarly, the Danubian goddess and horseman, or horsemen, form an iconographical unit which in itself identifies the participants. The unit includes not only the goddess and riders but the human or animal forms beneath the horses.

The goddess of the Danubian religion has the fish as the creature most closely associated with her. A fish appears on the tripod table in front of her on the London Museum roundel.[860] Occasionally, the fish replaces one of the enemies prostrate beneath the horseman.[861] On rare occasions it appears alone in the gables of the lead plaques.[862] As we have no name for the goddess, there has been much speculation on the subject. Manfred Oppermann summed up the suggestions put forward: according to various scholarly theories she is to be identified as Artemis-Anahita-Cybele-Rhea-Venus-Diana Ephesiana as well as Demeter, Magna Mater, Selene, Artemis-Bendis, Despoina-Nemesis or Aphrodite Spandarmat.[863]

The Horsemen

The horsemen too keep their anonymity. Their costumes may vary; sometimes they are dressed in Oriental garb and sometimes as Roman soldiers. They often wear Phrygian caps. They may be followed by attendants or not and the right horseman in particular may have a human enemy underfoot who may at times be replaced by an animal. Ljubica Zotović has looked for a consistent pattern in these variations but has not succeeded in finding anything significant beyond the fact that the fish is only associated with the horseman on metal reliefs.[864] Other variations seem to elude categorization. Except as mounts for the riders, the horse makes no other appearance on the plaques and does not seem to have a place in the cult scene. This leaves unanswered the question as to why the two males are always represented mounted. There is no suggestion that the horses have any role to play in a theriomorphic representation of the two horsemen as is the case with the Celtic Mars. No plaques show horses alone representing the two riders. The significance of the horse may not be in any symbolic role it has to play but as the fitting companion and vehicle for a divine warrior — the inheritance of Hellenistic and Imperial attitudes toward riding.

Sol and Luna

The uppermost parts of the plaques are almost always reserved for Sol and Luna either as busts or symbols. On the single or double register reliefs, the busts may be placed directly above the figures of the goddess and horsemen. But on more ambitious works, the celestial deities have a register of their own. As a rule Sol appears on the left and Luna on the right. Sol often wears a rayed crown and Luna a crescent moon, so the identifications are quite certain.[865] The frequent representation of the celestial gods on the plaques is paralleled by their representation on monuments of other mystery cults, particularly the cult of Mithras in which the sun had a very close cultic relationship with the

Iranian god and was eventually identified with him.[866] The importance of Sol in the Danubian cult can be judged by the development of the type of lead plaque on which Sol dominates the upper scene and is shown riding in a quadriga in the middle of the register. This top register has been enlarged at the expense of the second level so that Sol, rather than the goddess and horsemen group, is the focal point of the plaque.

The iconographical forms of Sol and Luna appear to have been borrowed originally from Mithraic usage. The growth of the identification between Mithras and Sol in the Mithraic religion may have led to similar enhancement within the Danubian Rider cult since the latter seems to have borrowed many of its cultic rituals and probably, as some scholars believe, much of its philosophy and theology as well from Mithras.[867] Certainly, the rituals as they are represented on the plaques are reminiscent of what we know of Mithraic cult practice in many ways. And some of the symbols like the lion-krater-snake groups, the raven, the eagle and the cock have clear Mithraic associations.[868]

Using stylistic criteria, Dumitru Tudor dates the lead plaques mainly to the third century. The earliest, those with smooth column shafts,[869] are dated somewhere within the first half of the third century because the hairstyle of the goddess Luna is of the type frequently worn by the Syrian princesses, Julia Domna, Julia Maesa and Julia Mamaea.[870] Severus and his wife Julia Domna had themselves represented as Sol and Luna and it is likely that representation of the goddess with some of the characteristics of the Syrian empress was deliberate.

The Dioscuri

Some tablets, like a stone plaque from *Potaissa* in Dacia Superior, show the celestial gods at the edges of the register with the two snakes between them rearing up and facing what appears to be an egg in the centre between them.[871] The relief is a class A type. On a similar relief from the same place, the snakes face a krater in the middle of the register.[872] In a few cases it looks as if the busts have been completely replaced by the snakes.[873] The snakes are most likely to be identified with the Dioscuri for whom opposed snakes with an egg between them is a common symbol. Here again, we might add that there is no evidence that the horse ever played a similar symbolic role in Danubian Rider imagery.

The Dioscuri, in turn, are associated with the heavens and the stars so it is not surprising that in a syncretistic cult like this one, their symbols should represent the celestial world along with the busts of Sol and Luna or even that the two become interchangeable.[874]

Interpretation of the Plaques

According to Tudor's hypothesis, the division of the plaques into registers, particularly three registers, expresses the triple function of the goddess and riders: celestial, terrestrial and chthonic or eschatological.[875] The celestial imagery of the uppermost register, sometimes conflated with the scene of the goddess and riders is very clear. The goddess and riders

represent the terrestrial level. They are sometimes attended by other gods who look after worldly concerns — Mars depicted in Roman military dress, Nemesis who holds her hand to her mouth and inclines her head and Victory, all of whom represent concepts important to the earthly lives of the soldier devotees.

The lower levels represent the promises that the cult makes to its adepts. Sometimes, the cult's message is in the form of symbols, but often it is shown as groups of people involved in what must be the rituals themselves. On the plaques with four levels, this one is usually the third.

The representations of ritual acts recorded on the lower register are among the main reasons for determining that the Danubian Rider cult is a mystery cult. The reliefs of that other puzzling religion, the Thracian Rider cult, provide no indication as to whether there was any mystery element present at all. But the Danubian Rider reliefs, even without inscriptional evidence, give a reasonable indication of the character of the cult.

The main elements of the ritual scene as we saw them on the lead plaques from *Viminacium* are the killing of an animal and a banquet. The animal, certainly a ram, which is associated with the riders as the fish is with the goddess, is shown killed and hanging from a tree.

The *criobolium* and the *occultatio* take forms which are familiar from other mystery rites of the Roman period. The blood-letting of the *criobolium* was associated chiefly with the cult of Cybele. The type of ordeal represented by the *occultatio* was common to many cults especially Mithraism and the Isis cult where new *mystai* were required to show their courage in facing symbolic death, much as our reliefs seem to show.[876] However, ram-sacrifice may also have played a part in earlier Thraco-Dacian religion. A gold helmet dated to around 400 BC was a chance find at Coţofeneşti in Romania.[877] On the cheek pieces of this helmet a warrior is represented quite clearly sacrificing a ram.[878] While it is too fanciful to bring this into direct connection with the rider cult; nevertheless, it is possible that the ram as the sacred animal of a Daco-Thracian warrior and rider god long predates the development of the Imperial mystery religion. The form of sacrifice, but not the animal of sacrifice, was borrowed from the cult of Cybele.

There is little evidence for representation of actual rites on the votive artefacts of any of the other mystery cults. A Mithraic relief fragment from Ratiaria shows a figure holding a patera in one of his raised hands under one arch of an arcade. Since he does not seem to belong to any familiar Mithraic scene, it has been suggested that he is a priest or high ranking *mystes* about to make a sacrifice in the grotto.[879] Another, lost, relief from *Viminacium* may also have included a scene involving participation in the cult.[880]

A mosaic floor found at Trier which has been dated to the fourth century AD depicts what appears to be the rites of a mystery cult including the representation of a scene from the cult myth — the birth of the Dioscuri and Helen from the egg — balanced by a scene showing elements of the ritual itself. The mosaic is rectangular in shape and divided across the broad side into two square panels each of which is framed by medallions. Each medallion carries the figure of a named devotee or participant in the rite. The central panels, like the rider plaques, show the divine world in juxtaposition to the human one. The largest figures on the floor are the mythological group, presumably representing the cult myth. Leda stands next to an altar on which is an egg whose contents can be seen: three infants. Their names are written above them CASTOR, POLUS, AELENA. Over the altar is Jupiter, not in the form of a white swan but as a brown eagle.[881] Next to the altar on the left stands Agamemnon whose relation to the others is problematical.[882] Jacques Moreau believes the cult to be that of the goddess Nemesis.[883] Nemesis, like the Dioscuri, seems to have played a role in the Danubian cult as well.

The complementary central group on the lower half of the Trier mosaic shows the rite and not the gods. Its axis is aligned with the short side, while the mythological scene is aligned along the long axis of the floor. The lower group has thus been turned through 90 degrees. Inscriptions identify all the figures although the significance of the names, perhaps cult names, is unknown.[884] This differs from the rider plaques, as we have seen, where no names, cultic or otherwise, are recorded.

The Trier mosaic appears to show a mystery cult whose liturgy involves a banquet, procession of offerings and the ritual handling of an egg and bird. If some of these elements seem similar to Danubian Rider representations, the similarity is due to the form of the mystery ritual which was a feature of all mystery-type religions and which, indeed, goes a long way toward defining them as a group. What distinguishes the Trier mosaic cult and the Danubian Riders from the majority of mystery cults is the detail with which the acts of the rite have been recorded for all time. Wall paintings from Pompeii like the series in the Villa of Mysteries or the scene of the Isis ceremony now in the Naples Museum, show that representations in paint of rituals outside the state religion, even secret ones, were not unknown. The Trier mosaic may follow this tradition. But what particularly distinguishes the Danubian Rider plaques from all of these is their small size and portability which would, therefore, make them liable to fall into the hands of unbelievers. This may account for their lack of inscriptions.

The inclusion of such deities as Mars, Nemesis and Victory and the occasional representation of the two riders in military garb lend the Danubian Rider cult a distinctly military tone. The devotees of the cult would have been largely soldiers posted along the frontiers. Finds of reliefs at camp sites[885] confirm a military connection. But some of the plaques, including the single Gaulish find, have been discovered in domestic villas which could mean family worship as well.[886] None of the reliefs appears to show female initiation. Whether women were allowed to become initiated into the cult is not known. The fact that the principal deity was female and may have been, at some point, identified with the Great Mother or other great goddess figures, may have meant that female worship was accepted.

The end of the cult appears to have been gradual. It began to decline in the second half of the third century[887] and there seems then to have been a shift in its geographical centre of gravity from Dacia where it originated to the Pannonian provinces where the metal plaques were the dominant form of relief.[888] Undoubtedly, the withdrawal of the Romans from Dacia in AD 271 hastened the decline of this cult which depended so much on the military. Barbarian invasions of the new vulnerable towns of Dacia and the increasing barbarian activity in the whole Danube area would have slowly and fatally weakened the cult even before the influence of Christianity.[889]

The modern title, Danubian Rider cult, is, as we have seen, somewhat inaccurate since the central figure to whom worship was addressed was a goddess of the great or mother goddess type. Exactly what role the horsemen had is difficult to determine. Making analogies with the cult of the Dioscuri, they may have been protectors of the goddess and certainly were warriors and not hunters. Undoubtedly they would have been fighters for good over evil, bringers of divine victory who would also have brought earthly victory to soldier devotees. By extension, this victory became the victory over death for the initiates.[890] Several of the plaques have been found in tombs[891] but there is no evidence to suggest that the horsemen took the role of psychopomp and led the dead to the cultic paradise. Furthermore, the horses themselves seem to have played no demonstrable part in the cult activities. Nothing currently surmised about the cult suggests that it would have differed materially if the warriors had not been mounted. Of course, we might think otherwise if we knew the cult myth. But based on our present knowledge the horsemen seem well characterized by Ernest Will's comment that "il n'existe pas de dieux cavaliers, mais seulement des dieux representés à cheval et, plus exactement même, des dieux de peuples cavaliers".[892] The early Dacians like the Thracians were certainly *peuples cavaliers* and this is still reflected in the Imperial Danubian Rider cult.

Chapter 8

Conclusion

The Importance of the Greek Background

The strand that connects all the different manifestations of the horse and rider image across the breadth of the western Roman Empire is the constant use of established Greek rider imagery, whether it be borrowed second-hand by way of Rome or directly through Hellenistic sources in those areas, like Thrace, which were open to direct influence from Greece. Rider imagery is part of a much larger picture which shows the profound effect that the artistic achievement of Greece had on all who came into contact with it.

The reason for this becomes clearer if we look into the nature of the Greek achievement. What distinguishes the development of Greek art from that of the Romans or the Celts or, indeed, any other ancient people is summed up by Ranuccio Bianchi Bandinelli in his discussion of the development of perspective and other effects in painting:

> Such devices can be absorbed into the formal vocabulary of art only by a highly complex society in which generations of artists deliberately and consciously set themselves the same problem. Such, *par excellence*, was the world of Greek art, where formal progress is invariably accompanied by theoretical speculation (as subsequently during the European Renaissance), and a work of art results from the balance between irrational inspiration and rational theory.[893]

These developments then, which took place mainly during the latter two-thirds of the first millenium BC in Greece, were passed on as borrowings to other societies within the ancient world. Clearly traceable stages in the development of the human and animal forms can be observed only in Greek art. In all the other societies we have considered, these forms appear suddenly, full-blown, to be adapted to local needs without any sense of the theoretical underpinning which distinguishes the evolution of Greek art and later, as Bandinelli says, the art of the European Renaissance.

Leaving the Romans for a moment, we can see the contrast between the idea of evolutionary artistic development, on the one hand, and adaptation of style, on the other, in the contrast between Greek art and Egyptian art. In the case of the latter, the very early period, particularly the late Pre-Dynastic period, and first few dynasties show a reworking of the artistic conception of the human form, a reworking that may have been home grown but could have equally been borrowed from Mesopotamia, a region of considerable influence on the developing art of early Egypt. However, once a satisfying form had been developed — leaner and tauter than the Mesopotamian, but in terms of the solution to problems of perspective and the articulation of the human body, little different — it remained stable and virtually unchanged through three millenia. Individual experiments with greater illusionism in painting can be seen among tomb paintings particularly of the Eighteenth Dynasty. But the results of these experiments were not followed up and came to nothing because that element of 'rational theory' required by Bandinelli for artistic development is missing. Indeed, it is possible to say that what is required is a desire within the society as a whole to explore, and to appreciate exploration into, the development of form. In Egyptian society, except for the minor changes and refinements that make it possible to distinguish the art of one period from another, this desire never seems to have manifested itself.

The Greeks, by contrast, borrowed the formal representation of the human figure in sculpture, and possibly in painting as well, from the Egyptians, but they were not content with a limited adaptation of traditional types. In sculpture, sculptors first adopted the fully frontal poses of Egypt, but soon broke away. For painters, the traditional solution to representing three dimensions on a flat surface was to avoid the problem completely by using only views that were easily represented in two dimensions, e.g., frontal upper torso turned sideways at the waist to accommodate profile feet, frontal eye in profile head (unforeshortened frontal feet presented problems of representation as, for example, the pigeon-toed dead enemies on the Narmer Palette). But these composite images were quickly supplanted by new types, the results of the discovery of, and experimentation with, foreshortening. Vase painters of the late 6th century BC in Athens, for instance, worked closely together and in competition with each other to produce new and better solutions to the problems of adapting the human figure to a flat surface. The conscious and competitive nature of the enterprise and the way in which one artist drew upon the discoveries of another are preserved in the inscriptions produced by Keramicus painters like Euthymides who, on a pot with a particularly impressive figure, wrote *hos oudepote Euphronios*: 'as never Euphronios'.[894] Euthymides, thus, bragged of his triumph over the rival painter. This sense of working toward a preconceived goal, and working competitively, is what distinguished the development of Greek art from that of other nations.

The Romans were exposed to Greek art early in their history through the Etruscans and Magna Graecia as well as through Greece itself. However, the true impact on Rome of the Greek achievement came with the importation as booty of thousands of works of Classical and Hellenistic art as Rome's military conquests spread.[895] But while the Romans, particularly at the upper levels of society, came to value the works of art they had looted, and copies and variations were produced, the investigation of new artistic forms for their own sake continued to be the concern of mainly Greek artists rather than of Romans.

Thus, the forms of Roman art were based on Greek models which came to Rome by a variety of routes. The Romans in their turn took these same forms with them wherever they conquered or, indeed, traded so that a veneer of Hellenism was spread through the ancient world even as far as India, where both pure Hellenic and Roman influences can be detected.[896]

On their home ground, Bandinelli distinguishes between the Greek, particularly Hellenistic, veneer of the aristocratic and official art of Rome and a plebian Roman art which, although outwardly derived from the Greek tradition is more 'Roman' in that the balance between form and content which characterizes Greek art is very clearly lacking. This is the art of the Roman street signs and tombstones. The content is often lively and prosaic: a greengrocer's shop sign from Ostia, for example, with the produce on display and the shopkeeper busy with customers.[897] Not only is the subject not elevated, but the figures themselves do not obey the canons of proportion stipulated by the Greeks. Yet the figures are foreshortened convincingly and are clearly at the end of the development which so excited Euthymides and his co-workers. This undercurrent in Roman art, which Bandinelli identifies, is important for several reasons: first, because it shows distinct similarities with the art of the provinces in the lack of interest in form as an end it itself but rather as a vehicle for content. This is not an art with theoretical underpinnings. Secondly, the artisans who produced these works at Rome were very likely similar to the type of men who worked in the provinces also for the ordinary people. They would have lacked a deeper understanding of the forms they were copying and probably had very little interest in acquiring any such understanding.

In general terms, the Roman contribution was to take the forms of Greek art and turn them from their mainly religious subject matter to use in the development of a Roman political iconography. Although political reference was not new to Greek art, the Greeks had, as a rule, preferred to conceal real enemies behind mythological representations. Although heroic Celts could be found among the Amazons and giants of the Attalid monuments, the stark realism of Trajan's column was, it would appear, unacceptable. It may be that the realization of the value of sculpture and relief in the dissemination of Imperial propaganda was the result, in part, of exposure to Egyptian art where the tradition of royal glorification in stone went back millenia. A similar tradition is found in the court art of Achaemenid Persia, at Persepolis, for example. So such traditions of propagandistic art were long familiar in non-Greek contexts. What the Romans did was to take over the sophisticated Greek forms as a vehicle for the development and dissemination of their own state propaganda.

Craftsmen in the Empire

The spread of artistic forms would have been along the trade routes as well as by way of loot and plunder, but mainly through the movement of the artisans themselves across the Empire. The movement of artisans is difficult to trace. However, there seems little doubt that some craftsmen moved from job to job.[898] Greek craftsmen were clearly attracted to Rome by the lure of commissions from wealthy patrons. Signed works from Rome show that Greek, especially Athenian, names predominate. There are few Latin signatures.[899] The Venus Genetrix, created specifically to glorify the Julian house by Arcesilaus is a good example of Greek art in service to Roman ideas.[900]

Pliny's notice concerning the sculptor Zenodorus shows that the movement of Greek sculptors were not confined to Rome itself. Discussing the creation of colossal statues, Pliny notes that Zenodorus, most likely a travelling sculptor from the eastern provinces, made a gigantic statue of Hermes or Mercury for the Arverni in Gaul. It took ten years and cost 40,000,000 sesterces and so impressed the Emperor Nero that the artist was invited to create a colossal statue of the emperor himself.[901] Here then, is a clear case of an artist moving across the Empire as commissions dictate. The ancient cities of the East and the growing cities of Gaul and the West would have desired the services of competent craftsmen, particularly for the decoration of civic amenities in the Roman style and particularly if, as Alison Burford suggests, there was a chronic shortage of skilled labour during most periods in the ancient world.[902]

At the lower levels of society, it seems more likely that local craftsmen, immigrants or itinerant artisans of lesser skill travelling through the provinces, produced much of the work that has survived. There were also workshops that served various communities. In Chapter Six we discussed the Batkun-Glava Panega workshop which produced a distinctive series of Thracian Rider reliefs. Workshops in the Rhineland are known which manufactured many of the military tombstones found in that area.[903] They may have attracted local youngsters as apprentices. Two examples of inscriptions from Bath suggest the presence of both local and immigrant workers, although these two individuals may not have been contemporaries. One, Sulinus son of Brucet(i)us, dedicated altars at Cirencester and at Bath. On the latter he named himself as *scultor*. His name suggests that he may have been born at Bath. The other inscription is a dedication to Sulis from Priscus son of Tout(i)us, *lapidarius*, originally from the area around Chartres — a Carnutenian.[904] Thus, itinerant artists, immigrant artists, military artists and imported goods would have circulated artistic ideas and forms around the Empire. It is also possible that pattern books and other devices for transmitting designs were available to local craftsmen too.[905]

The spread of Graeco-Roman forms through the Empire can undoubtedly be traced to a variety of factors. The founding and building of Roman, particularly Imperial, towns in Gaul would have required artists for construction and decoration of civic amenities. Trade in Roman wares would have introduced painting, relief and mosaic. The Romanization of the upper and urbanized classes, in particular, in Celtic society would have inspired a taste for Graeco-Roman art and a desire to interpret indigenous culture, as, for example, religion, along Roman lines. The westernization of much of the modern third world provides some analogy with this process and shows too how unevenly the new cultural overlay is spread and also how quickly new generations accommodate themselves to the cultural changes. Edith Wightman's comment on how widespread the practice of erecting sculptural monuments was all down the social scale in Roman Gaul suggests this kind of phenomenon.[906]

The Relation to Celtic Art

The short discussion of the antecedents of Romano-Celtic art in Chapter One has suggested that with respect to figural art, the Celts, like the Romans themselves, did not evolve an indigenous artistic form of anything but the simplest kind. The representation of the human body in Celtic art does not show the kind of evolution we might expect if the Romano-Celtic imagery — the Eponas, the mounted gods — had sprung from experiments over centuries within Celtic art itself. Nor is there anything to suggest that once the Celts had borrowed the formula for human representation, they went on to develop it into something particularly their own, as the Greeks did with Egyptian sculpture. The reliefs and statues compare most closely in style and level of craftsmanship to Bandinelli's Roman plebian style, the interpretation of sophisticated state art by ordinary people.

By contrast, the clear affinity the Celts had for decorative art showed itself in the way that decorative motifs, although also often borrowed from Classical types, were transformed into something new and distinctively Celtic. This can be observed over and over again in Celtic metalwork with its intricate patterns and distinctly un-Classical tensions and distortions. The love for abstract design is obvious, also, in the way that Greek coins were copied by Celtic craftsmen and over time the integrity of the forms began to dissolve and the images to disintegrate into a series of patterns. This delight in abstract rather than the realistic form and the lack of any evidence of a coherent evolution of human representation make it extremely unlikely, if not impossible, that the Celts were drawing on an indigenous tradition in the representation of their gods during the Roman period. Similarly, although there is certainly evidence for a native tradition of figural art within the Thracian and Dacian regions, there is none for a developmental sequence which spans the period between the Letnitsa types, for example, and the Thracian Rider plaques. These latter, as we have seen, are more likely to have been directly influence by Hellenistic models.

Mars

Looking at the various representations of the horseman in the western Empire, we can see how, in each case, craftsmen sought their models within the established repertory of Graeco-Roman horsemen that had developed over the preceding centuries. The case of the Celtic Mars is a particularly difficult one to use as a starting point, because not all the monuments we have identified as 'Mars' can be proven to be so. The problem for the artist appears to have been that the god who was identified with the Roman Mars under the *Interpretatio Romana* was also, in Celtic lore, a rider. As the Roman Mars was never seen this way, adjustments were necessary when this aspect was to be emphasized. The most common representations of the Celtic Mars, as we saw in the case of Lenus Mars and Intarabus, was as the standing god of Graeco-Roman origin, nude after Greek types or cuirassed after Roman. The standing Mars possibly represents the most assimilated form, found at large cult sites frequented by Romans and Romanized Gauls. This may, however, be an unbalanced view, based as it is only on what has survived.

At Sougères-en-Puisaye (Yonne), remains of life-size statues of riders, one in armour, have been found. These may represent Mars mounted. But the evidence for the Celtic Mars at this and other Gaulish sites is based on the outcome of logical arguments rather than on actual proof. Similarly the evidence for identification of other mounted cuirassed figures, such as the little bronzes found in Britain, is of the same type. However, since similar small figurines of recognizable divine figures have been found in *lararia*, obviously for personal worship, it is likely that the little bronzes of horsemen, discovered as they often were on temple sites, also represent divine figures. The military costume suggests Mars or one of the Dioscuri. These latter, however, were less often represented in armour in the West than in the East.

The possible derivation of the small horsemen from Imperial prototypes — perhaps from statues of the type to be found in any of a number of civic centres throughout the Empire — also increases the likelihood that they are gods. They could have developed within workshops producing statuettes of reigning emperors, evolving from the kind of small copies of Imperial monuments which have been discovered on the continent. In his discussion of sculpture, Pliny suggests the intriguing possibility that among the Romans, such small statuettes were kept as personal amulets, for he tells us that Nero, among others, carried around a statuette of an Amazon, while Gaius Cestius carried his figurine even onto the battlefield.[907] The small figure of a Dioscurus found at Wroxeter referred to in Chapter Five may have served this way and the discovery of isolated figurines may point to personal loss or an impulse dedication to a particular god.

The impetus for the production of the little horsemen, however, may have been purely Celtic. For they can also be interpreted as an adaptation to Roman form of a tradition of horse amulets which reaches back to the Hallstatt period among the Celts. Numerous horse figurines, and brooches have been discovered from both Hallstatt and La Tène sites as described in Chapter One. These horses, unlike their Roman-inspired successors, tend to stand four-square and often display the distinctive Celtic stylization with elongated neck and torso. They could well be the ancestors of the little bronze riders of the Roman period and also of the horse and rider fibulae found on a number of sites in Britain. All these may thus be seen as new interpretations of an old tradition, but using Roman models.

Jupiter and the Giant

If the rider figures grouped under the heading 'mounted Mars' represent a very mixed collection and few firm conclusions, those known as the 'mounted Jupiter' contain no such ambiguities. Although there is no agreement as to the true name of the god represented, nevertheless the monuments form a homogeneous group, variations in style and quality notwithstanding. Here is a very good example of a non-Roman god with distinctive iconographical requirements for whom Graeco-Roman models have been pressed into service, in this case, we would argue, probably Hellenistic ones. We have seen above, the evidence for itinerant craftsmen, but the monuments themselves, because of the strong affinity with Graeco-Roman style of so many of them, point to artists who had been trained in the Graeco-Roman tradition. Such artists may have come from Rome itself or, what is more likely, the Romano-Celtic cities of Gaul and Germania. This raises the interesting question as to when and how the standard iconography for Jupiter and the giant developed. Although there is some variation, it is remarkably slight. Jupiter and the giant are clearly identifiable as an iconographical group. This is in contrast to the 'mounted Mars' motif which does not seem to have evolved a canonical form although this perception may only be the result of the accident of preservation. The Jupiter and giant, however, suggests a worked-out iconography which could be alternated with the Phidian seated Zeus/Jupiter as an acceptable way of recognizing the Celtic Jupiter. The wheel attribute, with which Celtic Jupiter figures are sometimes provided, may also have the same function, that is, to identify a given figure as this particular god. But the significance of the wheel is unclear as it only appears occasionally on these monuments. It may be analogous to the piloi of the Dioscuri which are only worn very occasionally by the twins in the West; standing figures of two nude young men holding the reins of their horses are sufficient to identify the Dioscuri without additional attributes.

Although, as we have seen, columns with riders were relatively common in the Roman Empire, the idea of using this form of monument for an important Celtic god must have occurred at a single time and place and then spread outward. The Great Mainz column dated to the second half of the first century[908] and the pillar of the *Nautae* of a slightly earlier date in Paris[909] have been suggested as prototypes for some of the iconography of the typical Jupiter column. Neither one includes any horsemen but the former suggests active and original sculptural production in the cites of the provinces and the latter that sculptors trained in the Roman tradition were adapting their skills to portrayal of Celtic deities alongside Roman ones. Thus, it seems plausible to think that the Jupiter and giant group is the result of the combination of several factors: the desire for a recognizable icon for an important Celtic deity; the presence of skilled sculptors who were able to make such an adaptation; and the wealth and desire for status in provincial cities or, indeed, among the provincial priesthood, which, once the new iconographical type was developed, caused it to spread across Gaul and Germania. That so complex a new iconographical form for the Celtic Jupiter was considered necessary also suggests the centrality of the giant — as friend or foe — to the portrayal of this god since it was the giant's presence which made necessary the modification to the standard Hellenistic and Imperial rider to better reflect the deity's nature. Stories about fights between gods and giants or monsters are an important part of much Indo-European myth. There is no reason to believe that such a story did not exist among the Celts as well. Here the image of the moment of triumph, the vanquishing of the giant, became the representation which distinguished this god from other mounted deities.

Epona

The development of the Epona iconography must have presented slightly different problems from those of the Celtic Jupiter. Like the Jupiter and giant groups, Epona's monuments are, in general, easily identifiable. Although, strictly speaking, it is not certain that all female figures riding or accompanied by horses represent Epona, nevertheless, the enormous similarity of one to another suggests strongly that we are looking at a single iconographical type and a single deity. Unlike Jupiter, however, Epona has no Roman or Greek counterpart from which a ready-made formula could have been taken for adaptation. The artists employed in formulating the Epona image could range widely in looking for models from which to adapt their new composition. Indeed, it appears that at one time or another they drew on almost the entire repertory of mounted female figures in the Graeco-Roman artistic vocabulary. This would explain the various postures of the mounted Epona.

It is not possible to know whether the first Epona was produced by a local artist trained in the Graeco-Roman tradition or an outsider. The observation by Pliny, discussed above, that the Arverni invited the Greek Zenodorus to create a gigantic Hermes or Mercury for them reinforces what some of the statues themselves already imply: that skilled foreigners were invited to create monuments of the highest quality. One can think, for example, of the Helenenberg youth, the fine statue that may represent Mars Latobius.[910]

That artists did not try to invent an entirely new image for Epona is probably a result of the way in which ancient artisans approached their craft. Novelty, particularly in religious imagery, was not necessarily a virtue. Even those artists who created the new iconography for Christianity drew on pagan representation. The forms remained the same while the content changed dramatically.[911] The same is true for the artists who looked for a way to represent Epona. As Alison Burford says, "Plagiarism was an unknown concept".[912] What was required was an empty vessel capable of being filled with new and distinctive contents. Changing Cybele's lions to horses or Europa's bull to a horse fulfilled that requirement. Once the first figures were produced, not only could craftsmen begin to mass produce them in workshops as required — the similarity of style among the series at La Horgne-au Sablon suggests a local workshop, for example — but the small size of so many of the icons meant that they themselves could be used as models for further figures. Itinerant craftsmen could easily add this figure to their repertory as it was so similar to established types.

The question also arises as to when and why the second Epona type, the seated goddess, was created. There seem to be connections with the army and it would be interesting to know whether, for some reason, the mounted figure was rejected. It may be that the seated goddess presented a more familiar image that made the Celtic goddess seem less alien to the army with its mixed ethnic origin. Whatever the reason, the choice of this alternative iconographical type, which was shared with the great mother goddesses, seems to suggest that some devotees, at least, were more comfortable with a goddess who was closer in type to the mature Cybele or the Celtic mothers than to the semi-nude ocean nymphs whose representation may also have served as a model for some of the reliefs and statuettes of Epona as rider. In general, the development of Epona's imagery presents a good example of the way in which the ancient craftsman went about creating an artistic vocabulary for a deity who had previously had none and gives us a small insight into the thought processes involved.

The Dioscuri

Unlike the deities discussed above, the Dioscuri were imported wholesale into the art of the Celtic parts of the Roman Empire. Inscriptions suggest that their figures often masked a pair of Celtic twin gods, but the image of the Dioscuri was not changed to make this in any way apparent. They suffered none of the adaptation that Jupiter underwent to make his image closer to whatever may have been conceived as the essence of the Celtic god. The adaptations made to Jupiter and the various forms that Mars seems to have taken, as well as the specifically Celtic alternative forms of such gods as Hermes, are attempts to combine two essentially different deities to suit the new political reality and also the demands of what, over the centuries, had become a hybrid Romano-Celtic population, particularly in the cities. The fact that the Dioscuri do not change perhaps can be seen as implying that their character as youthful riders was not very far from that of their Celtic counterparts. Although we cannot be certain that a pair of Celtic twins existed, the existence of the Germanic Alci, the Roman Romulus and Remus, and the Vedic Asvins, as well as the Dioscuri, shows that youthful twin gods were common in various other Indo-European pantheons.[913] In the case of the last two pairs there is also a strong association with horses, a likely element in the Celtic pattern as well, considering the importance we have already seen attached to horses in Celtic culture.

The representation of the Dioscuri also reflects the innate conservatism which is characteristic of most religious representation. The type was established during the Classical period and once it had become the dominant form of representation for the Dioscuri, it remained so throughout antiquity. Here again there is a parallel with Christianity which contains certain images which were established very early on in Christian history and survive to this day. We also noted that while the eastern part of the Empire accepted two types of Dioscuri — mounted and standing — as canonical, the West preferred only the standing. The reason for this may be that for the Romano-Celtic world, the standing youth with his horse was unambiguously a Dioscurus whereas a mounted figure could be confused with Jupiter or Mars or any other rider. Outside the Celtic regions, this ambiguity was perhaps less likely.

The eastern image of the Dioscuri as members of a group of three with a goddess, borrowed for the Danubian Riders, reflects the popularity of a divine triad involving two men and a woman. The mounted Dioscuri and their goddess have been found on reliefs in Lycia,[914] Thasos,[915] and Palmyra[916] and on coins of the Roman period from Alexandria[917] although the central figure can vary. A coin of Caracalla from Ephesus has the mounted brothers facing the Ephesian Artemis.[918] Whatever the interpretation of these images, their failure to find an echo in Rome and westward suggests that the pairing of the twins with a female, Helen or another, although certainly not absent,[919] was not significant in the West. This is particularly interesting as

the number three or triplication seems to have been so important in Celtic thinking.[920]

The Thracian Rider

The Thracian Rider does not belong to the Celtic world but is most probably an indigenous Thracian god and iconographically tied to Greece. Like the Celtic gods, however, very little is known about the Thracian Rider or his cult myth and practices. Only the art and a selection of inscriptions give any indication of the nature of the god. The iconography, the choice of elements, also tells something about the cult, but without written information even this is of limited value.

In artistic terms, we are not dealing with variations on a particular Roman prototype as among the Celts. Rather the influences come directly from Greece. Indeed, the Thracian Rider is most difficult to assess in terms of antecedents because his imagery deviates so little from the simple single rider composition whose history can be traced back to Archaic Greece. The rider is, then, a good example of a commonplace image which, by adaptation, became distinctive. It is thus also a good example of the way in which religious imagery works by particularizing the generic image through the addition of attributes and other specific elements. The ranks of medieval saints, all looking alike but each with his or her distinctive attributes, are the result of this same process. In the case of the Thracian Rider, a number of elements in the composition, not all of which appear at the same time, contribute to the identification. Among these are the tree, snake and altar, the female figures standing in front of the horse and the youthful face (although bearded riders do exist) and figure of the rider himself, all framed in a relatively small plaque. But even when these attributes are absent, representation of a single youthful rider in chiton or nude, on a plaque of the right size and date (approximately 30–50 cm. in width and second or third century in date) is enough to bring the Thracian Rider to mind. In other words, if the context is correct, the undifferentiated nature of the image is of considerably less importance. Nevertheless, the addition of attributes helps to confirm the identity even without inscription. And when the inscription identifies the god as other than Heros, we tend to assume a conflation of the two deities — a likelihood strengthened by atypical attributes put into the hands of typical Thracian Riders and inscriptions addressing the god by a double name. The rider as Apollo with a lyre is an instance of this. But despite a certain freedom in the use of attributes, there seem to be clear limits to identifiers, based, no doubt, on the nature of the god. The Thracian Rider is a hunter not a warrior. He kills only animals and he does not trample humans. These omissions distinguish him from the Danubian Rider in that god's early form. Both appear to derive from the common Greek horseman or, when accompanied by a compositional element placed in front of the horse, from two-thirds of a Dioscuric triad. But the use of distinctive attributes allows the viewer to distinguish between them.

The vehicle for representation of the Thracian Rider is most often the small plaque. Statues are extremely rare, whereas plaques have been found by the thousands. The plaques depict some scene from the Thracian Rider cult myth. Only a small variety of scenes are repeated which suggests that, like a mystery cult, the Thracian Rider religion had one significant cult myth which was always illustrated. Indeed, as we have seen, some scholars believe that the Thracian Rider cult was of the mystery type.[921] Certainly, the Thracian Rider appears frequently on tombstones which in itself could point to eschatological beliefs. The representation could be analogous to Mithras and the bull or the image of Attis with his lower body revealed by his open garments, both of which are associated with a central cult myth. This development of a representation which embodies in a single image the essence of the main religious narrative — the Christian crucifixion is a prime example — is in contrast to the traditional image inherited from the Classical period where the god's appearance did not bring to mind any one in particular of the stories which clustered around his or her name. The god's many deeds and stories could be illustrated in a variety of media, but the cult statue itself was of a more general nature. The advent of the mystery cult with its emphasis on a single myth of major importance introduced a new kind of cult image, one which represented the god not as a passive standing or seated figure, but in the act of guaranteeing the salvation which the cult promised to its devotees. This appears to be what the Thracian Rider is doing. However, as there is no clear evidence that the Thracian Rider was a true mystery god of the Mithraic type, it is possible that this new form of active representation came to be adopted by other more traditional cults. This may also be the case with the Jupiter and giant group which gives the same impression of being the illustration of a key narrative. Both may thus reflect, in a general way, the taste in religious imagery of their time.

The Danubian Riders

The one mystery cult closely associated in its pictorial imagery, at least, with horses is the Danubian Rider cult. Here is a true mystery cult. However, it is interesting that the divine epiphany, the representation of the riders and their goddess, is not of the narrative type, but depends heavily on the triadic Dioscuri and goddess group. Rather the mystery element is apparent in the additional scenes of the devotees involved in cultic rites which are often presented on registers below the riders and goddess. Surprisingly for a mystery cult, the details of initiation are not secret but carefully represented in continuous narrative in successive registers. More typically on Mithraic reliefs, for instance, the central image is supplemented with illustrations from the life of the god and his deeds.

The Danubian formulation, however, is not absolutely unique. We have already looked at the cult mosaic at Trier which too shows the rite and its participants. Also Christian examples of devotees can occasionally be found particularly in the catacombs. In the Catacomb of Callixtus are two pre-Constantinian scenes of baptism with a larger figure reaching out to a smaller and a eucharistic scene with a group of seven seated around a table with loaves and fishes which looks remarkably like the banqueting scene on some Danubian Rider plaques.[922] However, taken as a whole, there seems to be nothing known that is quite like these step by step pictorial accounts of mystery practice represented on the same small, portable, relief plaques as the images of the gods and goddess themselves.

The role of the horse in the cult is problematic. The Dioscuri model has, as we know, an alternative form in which the twin gods are standing but this was not used in any extant Danubian plaques of either the single or double god type. Other animals are represented on the plaques, such as the cock, and these are explained by analogy with similar representations on Mithraic artefacts. However, in the Danubian cult, the horse does not appear to belong to that group of elements: animals and objects shown on the lowest register and most likely associated with the metaphysical speculations of the cult. Rather the horse appears to be part of the equipment of the two warrior figures who flank the goddess. As we saw in Chapter Seven, these two are armed and on many plaques trample fallen men underfoot. The proximity too of deities like Nemesis, Victory and Mars reinforce the assumption of a warlike character for the cult itself. The pair of mounted warrior gods recalls the traditions which were associated both in Greece and Rome with the interventions of the Dioscuri in battle. We have already mentioned Lake Regillus, but similar stories come from Greek sources about two young warriors on white horses who turned the battle for the Locrians in c. 500 BC and the Spartans in 405.[923] While the Dioscuri are, to a certain extent, polyvalent, having other aspects to their powers beyond the military, the two Danubian deities may function as military saviours alone and for that reason are represented as mounted and trampling an enemy underfoot. It is, however, hard to reconcile the early single Danubian Rider plaques, the compositional emphasis of which is on the rider, with the later triad groups where the emphasis shifts quite perceptibly to the goddess and the action of the devotees points toward her primacy. The change may represent a change in the cult itself. The inclusion of Mithraic symbols and the appearance of the sun god, often shown quite large, suggests that this was a cult which borrowed heavily from others and in the process, the early or native elements may have lost their place to later fashions.

What is difficult to assess, given the ubiquity of the rider image, is the role the horse played within the mythology of any of these deities. Indeed, the results of this survey tend to blur the issue even further because it has shown how the horse came to overshadow the chariot as the favoured mode of transport for the gods and the upper classes and for this reason, it became a commonplace for statues of statesmen, emperors and gods to be represented mounted. In the case of the Celtic Mars, there is some likelihood that the horse was this god's animal avatar. In the case of Epona, the association of the horse and the goddess is beyond all question a close and significant one. The Dioscuri in Greek myth are characterized as riders in contrast to their elders who are charioteers. However, for the other three, the picture is not at all clear. Is the Thracian Rider a rider because he is a hunter and hunters chase their quarry on horseback or is there another meaning? Is Jupiter a rider because he is a warrior or because he has some special relation with the horse in general or his own horse in particular? One can think of Odin who rides the magical eight-legged horse Sleipnir as an example of the latter relationship.[924] However, questions such as these belong to a different type of study. Here we have tried to look at the artistic imagery and put it into its art historical context in order to gain some insight into the choices the artist had when the commissions were given and why he produced what he did.

The horseman was also a familiar figure in the art of the eastern Roman Empire. A future investigation could take the theme into Egypt from which examples of the Thracian Rider, for instance, are known[925] and into Mesopotamia and to the emerging Persian Empire of the Sassanians where, in the third century, the investiture of the first king of that dynasty by the god Ahura Mazda is depicted on a monumental rock relief where both participants are on horseback.[926] All these, like the art of the western Empire, are tied to the movement of Greek and Roman art through the ancient world in the wake of conquest, trade and cultural relations. For despite the difficulties of communication and travel, the striking unity of form during the Roman Empire shows how closely in touch, at least superficially, the various cultures really were.

Footnotes

1 Martin Price, *Coins of the Macedonians*, London, 1974, no. 22.
2 Emily Vermeule, *Greece in the Bronze Age*, Chicago, 1964, fig. 17.
3 *Ibid.*, 91–2.
4 *Ibid.*, 204–5, pl. XXXII, B, D.
5 J. K. Anderson, *Ancient Greek Horsemanship*, Berkeley, 1961, 10.
6 *Ibid.*, 6.
7 M. S. Hood, "A Mycenaean Cavalryman", *Annual of the British School at Athens*, XLVIII, 1953, 84, figs. 47–8.
8 *Ibid.*, 86–7.
9 Anderson, 13.
10 *Ibid.*, 10–13.
11 Vermeule, 222, pl. XLI F.
12 Bernhard Schweitzer, *Greek Geometric Art*, London, 1971, 156–9, figs. 194–6.
13 Vermeule, 292–3.
14 Fritz Schachermeyr, *Poseidon und die Entstehung des griechischen Götterglaubens*, Bern, 1950, 32.
15 Metropolitan Museum of Art, *Greek Art of the Aegean Islands*, New York, 1979, no. 70.
16 Pausanias, VIII, 25.4.
17 Walter Burkert, *Greek Religion*, Oxford, 1985, 138.
18 Schachermeyr, 15.
19 Oscar Broneer, "Hero Cults in the Corinthian Agora", *Hesperia*, XI, 1942, 139; Schachermeyr, 33.
20 G. M. A. Richter, *Attic Red-Figured Vases*, London, 1958, 159, fig. 121.
21 Nikolaos Yalouris, "Athena als Herrin der Pferde, *Museum Helveticum*, 1950, 19–101.
22 Burkert, 141.
23 John Boardman, *Greek Sculpture: the Classical Period*, London, 1985, fig. 97.
24 Yalouris, 60; John Boardman, *Athenian Black Figure Vases*, London, 1974, figs. 297, 301.2.
25 John Boardman, *Greek Art*, London, 1973, fig. 171.
26 Anderson, 10.
27 Schweitzer, 50, fig. 50.
28 *Ibid.*, 210, fig. 122.
29 Daphné Woysch-Meautis, *La répresentation des animaux et des êtres fabuleux sur les monuments funeraires grecs de l'époque archaïque à la fin du IV siècle av. J. C.*, Lausanne, 1982, 24; Donna Kurtz and John Boardman, *Greek Burial Customs*, London, 1971, 221, pl. 50.
30 Kurtz and Boardman, 86, fig. 15.
31 Woysch-Meautis, 25.
32 Boardman, *Classical Period*, 184, fig. 153.
33 Tonio Holscher, *Griechische Historienbilder des 4 und 5 Jahrhundert vor Chr.*, Wurzburg, 1973, 109.
34 *Ibid.*
35 John Boardman, *Greek Sculpture: the Archaic Period*, London, 1978, fig. 114.
36 Harald von Roques de Maumont, *Antike Reiterstandbilder*, Berlin, 1958, fig. 1b.
37 *Ibid.*, fig. 2b.
38 *Ibid.*, 14.

39 Price, 7.
40 *Ibid.*, nos. 16, 18.
41 *Ibid.*, no. 47.
42 Holscher, 104–6.
43 von Roques de Maumont, 21.
44 Wilhelm Kraiker, *Die Malerei der Griechen*, Stuttgart, 1958, 164.
45 Holscher, 162–5.
46 Apostolos Dascalakis, "La déification d'Alexandre le Grand en Égypte", *Studii Clasice*, IX, 1967, 103.
47 Pausanius, V, 20.10.
48 Caroline Houser, "Alexander's Influence on Greek Sculpture as Seen in a Portrait in Athens", *Macedonia and Greece*, Beryl Barr-Scharrar and Eugene Borza, eds., Washington, 1982, 236.
49 Chrysa Paliadeli in *The Search for Alexander*, Boston 1980, nos. 170–1.
50 von Roques de Maumont, 23.
51 *Ibid.*, 24.
52 Houser, 230.
53 See Heinrich Siedentopf, *Das hellenistische Reiterdenkmal*, Waldsassen/Bayern, 1968.
54 Richard Brilliant, *Gesture and Rank in Roman Art*, Memoirs of the Connecticut Academy of Arts and Sciences, 14, 1963, 47.
55 Livy, 2.14.
56 See Marjorie Mackintosh, "The Sources of the Horseman and Fallen Enemy Motif on the Tombstones of the Western Roman Empire", *Journal of the British Archaeological Association*, CXXXIX, 1986, 5–14.
57 Price, nos. 59–61, 63–4.
58 *Ibid.*, no. 69.
59 *Ibid.*, 26–7, no. 66.
60 *Ibid.*, nos. 67–8.
61 Niels Hannestad, *Roman Art and Imperial Policy*, Aarhus, 1986, 21.
62 *Ibid.*, 140.
63 *Ibid.*, 104–5.
64 Brilliant, 55.
65 Hannestad, 139.
66 Brilliant, 96, dates this statue soon after AD 89.
67 *Ibid.*, 111.
68 Holscher, 130
69 Stuart Piggott, *Ancient Europe*, Edinburgh, 1967, 182–3.
70 As, for example, in the Pontic-Caspian region including finds from the so-called Samara and Dneiper-Donets cultures. J.P Mallory, *In Search of the Indo-Europeans*, London, 1989, 206–8. For discussion of the earliest use of the horse among Indo-Europeans, see David W. Anthony and Dorcas R. Brown, "Origins of Horseback Riding", *Antiquity*, 65, 1991, 22–38.
71 Mallory, 119.
72 For the question of the Celts and their early history, see Mallory 106–7.
73 J. V. S. Megaw, *The Art of the European Iron Age*, Bath, 1970, 49, no. 17; but dated to 700 BC by Herbert Schutz *The Prehistory of Germanic Europe*, New Haven, 1983, 227. See also, M. E. Mariën, "Tribes and Archaeological Groupings of the La Tène period in Belgium: some Observations", in *The European Community in Later Prehistory: Studies in*

Honour of C. F. C. Hawkes, eds. J. Boardman, M. A. Brown and T. G. E. Powell, London, 1971, 214 for discussion of discontinuities.

74 Wilfried Menghin, *Kelten, Romer und Germanen: Archäologie und Geschichte*, Munich, 1980, 92, no. 89.

75 Piggott, 177, figs. xxvi b, xxxi.

76 Schutz, 223.

77 N. K. Sanders, *Prehistoric Art in Europe*, Harmondsworth, 1968, 214–5.

78 Bernhard Schweitzer, *Greek Geometric Art*, London 1969, nos. 128-9, 130-1, 172.

79 Sanders, 215, pl. 220.

80 Ferdinand Maier, "Quelques éléments stylistiques des bronzes animaliers des Celtes", *L'art celtique de la période d'expansion IVe et IIIe siècles avant notre ère*, P.-M. Duval and V. Kruta eds., Geneva, 1982, 88–9; compare particularly fig. 5.3 from Hradiště in Bohemia with fig. 2.2 from Beckersloh in Bavaria.

81 Barry Cunliffe, *Greeks, Romans and Barbarians: Spheres of Interaction*, London, 1988, 24–5.

82 Monique Clavel-Leveque, *Marseille grecque*, Marseille, 1977, 195.

83 René Joffroy, *Vix et ses Trésors*, Paris 1979, 75.

84 *Ibid.*, 187–8.

85 J.-J. Hatt, "Les cadres historiques de l'évolution de l'art celtique", in Duval and Kruta, eds., 27–9.

86 Ibid., 32.

87 Sanders, 227–31.

88 See for example, Sanders, 234; Venceslas Kruta, "Aspects unitaires et faciès dans l'art celtique du IVe siècle avant notre ère: l'hypothèse d'un foyer celto-italique" in Duval and Kruta, 35–49; Christian Peyre, "Y a-t-il un context italique au style de Waldalgesheim?" in Duval and Kruta, 51–82.

89 Sanders, 228.

90 Garrett S. Olmsted, *The Gundestrup Cauldron*, Brussels, 1979, 15.

91 Ibid, 20–3.

92 Ibid, 27, pls. 3, 11.

93 O. Klint-Jensen, "Foreign Influences in Denmark's Early Iron Age", *Acta Archaeologica*, XX, 1950, 119–57.

94 Olmstead, 90–1.

95 Sanders, 255.

96 T. G. E. Powell, "From Urartu to Gundestrup", in *Studies in Honour of C. F. C. Hawkes*, eds. J. Boardman, M. A. Brown and T. G. E Powell, London, 1971, 183–210; Sanders, 255–7.

97 Powell, 201; J.-J. Hatt, *Celts and Gallo-Romans*, London, 1970, pls. 50, 48.

98 R. F. Hoddinott, *The Thracians*, London, 1981, 141, fig. 135.

99 Powell, 201, Hatt, pl. 56.

100 Powell, 201, Hatt, pl. 60.

101 See Powell, 190–7 for a detailed discussion of Thracian stylistic elements on the Gundestrup cauldron.

102 A. Fol, B. Nikolov, R. F. Hoddinott, *The Thracian Treasure from Rogozen, Bulgaria*, London, 1986, no. 158.

103 *Ibid.*, 11.

104 Powell, 197–200.

105 Garrett Olmstead, 221–2, equates this scene with an episode from the Irish tale *Táin Bó Fraích* and the gigantic god with the hero Cú Chulainn; Hatt, pl. 55.

106 Stuart Piggott, *The Druids*, Harmondsworth, 1968, 179.

107 Powell, 202–3 and the basis for Garrett Olmstead's interpretation of the scenes on the cauldron. J.-J. Hatt, *Celts and Gallo-Romans*, 315, explains this scene as the "parade of Gallic army setting out to rescue the Mother Goddess. Human sacrifice to Teutates and offering of an uprooted tree".

108 Fol, Nikolov and Hoddinott, no. 158, 162; Hoddinott, *Thracians*, fig. 166.

109 Hoddinott, *Thracians*, fig. 115.

110 Paul Jacobsthal, *Early Celtic Art*, Oxford, 1944, no. 370, pl. 74.

111 Robert Hattatt, *Ancient and Romano-British Brooches*, Dorset, 1982, 16, fig. 68.

112 Sanders, pl. 300, bottom.

113 Powell, 205. But Olmstead, 50, argues for a Celtic origin.

114 Sanders, 253.

115 *Ibid.*, 256 and preferring the second century BC to the first.

116 Powell, 205.

117 *Ibid.*, 53–4 and also 93–102 for the logic of the proposed dates.

118 H. J. Rose, *Ancient Roman Religion*, London, 1948, 66–7; R. M. Ogilvie, *The Romans and Their Gods*, London, 1969, 78.

119 See Johan H. Croon, Die Ideologie des Marskultes unter dem Principat und ihre Vorgeschichte", *Aufstieg und Niedergang des römischen Welt*, II, 17.1, 1981, 260–1 for a summary and discussion of the controversy.

120 Ogilvie, 96.

121 *Ibid.*, 141; see Pierre Boyancé, *Études sur la Religion romaine*, Rome, 1972, 320; Rose, 210.

122 Rose, 215.

123 Giorgio Gualandi, "Marte", in *Enciclopedia dell'Arte antica*, Rome, 1961, 887.

124 Hiltrud Merten, "Der Kult des Mars in Trevererraum", *Trierer Zeitschrift*, 48, 1985, 12.

125 Ogilvie, 115.

126 Gualandi, 887.

127 Walter Burkert, *Greek Religion*, Oxford, 1985, 169–70.

128 Liliane Bodson, 'IEPA ZΩIA, Brussels, 1975, 152.

129 "Ares" in *Lexicon Iconographicum Mythologicae Classicae*, no. 44.

130 Pausanius, I, 8.4.

131 Boardman, *Classical Period*, fig. 223.

132 *Ibid.*, fig. 184.

133 Gualandi, 887.

134 *Ibid.*

135 Ariel Herrmann in *The Search for Alexander: an exhibition*, New York, 1980, nos. 4, 38.

136 John Reich, *Italy Before Rome*, Oxford, 1979, 93.

137 Stephanie Boucher, *Recherches sur les bronzes figurés de Gaule pré-romaine et romaine*, Rome, 1976, 132.

138 Stephanie Boucher, "Figurations de bronze Grèce et Gaule", *Revue archéologique*, 1975, 251.

139 *Ibid.*, 254.

140 Émile Thevenot, "L'interpretation 'gauloise' des divinités romaines: Mars gardien des calendriers celtiques", *Hommages à Albert Grenier*, Brussels, 1962, 1482–4.

141 But see Lothar Eckhart, "Mars Lauriacensis", *Jahreshefte des Österreichischen Archäologischen Institutes in Wien*, XLVIII, 1966–7, 16–39 and also *LIMC*, "Ares/Mars", 579.

142 Merten, 9.

143 *Ibid.*, 19–20, *CIL* XIII, 7661.

144 *Ibid.*, 24.

145 *Ibid.*, 50–1.

146 *Ibid.*, 52–3.

147 *Ibid.*, 54.

148 *Ibid.*, 60.

149 Germaine Faider-Feytmans, *Les bronzes romains de Belgique*, Mainz, 1972, nos. 52, 70.

150 *LIMC*, "Ares/Mars", no. 267.

151 *Ibid.*, no. 413.

152 Lothar Schwinden, "Der Tempelbizirk am Irminenwingert", *Trier: Augustusstadt der Treverer*, Mainz, 1984, 244.

153 Erich Gose, *Der gallo-römische Tempelbezirk im Altbachtal zu Trier*, Mainz, 1972, 96.

154 *Ibid.*, 4.

155 Emil Krüger, "Die gallischen und die germanischen Dioskuren II", *Trierer Zeitschrift*, XVI, 1941–2, 15.

156 *Ibid.*, 34–5, pl.4.

157 Hedwig Kenner, "Die Götterwelt der Austria Romana", Sonderdruck des *Jahreshefte des Österreichischen Archäologischen Institutes*, XLIII, 1956–8, 75, fig. 35.

158 Emil Krüger, "Die gallischen und die germanischen Dioskuren I", *Trierer Zeitschrift*, XV, 1940, 22.

159 Raymond Weiller, "Die Treverer-Munzprägung am Beispiel des Titelberges", *Trier: Augustusstadt der Treverer*, Mainz, 1984, 100–1.

160 Derek Allen, *The Coins of the Celts*, ed. Daphne Nash, Edinburgh, 1980, 141.

161 Fernand Benoit, *Mars et Mercure*, Aix-en-Provence, 1959, 86.

162 Fernand Benoit, *L'art primitif méditerranéen de la vallée du Rhône: La Sculpture*, Paris, 1945, pl. xiv.

163 *Ibid.*, pl. xv.

164 *Ibid.*

165 Isabelle Fauduet and Colette Pommeret, "Les fibules du sanctuaire des Bolards à Nuit-St. Georges (C. d'Or)", *Revue archéologique de l'Est et du Centre-Est*, 36, 1985, 63.

166 Émile Thevenot, *Sur les traces des Mars celtiques*, Bruges, 1955, 47–8.

167 Fauduet and Pommeret, 65.

168 Benoit, *Mars et Mercure*, 64.

169 Pierre Lambrechts, *Contributions à l'étude des divinités celtiques*, Bruges, 1942, 129.

170 Thevenot, *Sur les traces*, 48.

171 *Ibid.*, 37–41.

172 *Ibid.*, 39.

173 Émile Thevenot, *Divinités et sanctuaires de la Gaule*, Paris, 1968, 48.

174 Thevenot, *Sur les traces*, 104; *CIL* XII, 2204 and 1566.

175 *Ibid.*, 104.

176 Émile Espérandieu, *Recueil général des bas-reliefs de la Gaule romain*, I, Paris, 1907, no. 38.

177 Thevenot, *Sur les traces*, 108.

178 Thevenot, *Divinités*, 50.

179 Kenner, 70–1; *CIL* III 5320.

180 Herbert Schutz, *The Romans in Central Europe*, New Haven, 1985, fig. 140.

181 Kenner, 74.

182 *Ibid.*, 77, fig. 36.

183 *Ibid.*, 71.

184 M. V. Taylor, "A Roman Bronze Statuette from Northamptonshire", *Antiquaries Journal*, XXXVII, 1957, 71.

185 M. V. Taylor, "Statuettes of Horsemen and Horses and Other Votive Objects from Brigstock, Northants", *Antiquaries Journal*, XLIII, 1963, 264–5.

186 Hazel Wheeler, "Two Roman Bronzes from Brigstock, Northants", *Antiquaries Journal*, LXI, 1981, 309.

187 E. Greenfield, "The Romano-British Shrines at Brigstock, Northants", *Antiquaries Journal*, XLIII, 1963, 239.

188 *Ibid.*, 231, fig. 2; 236, fig. 3.

189 M. J. T. Lewis, *Temples in Roman Britain*, Cambridge, 1966, 80.

190 Greenfield, 238.

191 Taylor, 1963, 267.

192 Martin Henig, *Religion in Roman Britain*, London, 1984, figs.12, 15.

193 *Ibid.*, fig. 14.

194 Miranda Green, *A Corpus of Religious Material from the Civilian Areas of Roman Britain*, BAR no. 21, 1976, 210, pl. X a, b, c; Henig, 138–41, fig. 14.

195 *Journal of Roman Studies*, XLIII, 1953, 118, pl. xxiii.

196 Anne Ross, *Pagan Celtic Britain*, London, 1967, 29–30 and more recently: Ralph Merrifield, *The Archaeology of Ritual and Magic*, London, 1987, 45–8.

197 G. C. Boon, "Some Romano-British Domestic Shrines and their Inhabitants", *Rome and her Northern Provinces*, Gloucester, 1983, 33–55.

198 *Ibid.*, pl. vii, for example.

199 E. J. W. Hildyard, "Another Roman Bronze Statuette", *Antiquaries Journal*, XXXVIII, 1958, 246.

200 For example: H. Rolland, *Bronzes antiques de Haute Provence*, Paris, 1965, no. 245 in the museum at Avignon — a horse standing on a base where the sites of attachment are visible on the horse's flanks; no. 246, a horse at Avignon perhaps of Roman workmanship which was found with a rider that has since disappeared. It was apparently similar to no. 104 now in Rouen catalogued in É. Espérandieu and H. Rolland, *Bronzes antiques de la Seine-Maritime*, Paris, 1959. Annalis Leibundgut, *Die römischen Bronzes der Schweiz*, II, Mainz, 1977, no. 42 from Avenches — a saddled horse with a large round hole in its back where a separately cast rider must have sat. A. N. Zadoks-Josephus Jitta, W. J. T. Peter, W. A. van Es, *Roman Bronze Statuettes from the Netherlands*, Groningen, 1967, no. 49 from Makkum in Friesland — a horse with a joint running down the centre of its flanks. It seems likely that the join was covered by the legs of the rider.

[201] Germaine Faider-Feytmans, *Recueil des bronzes de Bavai*, Paris 1957, no. 89.

[202] Robert Fleischer, *Die römischen Bronzen aus Österreich*, Mainz, 1967, no. 189.

[203] von Roques de Maumont, 22–3.

[204] *Ibid.*, 19.

[205] *Ibid.*, 22–3.

[206] *Ibid.*, 22.

[207] Annabel Lawson, "A Fragment of Life-Size Bronze Equine Statuary from Ashill, Norfolk", *Britannia*, XVII, 1986, 334.

[208] For example, Zadoks-Josephus Jitta, no. 49; Faider-Feytmans, *Bavai*, no. 140; Faider-Feytmans, *Belgique*, no. 97; Leibundgut, no. 64.

[209] Harold Mattingly, *Coins of the Roman Empire in the British Museum*, I, London, 1923: Claudius, nos. 122, 188.

[210] von Roques de Maumont, 26, fig. 12.

[211] Herrmann, 123, no. 46.

[212] von Roques de Maumont, no. 32.

[213] Leaving aside those showing strong Celtic influence: Zadoks-Josephus Jitta, nos. 50, 51, 74; Faider-Feytmans, *Bavai*, no. 139; Rolland, nos. 186, 245–6, 297–8; Espérandieu and Rolland, nos. 103–4.

[214] von Roques de Maumont, 23–4.

[215] *Ibid.*, fig. 18.

[216] *Ibid.*, 36; also see Chapter Six for a discussion of the distinctions between Greek and Roman horses.

[217] *Ibid.*, 30–1.

[218] *Ibid.*, fig. 14.

[219] Rolland, no. 186.

[220] von Roques de Maumont, 47.

[221] For example, Mattingly, Claudius: no. 2; von Roques de Maumont, Trajan: 27a, Antoninus Pius: 28b where the front leg of the horse just touches the ground instead of being raised.

[222] I. A. Richmond and R. P. Wright, *The Roman Inscribed and Sculptured Stone in the Grosvenor Museum, Chester*, Chester, 1955, no. 99.

[223] See Lawson, 333–338.

[224] Espérandieu and Rolland, no. 104.

[225] Rolland, no. 246.

[226] Krüger, II, 34–5.

[227] *VCH* Suffolk, i, 312; *RIB*, 213.

[228] Zadoks-Josephus Jitta, no. 49.

[229] Faider-Feytmans, *Belgique*, no. 97.

[230] *Archaeological Journal*, XX, 1863, 186–7.

[231] Green, 172.

[232] *Ibid.*, 170.

[233] John Wacher, *The Coming of Rome*, London, 1979, fig. 1(f).

[234] Derek Allen, *An Introduction to Celtic Coins*, London, 1978, no. 114.

[235] Communication from Mr. E. Price of Frocester Court.

[236] Megaw, no. 306c.

[237] Paul-Marie Duval, *Les Celts*, Paris, 1977, nos. 389–90.

[238] Simone Scheers, *Les monnaies gauloises de la collection A. Danicourt à Peronne (Somme)*, Brussels, 1975, no. 199.

[239] Although the plaque was associated with the excavated material from Margidunum (East Bridgfort in Notts.),

its origins are in fact obscure. See Malcolm Todd, *Britannia*, II, 1971, 232.

[240] D. B. Charlton and M. M. Mitcheson, "Yardhope, a Shrine to Cocidius?", *Britannia*, XIV, 1983, 143–53.

[241] S. A. Butcher in Roger Leech, "The Excavation of a Romano-Celtic Temple on Lamyatt Beacon", *Britannia*. XVI, 1986, 319.

[242] For example, Allen, *Introduction*, nos. 53, 55.

[243] Schutz, *Germanic Europe*, figs. 139–40.

[244] Megaw, no. 187.

[245] Martin Henig in Roger Leech, "The Excavation of a Romano-Celtic Temple on Lamyatt Beacon", *Britannia*, XVI, 1986, 274 no. 1; 277 no. 4.

[246] *Ibid.*, 274–81.

[247] Leech, 270.

[248] S. A. Butcher, "Enamels from Roman Britain", *Ancient Monuments and their Interpretation*, London, 1977, 54–5.

[249] Butcher, *Britannia*, 317.

[250] D. R. Wilson, "Temples in Great Britain", *Caesarodunum*, 8, 1973, 31.

[251] Butcher, *Ancient Monuments*, 44.

[252] Frank Jenkins, "The Finds, Nor'nour", *Archaeological Journal*, CXXIV, 1967, 19.

[253] Henig, *Religion*, 150, fig. 71.

[254] R. A. H. Farrer, "Rider Relief from Whitcombe", *Proceedings of the Dorset Natural History and Archaeology Society*, 86, 1964, 103. Most recently, Martin Henig, "The Rider Relief from Whitcombe" in G. M. and G. N. Aitken, "Excavations at Whitcombe, 1965–1967", *PDNHAS*, 112, 1990, 70–1.

[255] *Ibid*, 104.

[256] For example on Imperial coins: von Roques de Maumont, 27b, a coin of Trajan shows the emperor on a galloping horse trampling an enemy of the Dexileos type. As a divine motif, see the Thracian Rider reliefs, Chapter Six.

[257] Farrer, 104.

[258] For example, Graham Webster, *The Roman Imperial Army of the First and Second Centuries AD*, London, 1969, pl. II.

[259] Espérandieu, no. 6044.

[260] Mattingly, pls. 42–3.

[261] Karl-Joseph Gilles in *Trier: Kaisarresidenz und Bischofssitz*, Mainz, 1984, pl. 26b.

[262] André Grabar, *Christian Iconography and a Study of its Origins*, London, 1969, pl. 125.

[263] von Roques de Maumont, 70, fig. 36b.

[264] Eckhart, 26.

[265] Martin Henig and Timothy Ambrose, "A New Roman Rider-Relief from Stragglethorpe, Lincolnshire", *Britannia*, XI, 1980, 135–8.

[266] Mathilde Schleiermacher, *Römische Reitergrabsteine*, Bonn, 1984, no. 80.

[267] *LIMC*, "Ares/Mars", no. 487 and no. 488 the same subject from Toulouse.

[268] Schutz, *Romans*, 130, fig. 145 cuirassed Mars and fig. 146 nude Mars.

[269] H. M. Taylor and J. Taylor, *Anglo-Saxon Architecture*, II, Cambridge, 1965, 596.

[270] See Henig and Ambrose, 138.

[271] Barry Cunliffe, *Fishbourne: a Roman Palace and its Garden*, London, 1971, pl. I, figs. 51–2.

272 Barry Cunliffe, *Roman Bath*, Oxford, 1969, 14, fig. 3.
273 A drawing of the reconstructed column from Cannstatt is in Lambrechts, *Contributions*, 81, fig. 1.
274 For example, Espérandieu, no. 31 from 1931 Supplement (Schierstein); no. 5777 (Mainz).
275 *Ibid.*, no. 76-1931 Sup. (Butterstadt); no. 4557 (Hommert).
276 *Ibid.*, no. 5690.
277 *Ibid.*, no. 76-1931 Sup. (Butterstadt), for example.
278 Gerhard Bauchhenss and Peter Noelke, *Die Jupitersäulen in den germanischen Provinzen*, Cologne and Bonn, 1981, 70.
279 *Ibid.*, map 1.
280 Gilbert Picard, "Imperator Caelestium", *Gallia*, XXXV, 1977, 90.
281 Bauchhenss and Noelke, 15.
282 *Ibid.*, 14.
283 Thevenot, *Divinités*, 28.
284 Gerhard Bauchhenss, *Jupitergigantensäulen*, Stuttgart, 1976, 11.
285 *Pharsalia*, I, 448–51.
286 Bauchhenss and Noelke, 79–80.
287 *Ibid.*, 80–1.
288 For a detailed study of the wheel-god see: Miranda Green, *The Wheel as a Cult Symbol in the Romano-Celtic World*, Brussels, 1984.
289 Bauchhenss and Noelke, 24.
290 Edith Wightman, *Roman Trier and the Treveri*, London, 1970, 225.
291 Lambrechts, 88; Émile Thevenot, "Les monuments de Jupiter à l'anguipède dans la cité des Eduens", *Mémoires de la Commission des Antiquités du Department de la Côte d'Or*, XXI, 1936–9, 488.
292 Bauchhenss and Noelke, 21–2.
293 *Ibid.*, 22.
294 Ann Roes, "L'animal au signe solaire", *Revue archéologique*, 6 ser., XII, 1938, 153–82.
295 See Martin Henig, *A Corpus of Roman Engraved Gemstones from British Sites*, Oxford, 1974, no. 426; Francis Vian, *Répertoire des gigantomachies figurées dans l'art grec et romain*, Paris, 1951, no. 498, described as a modern replica of a Hellenistic original.
296 Marianne Maaskant-Kleibrink, *Catalogue of the Engraved Gems in the Royal Coin Cabinet, The Hague*, The Hague, 1978, no. 401a, b.
297 See, for example, Mackintosh, *JBAA*, pls. IA, IB, IIA.
298 Wilhelm Weber, *Die ägyptische-griechischen Terrakotten*, Berlin, 1914, nos. 336–7.
299 Micheline Rouvier-Jeanlin, *Les figurines gallo-romaines en terre cuite au Musée des Antiquités nationales*, Paris, 1972, no. 522.
300 Weber, 200.
301 Bernard Andreae, *Laokoön und die Grundung Roms*, Mainz, 1988, 69.
302 Margarete Bieber, *The Sculpture of the Hellenistic Age*, New York, 1961, 77, figs. 268–71.
303 *Ibid.*, 78.
304 Steven Lattimore, *The Marine Thiasos in Greek Sculpture*, Los Angeles, 1986, fig. 3.
305 Bieber, 113.
306 *Ibid.*, 115.
307 Vian, 6.
308 Joseph Fontenrose, *Python: a Study of Delphic Myth and its Origins*, Berkeley, 1980, 77.
309 Vian, pl. I, no. 4; Fontenrose, fig. 3.
310 Boardman, *Classical Period*, fig. 89.
311 Bieber, fig. 435.
312 T. B. L. Webster, *Hellenistic Art*, London, 1967, 116.
313 Bieber, 115.
314 *Ibid.*, 105; Vian, no. 40.
315 *Ibid.*, 165, fig. 706.
316 Vian, nos. 46, 48, 55.
317 Bieber, fig. 460.
318 *Ibid.*, fig. 467.
319 Baldassare Conticello, "Sul gruppo di Scilla e della nave nel Museo de Sperlonga", *Alessandria e il mondo ellenistico-romano*, Bonacasa and di Vita, eds., vol. VI, 1984, fig. 1, photos lxxxvi, lxxxvii.
320 *Ibid.*, 623.
321 Andreae, 102.
322 Achille Adriani, *Repertorio d'arte dell'Egitto greco-romano*, vol. II, Palermo, 1961, no. 75, pl. 52.
323 *Ibid.*, 20.
324 Lattimore, fig. 39.
325 Adriani, 20.
326 Boardman, *Archaic Period*, fig. 197.
327 Lattimore, 57.
328 Bieber, figs. 74–5.
329 *Ibid.*, 40, fig. 102.
330 Bauchhenss and Noelke, pl. 99; Noelke, no. 203.
331 Andreae, figs. 19–20, 22–4.
332 Bauchhenss and Noelke, 97; Espérandieu, nos. 76-1931 Sup., 4557, 5606.
333 Mackintosh, *JBAA*, pl. IIIA.
334 Bernhard Schweitzer, "Späthellenistische Reitergruppen", *Jahrbuch des Deutschen Archäologischen Instituts*, LI, 1936, figs. 3–4.
335 *Ibid.*, pl. 165.
336 Bauchhenss and Noelke, map 4.
337 Espérandieu, no. 5999.
338 *Ibid.*, no. 480-1931 Sup.
339 *Ibid.*, no. 6104.
340 *Ibid.*, no. 388-1931 sup.; similar no. 380 also from Pforzheim.
341 Bauchhenss and Noelke, no. 495, pl. 45, 1.
342 Espérandieu, no. 407-1931 Sup.
343 *Ibid.*, no. 4900.
344 *Ibid.*, no. 5246.
345 Bieber, figs. 530–3.
346 Andreae, 146–7.
347 *Ibid.*, 180–1.
348 Andrew Stewart, *Skopas of Paros*, Park Ridge (New Jersey), 1977, 74.
349 *Ibid.*
350 Bauchhenss and Noelke: Noelke, no. 17.
351 Lambrechts, 91–3.
352 Espérandieu, no. 6090.
353 Herbert Schutz, *Prehistory*, pls. 225–6.
354 J.-J. Hatt, *Celts and Gallo-Romans*, pl. 45.
355 Fernand Benoit, *Les mythes de l'outre-tombe*, Brussels, 1950, fig. 4.
356 Rannuccio Bianchi Bandinelli, *Rome: The Late Empire*, London, 1971, fig. 130, for example.
357 Bauchhenss and Noelke, 352–3.
358 Siedentopf, 23.

359 *Ibid.,* 20.

360 *Ibid.,* 63.

361 Siedentopf, 36–8, figs. 2, 8.

362 von Roques de Maumont, fig. 45.

363 Siedentopf, 71–2.

364 *Ibid.,* 71.

365 Schweitzer, fig. 2.

366 Bieber, 146.

367 *Ibid.,* fig. 21.

368 *Ibid.,* 73–8.

369 *Ibid.,* 32–3.

370 Weber, nos. 82–5.

371 Espérandieu, 407-1931 Sup.

372 *Ibid.,* 260–1.

373 Vian, nos. 537, 539.

374 Celtic stem *epo,* horse. Cognate with Greek *hippos* and Latin *equus.* See K. M. Linduff, "Epona: A Celt Among the Romans", *Latomus,* XXXVIII, 1979, 820.

375 *Ibid.,* 820–1.

376 For example in M. Rouvier-Jeanlin, *Les figurines gallo-romaines en terre cuite au Musée des Antiquités nationales,* Paris, 1972, nos. 436–40.

377 *Ibid.,* nos. 306–424.

378 Thevenot, *Divinités,* 185.

379 Émile Thevenot, "Les monuments et le culte d'Épona chez les Eduens", *L'Antiquité Classique,* XVIII, 1949, 396; Linduff, 834.

380 René Magnen and Émile Thevenot, *Épona, déesse gauloise des chevaux,* Bordeaux, 1953, catalogue nos. 113, 114.

381 Fernand Benoit, *Les mythes de l'outre-tombe: le cavalier à l'anguipède et l'écuyère Épona,* Brussels, 1950.

382 Magnen and Thevenot, no. 39.

383 *Ibid.,* no. 5.

384 *Ibid.,* no. 14.

385 Salomon Reinach, "Epona", *Revue Archéologique,* XXVI, 3 ser., 1895, 171; Magnen and Thevenot, no. 41.

386 J.-Cl. Papinot, *Gallia,* XLIII, 1985, 507–8, fig. 26.

387 Linduff, fig. 1; Magnen and Thevenot, 65.

388 E. M. Wightman, *Gallia Belgica,* London, 1985, xii–xiii.

389 Peter Salway, *Roman Britain,* Oxford, 1981, 669.

390 Magnen and Thevenot, no. 3.

391 *Ibid.,* no. 1.

392 Thevenot, "Les monuments", 388.

393 Linduff, fig. 1.

394 Wilhelm Schleiermacher, "Studien an Göttertypen der römischen Rheinprovinzen", *23 Bericht der Römisch-Germanischen Kommission,* 1934, 126–35; Linduff, 820–5.

395 Linduff, 823.

396 W. Schleiermacher, 127.

397 *Ibid.*

398 Linduff, 823.

399 Benoit's thesis of a Danubian origin for Epona has received no support. See Pierre Lambrechts, "Divinités équestres celtiques ou défunts héröisés?" *L'Antiquité Classique,* XX, 1951, 125–6.

400 Linduff, 823.

401 Cunliffe, *Greeks, Romans and Barbarians,* 134.

402 Wightman, 56.

403 MacKendrick, *Roman France,* London, 1971, 118–9.

404 *Ibid.*

405 *Ibid.,* 53.

406 Wightman, 80.

407 *Ibid.*

408 *Ibid.,* 176.

409 Linduff, 825–32.

410 Magnen and Thevenot, nos. 20–1; England and Scotland not two in England as Linduff, 831: RIB 1777 (Carvoran), RIB 2177 (Auchendavy).

411 Green, *Corpus:* South Collingham, 167, Alchester, 175; Caerwent, 183; Colchester, 216.

412 W. Schleiermacher, 130.

413 *Ibid.,* 130–1.

414 There is no good evidence that Epona was the poor horseman's answer to his officers' worship of Mithras as Kathryn Linduff suggests (836). The religious situation was far more complex than this and the number of artefacts relating to Epona actually found in clear military contexts is too small to adequately support such conclusions.

415 Magnen and Thevenot, no. 77.

416 Elfriede Brandt, *Antike Gemmen in Deutschen Sammlungen,* I, Stattliche Münzsammlung München ii, Italische Gemmen, Munich, 1970, no. 842.

417 W. Schleiermacher, 132, figs., 13.1, 2.

418 *Ibid.,* 132.

419 Reinach, 188–9.

420 W. Schleiermacher, 133.

421 Metamorphosis, III, 27.

422 Thevenot, "Les monuments", pl. II.1.

423 *Ibid.,* 388; Pierre Lambrechts, "La colonne du dieu-cavalier au géant et le culte des sources en Gaule", *Latomus,* VIII, 1949, 145–58.

424 Magnen and Thevenot, no. 37.

425 *Ibid.,* no. 79.

426 J. Charbonneaux, R. Martin and F. Villard, *Hellenistic Art 330–50 BC,* London, 1973.

427 *Ibid.,* fig. 192.

428 John Morris, *Londinium,* London, 1982, fig. 9.

429 Pliny, NH, XXXV, 36; Friederike Naumann, *Die Ikonographie der Kybele in der phrygischen und der griechischen Kunst,* Tübingen, 1983, 233.

430 Maarten J. Vermaseren, *Cybele and Attis,* London, 1977, pl. 37.

431 *Ibid.,* 53.

432 *Ibid.,* 38.

433 Elmar Schwertheim, *Die Denkmäler orientalischer Gottheiten im römischen Deutschland,* Leiden, 1974, no. 20.

434 Magnen and Thevenot, nos. 73, 73bis and Rouvier-Jeanlin, no. 474, for example.

435 Eva Zahn, *Europa und der Stier,* Würzburg, 1983, pl. 30.2.

436 Maaskant-Kleibrink, no. 551.

437 Charbonneaux et al., fig. 179.

438 Zahn, no. 114.

439 *Ibid.,* no. 104.6.

440 G. W. Meates, *The Roman Villa at Lullingstone, Kent,* Kent Archaeological Society, 1979, vol. I, frontispiece and pls. XV a, b.

441 Boardman, *Archaic Period,* fig. 208.3.

442 For example, Zahn, no. 89.

443 *Ibid.*, no. 104.6.

444 Rouvier-Jeanlin, 32.

445 Magnen and Thevenot, no. 156; Espérandieu, no. 8227. Espérandieu comments on the unusual treatment of the horse's head.

446 Charbonneaux, figs. 163–4.

447 Magnen and Thevenot, no. 38.

448 *Ibid.*, no. 100.

449 For example, *ibid.*, nos. 79, 83, 93. A mosaic found at Autun has a circular central *emblema* in which is a group composed of Bellerophon killing the chimera. The main section of the picture is missing but it has been restored to show the hero riding side-saddle. This is probably to accommodate the fact that the head, which is well-preserved, is rendered frontally. Bellerophon's mantle is also preserved and this billows out around his head like Epona's scarf. The mosaic is dated to the second half of the second century. The unexpected similarity between elements of the Bellerophon composition and the most common Epona type in this area may be coincidental or it may be an indication of a particular local taste. H. Stern and M. Blanchard-Lemée, *Recueil général des mosaiques de la Gaule*, II.2, Paris, 1975, no. 233.

450 Maarten J. Vermaseren, *Corpus Cultus Cybelae Attidisque*, III, Leiden, 1977, nos. 330, 439, 440, for example. Hereafter, *CCCA*.

451 Steven Lattimore, *The Marine Thiasos in Greek Sculpture*, Los Angeles, 1986, 28.

452 John R. Clarke, *Roman Black-and-White Figural Mosaics*, New York, 1979, fig. 48.

453 David Smith in *A Handbook of Roman Art*, Martin Henig, ed., London, 1983, 122.

454 Erika Zwierlein-Diehl, *Die Antiken Gemmen des Kunsthistorischen Museums in Wien*, I, Munich, 1973, nos. 252–8, especially 255.

455 Brandt, pt. III, no. 2730.

456 *Ibid.*, no. 2732.

457 D. E. Strong, *Greek and Roman Gold and Silver Plate*, London, 1966, pl. 62b.

458 Boardman, *Black Figure Vases*, 217.

459 Thevenot, "Les monuments", 391, pl. IV.1.

460 Magnen and Thevenot, no. 114. Espérandieu's numerical designations are used in the text because he illustrates all the monuments from La Horgne-au-Sablon together. Magnen illustrates only a few making comparisons difficult.

461 Magnen and Thevenot, nos. 186–7.

462 *Ibid.*, nos. 114, 186–8.

463 *Ibid.*, no. 190.

464 *Ibid.*, no. 185.

465 *Ibid.*, no. 183.

466 *Ibid.*, no. 200.

467 In central Gaul, a relief of one of the Dioscuri standing by his horse was found at Alise-Ste-Reine. See Joel Le Gall, *Alésia*, Guides archéologique de France, 1985, fig. 38.

468 Magnen and Thevenot, nos. 200, 200bis, 201–3.

469 See above note 411.

470 Gerard Nicolini, *Gallia*, XXXIII, 1975, 381–2, fig. 25.

471 Magnen and Thevenot, 57.

472 *Ibid.*, no. 201.

473 *Ibid.*, nos. 78 and 54.

474 Espérandieu, no. 1608.

475 W. Schleiermacher, 127.

476 Catherine Johns, "A Roman Bronze Statuette of Epona", *British Museum Quarterly*, XXXVI, 1971–2, 38.

477 Magnen and Thevenot, no. 217.

478 *Ibid.*, no. 218.

479 *Ibid.*, no. 18.

480 *Ibid.*, no. 207.

481 *Ibid.*, no. 6.

482 W. Schleiermacher, 134.

483 Vermaseren, *Cybele and Attis*, 15.

484 R. M. Dawkins, *The Sanctuary of Artemis Orthia at Sparta*, London, 1929, pls. XCI.1, XCI.2, XCII.2, for example.

485 Vermaseren, *Cybele and Attis*, 33–4, 72; Naumann, 159–60.

486 Vermaseren, *Cybele and Attis*, 33.

487 John Boardman, *Greek Art*, London, 1973, 134, fig. 137.

488 Rouvier-Jeanlin, Abundance seated: nos. 436–40; Minerva seated: no. 471; Mother goddesses seated: nos. 306–424.

489 For example, Espérandieu, nos.1528 and 1779.

490 For the seated Isis in the West: Tran Tam Tinh, *Isis Lactans*, Leiden, 1973, 11–2.

491 Other deities flanked by animals were current in the Roman Empire, but the form tended to be used for Oriental gods and goddesses. The most famous figure of the Ephesian Artemis was sometimes flanked by deer. On a stele from Izmir now in the Ryksmusem van Oudheden in Leiden, Artemis, identified as Artemis Anaitis in the form of the Ephesian Artemis, stands between a stag and a doe which are both facing away from her. On the register above her is the sun god. Robert Fleischer, *Artemis von Ephesos und Verwandete Kultstatuen aus Anatolien und Syrien*, Leiden, 1973. A statue of Jupiter Heliopolitanus of a type similar to the Artemis stands with a bull on either side of him (*Ibid.*, pl. 157).

492 See Eva and John Harris, *The Oriental Cults of Roman Britain*, Leiden, 1965, 96–7, 99, 100.

493 Vermaseren, *Cybele and Attis*, 131.

494 Schwertheim, 300.

495 *Ibid.*, 303.

496 Schwertheim, 303.

497 The guide book to the Saalburg points out that not only were there a Mithraeum and a Metroön but also a temple to Jupiter Dolichenus and a Gaulish sanctuary. These have been identified by inscriptions found on the site. The number of temples on this one site shows that the religious life on the frontier was very rich and varied. See Saalburgmuseum, *Saalburg-Roman Fort*, Saalburg-Kastell, 1984, 15.

498 Vermaseren, *Cybele and Attis*, 140.

499 At Naix, dated 210-211 (Magnen and Thevenot, no. 6); at Soleure in Switzerland, dated 219 (Magnen and Thevenot, no. 7); and later at Thil-Châtel, dated 250-251 (Magnen and Thevenot, no. 5) and at Mainz, undated (Magnen and Thevenot, no. 10).

500 Vermaseren, *Cybele and Attis*, 140–1.

501 Magnen and Thevenot, no. 46.

502 Johns, 38.

503 *Ibid.*, 40.

504 *Ibid.*, 38.

505 *Ibid.*, 40.

506 *Ibid.*

507 Vermaseren, *CCCA*, III, no. 148.

508 *Ibid.*, no. 350; similar: 202–3, 265, 340, 397, 427–32, 434–5.

509 Vermaseren, *Cybele and Attis*, pl. 77.

510 Magnen and Thevenot, no. 211.

511 *Ibid.*, no. 207.

512 *Ibid.*, no. 217.

513 *Ibid.*, no. 219.

514 *Ibid.*, no. 216.

515 *Ibid.*, no. 208.

516 *Ibid.*, no. 215.

517 *Ibid.*, no. 48.

518 Wightman, pl. 37, for example.

519 Graham Webster, *The British Celts and their Gods under Rome*, London, 1986, pl. 6.

520 Schutz, *Romans*, figs. 70–1.

521 Magnen and Thevenot, no. 213.

522 *Ibid.*, no. 214.

523 Michel Labrousse, *Gallia*, XXXIV, 1976, 486.

524 *Ibid.*

525 Magnen and Thevenot, no. 2.

526 Magnen and Thevenot suggest dates for only nine figures and nine inscriptions.

527 Burkert, 212.

528 *Iliad*, 3.237, Richmond Lattimore, trans., Chicago, 1961, 106.

529 Carl Kerényi, *The Gods of the Greeks*, Harmondsworth, 1958, 94–5.

530 Burkert, 212–3.

531 Livy, II, 20.

532 R. M. Ogilvie, *Early Rome and the Etruscans*, London, 1976.

533 Paul Faure, "Les Dioscures à Delphes", *Antiquité Classique*, LIV, 1985, 63.

534 See Boardman, *Archaic Period*, fig. 70.

535 Antoine Hermary in *Lexicon Iconographicum Mythologicae Classicae*, III, 591. Hereafter *LIMC*.

536 Boardman, *Archaic Period*, fig. 114.

537 Hermary, 591.

538 *Corpus Vasorum Antiquorum*, Oxford, I, pl. 29, 1.

539 Hermary, 591.

540 *Ibid.*, 591–2.

541 *Ibid.*, 592; see also Susan Guettel Cole, *Theoi Megaloi: the Cult of the Great Gods at Samothrace*, Leiden, 1984, 78–9.

542 Hermary, 592.

543 See, for example, Fernand Chapouthier, *Les Dioscures au service d'une déesse*, Paris, 1935, nos. 76, 79–85.

544 Hermary, 592.

545 Françoise Gury, *LIMC*, III, 629.

546 This subject has been much studied particularly by the followers of Georges Dumézil, e.g., Robert Schilling, *Rites, cultes, dieux de Rome*, Paris, 1979, 338–53; Donald Ward, "The Separate Functions of the Indo-European Divine Twins", in *Myth and Law among the Indo-Europeans*, London, 1970, 193–202.

547 R. Ross Holloway, *The Archaeology of Early Rome and Latium*, London, 1994, 130, 134, fig. 10.6.

548 Holloway, 134.

549 Gury, 609.

550 *Ibid.*, 629.

551 A. B. Cook, *Zeus*, Cambridge, 1925, II, 442.

552 Will, 114.

553 *Ibid.*

554 von Roques de Maumont, 15–6, fig. 5.

555 Boardman, *Classical Period*, fig. 22.

556 *Ibid.*, fig. 92.

557 For example, Salomon Reinach, *Répertoire des reliefs grecs et romaines*, Paris, 1909, nos. 415.1, 415.4, 416.2, 534.4.

558 Gury, 630.

559 Hermary, 592.

560 Gury, 630.

561 Licia Borrelli Vlad, Giulia Fogolari and Anna Guidi Toniato, "The stylistic problem of the Horses of San Marco", *The Horses of San Marco*, trans., J. and V. Wilton-Ely, Milan, 1979, 27, fig. 53.

562 *Ibid.*, fig. 52.

563 *LIMC*, 'Castores', nos 40–53.

564 *Ibid.*, nos. 80–90.

565 Chapouthier, for example, 6, 9, 10, 11.

566 Paul-Marie Duval, *Resumé du Paris Antique*, Paris, 1972, 27.

567 Espérandieu, no. 3133.

568 Diodorus Siculus, IV, 56, 3; see Jan de Vries, *La religion des Celts*, Paris, 1977, 119–20; Krüger, 1–9.

569 Krüger, II, 31.

570 See de Vries, 120–1.

571 *Ibid.*

572 Tacitus, *Germania*, 43, H. Mattingly, trans., Harmondsworth, 1948, 136.

573 Krüger, I, nos. 1, 2.

574 *Ibid.*, Pollux: nos. 23–5 (all from Spain); Castor: nos. 5, 8, 16.

575 *Ibid.*, no. 11.

576 *Ibid.*, no. 15.

577 *Ibid.*, no. 10.

578 *Ibid.*, no. 20.

579 *Ibid.*, 26.

580 Paul-Marie Duval, *Les dieux de la Gaule*, Paris, 1976, 87.

581 Krüger, II, no. 37, fig. 24a, b.

582 Chapouthier, no. 26, a fresco from the Fayum in Egypt and no. 54, a coin issued by Hadrian at Alexandria.

583 Krüger, I, no. 20.

584 Chapouthier, no. 72.

585 Krüger, II, 26, no. 61.

586 *Ibid.*, 27, no. 63.

587 Bauchhenss and Noelke, 57.

588 Gerard Bauchhenss, "Die Grosse Jupitersäule aus Mainz", *Corpus Signorum Imperii Romani*, Mainz, 1984, 14.

589 Krüger's contention that the Jupiter columns were German and that the Dioscuri were the Germanic Alci mentioned by Tacitus has long been dismissed.

590 Bauchhenss and Noelke, 52.

591 Krüger, II, no. 58, fig. 46.

592 *Ibid.*, 25.

593 Magnen and Thevenot, nos. 48 from Alise-Ste. Reine and 215 from Beihingen.

594 Bauchhenss and Noelke, 57–8.

595 *Ibid.*, 58.

596 *Ibid.*

597 *Ibid.*

598 J.-J. Hatt, *La tombe gallo-romaine*, Paris, 1951, 114-5; LIMC, "Castores", no. 80; Espérandieu no. 124–5.

599 Hatt, *La tombe* 114.

600 Franz Cumont, *Récherches sur le symbolisme funéraire des Romains*, Paris, 1942, 64–5.

601 Hatt, *La tombe*, 115.

602 *Ibid.*

603 Krüger, I, no. 30, fig. 14; E. no. 4359.

604 Krüger, I, 22.

605 *LIMC*, "Castores": 78–9, 97–100, 101–2.

606 Espérandieu, no. 96.

607 Espérandieu, no. 133.

608 Krüger, I, no. 14.

609 *Ibid.*, 11.

610 Gury, 632.

611 Cumont, 86–7.

612 *Ibid.*, 91.

613 Espérandieu, no. 169.

614 Michael Speidel, *The Religion of Iuppiter Dolichenus in the Roman Army*, Leiden, 1978, 1.

615 Pierre Merlat, *Jupiter Dolichenus*, Paris, 1960, 94.

616 See above note 614.

617 Speidel, 4.

618 *Ibid.*, 75.

619 *Ibid.*, 39.

620 Merlat, 37–8.

621 Speidel, pl. 12.

622 *Ibid.*, pl. 6.

623 *Ibid.*, pl. 8, described in detail in Pierre Merlat, *Répertoire des inscriptions et monuments figurés du culte de Jupiter Dolichenus*, Paris, 1951, no. 50.

624 Merlat, *Jupiter Dolichenus*, 93.

625 *Ibid.*, 91, n. 4.

626 Merlat, *Répertoire*, 303, no. 311.

627 Merlat, *Jupiter Dolichenus*, 38.

628 *Ibid.*, 39.

629 J. M. C. Toynbee, *Art in Roman Britain*, London, 1962, 164, fig. 95.

630 Ian Richmond, "Roman legionaries at Corbridge, their supply-base, temples and religious cults", *Archaeologia Aeliana*, 4 ser. XXI, 1943, 179–85.

631 *Ibid.*, 186–7.

632 *Ibid.*, 187–8.

633 J. M. C. Toynbee, *Art in Britain under the Romans*, Oxford, 1964, 140.

634 Krüger, I, 18; Espérandieu, no. 340; *LIMC* "Castores", no. 43.

635 *Journal of the Roman Society*, XLVIII, 1958, 144; Toynbee, *Art in Britain*, 159; *Id.*, *The Roman Art Treasures from the Temple of Mithras*, London and Middlesex Archaeological Society, Special Paper no. 7, London, 1986, 34–6, pl. 19.

636 *Ibid.*

637 *Ibid.*, 297.

638 *LIMC*, "Castores": nos. 19–20.

639 Martin Henig, Graham Webster and Robert Wilkins, "A bronze Dioscurus from Wroxeter and its fellow from Canterbury", *Antiquaries Journal*, LXVII, part ii, 1987, 360–2, pl. XXX.

640 *Ibid.*, 361.

641 Pliny 35, XVIII, 48 where *signum* is translated as 'figurine' rather than signet ring, medallion or brooch: H. Rackham in *Natural History*, Loeb Classical Library, IX, 162–3.

642 Henig *et al.*, *Antiquaries Journal*, 362.

643 Toynbee, *Art in Roman Britain*, 297.

644 *LIMC*, "Castores", no. 25.

645 Espérandieu, no. 6231.

646 Krüger, II, 71–2, no. 52.

647 Chapouthier, 129–51.

648 See, for example, Martin Nilsson, *The Mycenaean Origin of Greek Mythology*, New York, 1963, 73.

649 For example, Chapouthier, figs. 20–2.

650 Hermary, 593.

651 R. M. Dawkins, *The Sanctuary of Artemis Orthia at Sparta*, London, 1929, pls. XCI.1, 2; XCII.2 and XCV.

652 Chapouthier, 185–228.

653 *Ibid.*, nos. 37–54, for example.

654 *Ibid.*, nos. 77–8.

655 *Ibid.*, 97–8.

656 *Ibid.*, 46.

657 *Ibid.*, 99.

658 Louis Robert, *Antiquité Classique*, 1973.

659 Chapouthier, no. 12.

660 *Ibid.*, 35.

661 *Ibid.*, 285.

662 Aleksandrina Cermanović-Kuzmanović, "Die Denkmäler des thrakischen Heros in Jugoslavien und das Problem des thrakischen Reitergottes", *Archaelogica Iugoslavica*, IV, 1963, 41.

663 Gawril Kazarow, *Die Denkmäler des thrakischen Reitergottes in Bulgarien*, Budapest, 1938, no. 754.

664 Chapouthier, 234.

665 Chapouthier, no. 61.

666 Gabriella Bordenache "Histria alla luce del suo materiale scultoreo", *Dacia*, V, 1961, 199–200; D. M. Pippidi and E. Popescu, "Les relations d'Istros and d'Apollonie du Pont à l'époque hellenistique", *Dacia*, III, 1959, 235.

667 Ernest Will, *Le relief cultuel greco-romain*, Paris, 1955.

668 Another pair of Dioscuri have been added to the corpus recently after a re-evaluation of two youthful male figures found in Boulogne. The statues represent two young men wearing only mantles and pointed caps. The original discoverers wanted them to be the Mithraic figures Cautes and Cautopates in keeping with their presumed discovery of the walls of a Mithraeum. However, Eric Belot argues convincingly that the excavators were mistaken in their identification of a local Mithraeum and that the twin statues are the Dioscuri. Indeed, that the mistake was ever made and then perpetuated, given the clear resemblance of the pair to other Dioscuri figures but not to Mithraic dadophors, seems very strange. Eric Belot, "Dioscures ou dadophores? A propos des sculptures 'mithraiques' et du 'Mithraeum' de Boulogne-sur-Mer. Présence des cultes orientaux à Boulogne et en Morinie", *Revue du Nord-Archéologie*, LXXII, 1990, 135–62.

669 Manfred Oppermann, "Zu einigen Weihdenkmälern mit der Darstellung des thrakischen Reitergottes aus der

SR Rumänien und der VR Bulgarien", *Klio*, LV, 1973, 197.

[670] Cermanović-Kuzmanović, 47.

[671] *Iliad*, 10.434–8, Lattimore trans.

[672] Mihail Vasilescu, "Les Thraces dans les épopées homeriques", *Actes du II Congrès International de Thracologie*, I, Bucarest, 1980, 156–60; G. S. Kirk, *Homer and the Epic*, Cambridge, 1965, 214.

[673] Vasilescu, 160–1.

[674] Stanley Casson, *Macedonia, Thrace and Illyria*, Oxford, 1926, 249.

[675] *Ibid.*, 196.

[676] Yordanka Youroukova, *Coins of the Ancient Thracians*, BAR Supplementary series, 4, 1976, 68, nos. 15 and 16.

[677] *Ibid.*, 76, no. 68.

[678] Cermanović-Kuzmanović, 47.

[679] Kazarow, 15.

[680] Nubar Hampartumian, *Corpus Cultus Equitis Thracii: Moesia Inferior (Romanian Section) and Dacia*, Leiden, 1979, no. 45. (Hereafter *CCET*, IV.)

[681] Oppermann, 204.

[682] *CCET*, IV, 9.

[683] Cermanović-Kuzmanović, 44.

[684] See note 679.

[685] For example, N. Gudea, "Un relief al cavalerului trac la Pojejena", *Studii şi Cercetari de Istorie Veche şi Arheologie*, XXII, 1971, 345–9.

[686] Kazarow, 5.

[687] *Ibid.*, 5–6.

[688] *Ibid.*, 6.

[689] *Ibid.*

[690] *Ibid.*, 6–7.

[691] *Ibid.*, 7.

[692] *Ibid.*, Margarita Tacheva-Hitova, "Wesenzüge des Sabazioskultes in Moesia Inferior und Thracia", *Hommages à Maarten J. Vermaseren*, III, Leiden, 1978, 1225.

[693] Kazarow, 8–9.

[694] Cermanović-Kuzmanović, 48.

[695] Franz Glaser, *Die römische Stadt Teurnia*, Klagenfurt, 1983, 61, no. 39.

[696] Kazarow, 9.

[697] Maria Coja, "Terres cuites d'époque hellenistique représentant le cavalier trace trouvée à Histria", *Dacia*, n.s., XVIII, 1974, 283–4.

[698] *Ibid.*, 284.

[699] *Ibid.*, 285.

[700] *CCET*, IV, 6.

[701] *Ibid.*, 5.

[702] Zlatozora Gončeva and Manfred Oppermann, *Corpus Cultus Equitis Thracii: Monumenta Orae Ponti Euxini Bulgariae*, I, Leiden, 1979, nos. 80, 81. (Hereafter, *CCET*, I.)

[703] *Ibid.*, 62.

[704] *Ibid.*, no. 28.

[705] *Ibid.*, no. 97, 71–2.

[706] Manfred Oppermann, "Zum Kult des thrakischen Reiters in Bulgarien", *Thracia*, III, Sofia, 1974, 353.

[707] Ivan Venedikov, *Thracian Treasures from Bulgaria*, London, 1976, 63.

[708] Petre Alexandrescu, "Le group de trésors thraces du horde des Balkans", I, *Dacia*, n.s., XXVII, 1983, 59–61.

[709] *Ibid.*, 61.

[710] *Ibid.*, 66.

[711] Will, 66–89.

[712] Coja, 284.

[713] See above, note 695.

[714] Will, 79.

[715] *Ibid.*, 80.

[716] *Ibid.*, 81.

[717] Henri Frankfort, *The Art and Architecture of the Ancient Orient*, Baltimore, 1954, 152; see also Will, 88, n. 1.

[718] For example, R. D. Barnett, *Assyrian Palace Reliefs*, London, n.d., pl. 82.

[719] Will, 73, fig. 5.

[720] Will, 86.

[721] *Ibid.*

[722] *Ibid.*, 87–8.

[723] *CCET*, I, no. 81.

[724] Oppermann, *Klio*, 197–213; *Id.*, *Thracia*, 353–62.

[725] Oppermann, *Thracia*, 354–5.

[726] *Ibid.*, 356.

[727] *Ibid.*, 355–8.

[728] Oppermann, *Klio*, 197ff.

[729] *CCET*, IV, 5.

[730] *Ibid.*, 7

[731] *Ibid.*, 6.

[732] Radu Vulpe, "Ex-voto au cavalier trace provenant de Callatis", *Dacia*, n.s., VIII, 1964, 339.

[733] Casson, 193–4.

[734] Vulpe, 340.

[735] Dumitru Berciu, *Daco-Romania*, Geneva, 1978, 25.

[736] Herodotus, IV, 93.

[737] *CCET*, IV, 6.

[738] Constantin Scorpan, *Cavalerul trac*, Constanţa, 1967, 4–5.

[739] Venecia Ljubenova, "Ein thrakisches Heiligtum aus der römischen Epoche beim Dorf Daskalovo, Bezirk Pernik", *Thracia*, III, Sofia, 1974, 369.

[740] *Ibid.*, 369–70.

[741] *Ibid.*, 370.

[742] *Ibid.*, 370–3.

[743] *Ibid.*, 373–6.

[744] *Ibid.*, 373.

[745] *Ibid.*, 376–7.

[746] *Ibid.*

[747] *CCET*, I, 60.

[748] Zlatozora Gončeva and Manfred Oppermann, *Corpus Cultus Equites Thracii: Monumenta inter Danubium et Haemum Reperta*, II, pt. 2, 1984, 4–5. (Hereafter *CCET*, II.2.)

[749] *CCET*, I, no. 8.

[750] Zlatozora Gončeva and Manfred Oppermann, *Corpus Cultus Equites Thracii: Monumenta inter Danubium et Haemum Reperta*, II, pt. 1, 1981, nos. 195, 242, 303. (Hereafter *CCET*, II.1.)

[751] *Ibid.*, no. 335.

[752] *CCET*, II.2, no. 119.

[753] Scorpan, 5.

[754] Oppermann, *Klio*, 200.

[755] *CCET*, IV, 47.

756 D. M. Pippidi, "Note de Lectură: Peşti şi pescari la Istros şi la Odessos", *Studii Clasice*, VII, 1965, 327; *CCET*, I, no. 33, type A.

757 Zlatozora Gončeva, "Le culte d'Apollon en Thrace", *Pulpudeva*, I, Plovdiv, 1974, 217.

758 *Ibid.*, 215.

759 *CCET*, II.2, no. 457.

760 *Ibid.*, no. 483.

761 *Ibid.*, no. 460.

762 *CCET*, I, no. 8.

763 *Ibid.*, no. 111.

764 *CCET*, II.2, no. 542.

765 Ljubenova, 374.

766 *CCET*, II.1, no. 302.

767 *CCET*, II.2, no. 449.

768 *CCET*, I, 79–80, no. 111.

769 *CCET*, II.2, no. 542.

770 Margarita Tacheva-Hitova, *Eastern Cults in Moesia Inferior and Thracia*, Leiden, 1983, 165.

771 *Ibid.*, 188.

772 Cermanović-Kuzmanović, 45–6.

773 Aleksandrina Cermanović-Kuzmanović, *Corpus Cultus Equites Thracii: Monumenta intra Fines Iugoslaviae Reperta*, V, Leiden, 1982, nos, 66, 88 (Hereafter, *CCET*, V.)

774 Cermanović-Kuzmanović, 44.

775 Kazarow, no. 557.

776 *CCET*, V, 16, no. 23.

777 *CCET*, II.2, no. 570.

778 Kazarow, 13, no. 754.

779 Oppermann, *Klio*, 202.

780 *CCET*, IV, no. 144.

781 *Ibid.*, no. 33.

782 *Ibid.*, no. 34.

783 *Ibid.*, no. 92. In the Pontic coastal cities, Dionysus seems to have appeared frequently with the Thracian Rider. The situation in the hinterlands of Thrace may have been different. Gawril Kazarow discusses two reliefs from Bulgaria with Dionysus represented together with the Rider (nos. 505 and 852), but there appear to be no inscriptions or other means of reliably identifying Dionysus on these Rider reliefs in Thrace. This is particularly perplexing as Dionysus is thought by some scholars to have originated in Thrace or possibly Phrygia (G. S. Kirk, *The Nature of the Greek Myths*, Harmondsworth, 1974, 128; W. C. K. Gutherie, *The Greeks and Their Gods*, Cambridge, 1950, 32, no. 1).

784 *CCET*, IV, nos. 13, 187.

785 *Ibid.*, no. 199.

786 *Ibid.*, no. 37; Tacheva-Hitova, *Eastern cults*, 98, no. 55a.

787 Scorpan, 11.

788 For example, Cermanović-Kuzmanović, 43.

789 Scorpan, 11.

790 *Ibid.*, 5–6.

791 *CCET*, I, no. 25; *CCET*, II.1, no. 379.

792 R. F. Hoddinott, *Bulgaria in Antiquity*, London, 1975, 51.

793 Kazarow, 12.

794 For example *CCET*, IV, no. 157.

795 *Ibid.*, no. 53.

796 Cermanović-Kuzmanović, 52.

797 Venedikov, no. 275.

798 *CCET*, IV, 10–11.

799 *CCET*, V, no. 81.

800 *CCET*, IV, no.1.

801 *Ibid.*, no. 3.

802 Cermanović-Kuzmanović, 34.

803 *CCET*, IV, 29–31.

804 Georges Seure, "ΝΕΟΣ ῾ΗΡΩΣ, ΚΟΥΡΟΣ ῾ΗΡΩΣ", *Revue des études grecques*, XLII, 1929, 246.

805 Berciu, 108, figs. 101, 106.

806 P. A. Holder, *The Roman Army in Britain*, London, 1982, 13.

807 See Mackintosh, *JBAA*, pl. IIB; for Thracian names, CCET, IV, 83.

808 Eight have inscriptions but none are of a votive character. Only three have been deciphered successfully. See Dumitru Tudor, *Corpus Monumentorum Religionis Equitum Danuuinorum*, II, Leiden, 1976, 72. (Hereafter *CMRED*.)

809 *Ibid.*, 72–4.

810 *Ibid.*, 55.

811 *Ibid.*, 60.

812 Kurt Gschwantler, "Donaureiter Reliefs in Österreich", Römisches Österreichisches Jahreschrift des Österreichischen Gesellschaft für Archäologie, XI-XII, 1983–4, 107–43.

813 *CMRED*, I, no. 173 and II, 60.

814 Gschwantler, 117; *CMRED*, II, 60.

815 *CMRED*, II, 60.

816 András Mócsy, *Pannonia and Upper Moesia*, London, 1974, 31.

817 *Ibid.*, 246.

818 *CMRED*, I, no. 180.

819 *CMRED*, I, no. 1.

820 Manfred Oppermann, "Thrakische und danubische Reitergötter", *Die orientalischen Religionen in Romerreich*, Leiden, 1981, 519.

821 *CMRED*, I, 1.

822 Oppermann, 519.

823 *CMRED*, II, 83.

824 Herodotus, IV, 94–6; V, 7.

825 Hadrian Daicoviciu, *Dacia de la Burebista la cucerirea romană*, Bucarest, 1972, 204–5.

826 *Ibid.*, 215.

827 *Ibid.*, 206–7. See also Hoddinott, *Thracians*, 81, 152–4 for an English account.

828 *Ibid.*, 215.

829 Berciu, 50–1.

830 Will, 274.

831 *CMRED*, II, 50; Will, 89; Oppermann, 519.

832 Oppermann, 518.

833 Tudor, no. 1, for example.

834 Tudor, no. 71.

835 For example, Tudor nos. 2, 7 from *Apulum*; no. 71 from Almus (Bulgaria); no. 90 from Zaldapa.

836 Tudor, no. 64, Moesia Superior.

837 Marjorie Mackintosh, "Roman Influences on the Victory Reliefs of Shapur I of Persia", *California Studies in Classical Antiquity*, 6, 1973, 181–203, especially pl. 7.

838 Tudor, no. 183.

839 P. R. Bienkowski, *Die Darstellungen der Gallier in der hellenistischen Kunst*, Vienna, 1908, fig. 133.

840 Tudor, no. 66. Compare Mackintosh, *JBAA*, pl. IIIA, B.
841 Marta Giacchero, "Santuari indigeni nell'impero romano: i cavalieri danubiani e il cavaliere trace", *Contributi dell'instituto di storia antica dell' Università del Sacro Cuore*, IX, 1973, 170.
842 Mackintosh, *JBAA*, nos. 3 and 4: Chester; 10 and 11: Kirkby Thore; 15: Paris — all have suggested dates around the third century AD.
843 *CMRED*, II, 81.
844 Oppermann, 520.
845 *CMRED*, 80.
846 *Ibid.*, 81.
847 *Ibid.*, no. 181; Toynbee, *Temple of Mithras*, 36–9, no. 14, pl. XL.
848 Chapouthier, catalogue nos. 8, 13, 16–8, 33, 40, 51–2, 57, 68, 70.
849 Ljubica Zotović, "Les éléments orientaux dans le culte des cavaliers danubiens et quelques nouveaux aspects de ce culte", *Hommages à Maarten J. Vermaseren*, III, Leiden, 1978, 1354.
850 *CMRED*, II, 96; I, 96, 98, 102, 103.
851 *CMRED*, II, 60.
852 Edward Ochsenschlager, "Lead Plaques of the Danubian Horsemen Type at Sirmium" in Ochsenschlager and Popović, *Sirmium* II, Belgrade, 1971, 55.
853 Gschwantler, 109.
854 The description follows Gschwantler, 130–2.
855 *CMRED*, I, no. 29.
856 *Ibid.*, no. 188.
857 *Ibid.*, no. 95.
858 On the development of the *taurobolium* see Robert Duthoy, *The Taurobolium: its Evolution and Terminology*, Leiden, 1969.
859 Chapouthier, 134.
860 *CMRED*, II, 103.
861 *Ibid.*, 119; I, nos. 127, 132–3, 135.
862 Zotović, 1359; *CMRED*, I, no. 173.
863 Oppermann, 522.
864 Zotović, 1367–8.
865 *CMRED*, II, 182.
866 See Petar Selem, *Les religions orientales dans la Pannonie romaine*, Leiden, 1980, 167 where he traces the change in Pannonia from dedications to *Deo Invicto Mithrae* to those calling on *Deo Soli Invicto Mithrae*.
867 Ochsenschlager, 58–9; Zotović, 1351–78; see also Leroy Campbell, *Mithraic Iconography and Ideology*, Leiden, 1968.
868 Ochsenschlager, 60–1; *CMRED*, II, 217–8, 227–31, 286.
869 *CMRED*, I, nos. 68–9, 132, 134, 141–5, 163, 168, 180, 185; Ochsenschlager's type IA.
870 *CMRED*, II, 82.
871 *CMRED*, I, no. 9.
872 *Ibid.*, no. 10.
873 *Ibid.*, nos, 45–6.
874 *CMRED*, II, 164–5.
875 *Ibid.*, 279.
876 *CMRED*, II, 246–8.
877 Hoddinott, *Thracians*, 100.

878 See Ivan Mazarov, "Sacrifice of a Ram on the Thracian Helmet from Coţofeneşti", *Pulpudeva*, 3, 1978, 81–101.
879 Ljubica Zotović, Les cultes orientaux sur le territoire de la Mésie Superiéure, Leiden, 1966, 25 and no. 3.
880 *Ibid.*, no. 15.
881 Jacques Moreau, *Das Trierer Kornmarktmosaik*, Cologne, 1960, 10.
882 See Moreau, 20–22.
883 *Ibid.*, 7ff., pls. 1, 2 and I, II.
884 *Ibid.*, 12.
885 *CMRED*, I, nos. 21, 32, 60–1, 118.
886 *Ibid.*, nos. 66, 155, 166, 180.
887 *CMRED*, II, 83.
888 Oppermann, 521.
889 *CMRED*, II, 83.
890 Giacchero, 182.
891 *CMRED*, I, nos. 56, 65.
892 Will, 105.
893 Ranuccio Bianchi Bandinelli, *Rome: the Centre of Power*, trans. P. Green, London, 1970, 108–9.
894 R. M. Cook, *Greek Painted Pottery*, London, 1960, 255.
895 Bandinelli, 30–38; Pliny 35, XVI 36–7.
896 See for example, W. W. Tarn, *The Greeks in Bactria and India*, Cambridge 1951; Benjamin Rowland, "Rome and Gandhara", *East and West*, IX, 1958, 199–208; Hugo Buchthal, "The Common Classical Sources of Buddhist and Christian Narrative Art", *JRAS*, 1943, 137–48.
897 Bandinelli, 63, ill. 69.
898 Alison Burford, *Craftsmen in Greek and Roman Society*, London, 1972, 62–5.
899 J. M. C. Toynbee, "Some Notes on Artists in the Roman World", *Latomus Collection* VI, Brussels, 21–6.
900 Toynbee, 21–2; Pliny 35, XLIV, 156.
901 Toynbee, 27; Pliny, 34, XVIII, 45–7.
902 Burford, 66–7.
903 See for example, Ernst Gerster, *Mittelrhenische Bildhauwerkstätten im 1. Jahrhundert n. Chr., Bonn*, 1938.
904 Anthony Birley, *The People of Roman Britain*, London, 1979, 130.
905 Kurt Weitzmann believes an important role in the transmission of imagery was played by illustrated books, *Illustrations in Role and Codex*, Princeton, 1947, 6–7, 24, 32.
906 Wightman, 176.
907 Pliny, 35, XVIII, 48.
908 Bauchhenss, *Jupitergigantensaülen* 12–3.
909 See J.-J. Hatt, "Les monuments gallo-romaines de Paris et les origines de la sculpture votive en Gaule romaine", *Revue archéologique*, 6 ser, XXIX, 1952, 68–83.
910 Kenner, 74.
911 See, for example, Michael Gough, *The Origins of Christian Art*, London, 1973 or Ernst Kitzinger, *Byzantine Art in the Making*, London 1977. Both outline the role played by pagan prototypes in the formulation of Christian art.
912 Burford, 96.

913 See for example, Robert Schilling, "Romulus l'élu et Rémus le réproveé", *Rites, cultes, dieux de Rome*, Paris, 1979, 103–20.

914 Chapouthier, 40, no. 18.

915 Chapouthier, 29–30, no. 70.

916 Chapouthier, 35–6, no. 13.

917 Chapouthier, 62, nos. 51–2.

918 Chapouthier, 75–7, no. 68.

919 Robert Schilling, "Les 'Castores' romains", *Rites, cultes, dieux de Rome*, Paris, 1979, 344-7.

920 A notion explored, for example, by W. Deonna "Trois, Superlatif Absolu", *Antiquité Classique*, 23, 1954, 403–28.

921 Cermanović-Kuzmanović, 45-6.

922 Gough, 42–5, figs. 42–4.

923 Schilling, "Les 'Castores' romaines", 340–1.

924 H. R. Ellis Davidson, *Gods and Myths of Northern Europe*, London, 1964, 26.

925 Catalogue of the Exhibition, *Romans and Barbarians*, Boston Museum of Fine Arts, no. 49.

926 W. Hinz, *Altiranische Fund und Forschungen*, Berlin, 1969, pls. 60–8.

Bibliography

Adriani, Achille, *Repertorio d'arte dell'Egitto greco-romano*, Palermo, 1961.

Aitken, G. M. and Aitken, G. N., "Excavations at Whitcombe, 1965–1967", *Proceedings of the Dorset Natural History Society*, 1990, 57–94.

Alexandrescu, Petre, "Le group de trésors thraces du horde des Balkans," I, *Dacia*, n. s., XXVII, 1983, 44–66.

Allen, Derek, *The Coins of the Celts*, ed. Daphne Nash, Edinburgh, 1980.

————, *An Introduction to Celtic Coins*, London, 1978.

Anderson, J. K., *Ancient Greek Horsemanship*, Berkeley, 1961.

Andreae, Bernard, *Laokoön und die Gründung Roms*, Mainz, 1988.

Anon., *Archaeological Journal*, XX, 1863.

Anon., *Journal of Roman Studies*, XLIII, 1953.

Anon., *Journal of Roman Studies*, XLVIII, 1958.

Anthony, David W. and Brown, Dorcas R., "Origins of Horseback Riding", *Antiquity*, 65, 1991, 22–38.

"Ares" in *Lexicon Iconographicum Mythologicae Classicae*.

Bandinelli, Ranuccio Bianchi, *Rome: The Centre of Power*, trans. P. Green, London, 1970.

————, *Rome: The Late Empire*, trans. P. Green, London, 1971.

Barnett, R. D., *Assyrian Palace Reliefs*, London, n.d.

Bauchhenss, Gerhard, *Jupitergigantensäulen*, Stuttgart, 1976.

———— and Noelke, Peter, *Die Jupitersäulen in der germanischen Provinzen*, Cologne and Bonn, 1981.

Benoit, Fernand, *L'art primitif méditerranéen de la vallée du Rhône: la sculpture*, Paris 1945.

————, *Mars et Mercure*, Aix-en-Provence, 1959.

————, *Les mythes de l'outre-tombe: le cavalier à l'anguipède et l'écuyère Epona*, Brussels, 1950.

Berciu, Dumitru, *Daco-Romania*, Geneva, 1978.

Bieber Margarete, *The Sculpture of the Hellenistic Age*, New York, 1961.

Bienkowski, P. R., *Die Darstellungen der Gallier in der hellenistischen Kunst*, Vienna, 1908.

Birley, Anthony, *The People of Roman Britain*, London, 1979.

Boardman, John, *Athenian Black Figure Vases*, London, 1974.

————, *Greek Art*, London, 1973.

————, *Greek Sculpture: the Archaic Period*, London, 1978.

————, *Greek Sculpture: the Classical Period*, London, 1985.

Bodson, Liliane, *'IERA ZΩIA*, Brussels, 1975.

Boon, G. C., "Some Romano-British Domestic Shrines and their Inhabitants", *Rome and her Northern Provinces*, Gloucester, 1983, 33–55.

Bordenache, Gabriella, "Histria alla luce del suo materiale scultoreo", *Dacia*, V, 1961, 185–212.

Boston Museum of Fine Arts, *Romans and Barbarians*, Catalogue of the Exhibition.

Boucher, Stephanie, "Figurations de bronze Grèce et Gaule", *Revue archéologique*, 1975, 251–66.

————, *Recherches sur les bronzes figurés de Gaule pré-romaine et romaine*, Rome, 1976.

Boyancé, Pierre, *Études sur la religion romaine*, Rome, 1972.

Brandt, Elfriede, *Antike Gemmen in Deutschen Sammlungen*, I, Munich, 1970.

Brilliant, Richard, *Gesture and Rank in Roman Art*, Memoirs of the Connecticut Academy of Arts and Sciences, 14, 1963.

Broneer, Oscar, "Hero Cults in the Corinthian Agora", *Hesperia*, XI, 1942, 128–61.

Buchthal, Hugo, "The Common Classical Sources of Buddhist and Christian Narrative Arts", *Journal of the Royal Asiatic Society*, 1943, 137–48.

Burford, Alison, *Craftsmen in Greek and Roman Society*, London, 1972.

Burkert, Walter, *Greek Religion*, Oxford, 1985.

Butcher, S. A., "Enamels from Roman Britain", *Ancient Monuments and their Interpretation*, London, 1977.

Campbell, Leroy, *Mithraic Iconography and Ideology*, Leiden, 1968.

Casson, Stanley, *Macedonia, Thrace and Illyria*, Oxford, 1926.

Cermanović-Kuzmanović, Aleksandrina, *Corpus Cultus Equites Thracii, V: Monumenta intra Fines Iugoslaviae Reperta*, Leiden, 1982.

————, "Die Denkmäler des thrakischen Heros in Jugoslavien und das Problem des thrakischen Reitergottes", *Archaeologica Jugoslavica*, IV, 1963, 31–58.

Chapouthier, Fernand, *Les Dioscures au service d'une déesse*, Paris, 1935.

Charbonneaux, J., Martin, R., and Villard, F., *Hellenistic Art 330–50 BC*, London, 1973.

Charlton, D. B., and Mitcheson, M. M., "Yardhope, a Shrine to Cocidius?", *Britannia*, XIV, 1983, 143–53.

Clavel-Leveque, Monique, *Marseille grecque*, Marseille, 1977.

Clark, John R., *Roman Black-and-White Figural Mosaics*, New York, 1979.

Coja, Maria, "Terres cuites d'époque hellenistique representant le cavalier trace trouvées à Histria", *Dacia*, n.s., XVIII, 1974, 283–8.

Cole, Susan Guettel, *Theoi Megaloi: the Cult of the Great Gods at Samothrace*, Leiden, 1984.

Conticello, Baldassare, "Sul gruppo di Scilla e della nave nel Museo de Sperlonga", *Alessandria e il mondo ellenistico-romano*, Bonacasa and diVita, eds., 1984, 611–24.

Cook, A. B., *Zeus*, II, Cambridge, 1925.

Cook, R. M., *Greek Painted Pottery*, London, 1960.

Croon, Johan H., "Die Ideologie des Marskultes unter dem Principat und ihre Vorgeschichte", *Aufstieg und Niedergang des römischen Welt*, II, 17.1, 1981, 246–75.

Cumont, Franz, *Recherches sur le symbolisme funéraire des Romains*, Paris, 1942.

Cunliffe, Barry, *Fishbourne: A Roman Palace and its Garden*, London, 1971.

————, *Greeks, Romans and Barbarians: Spheres of Interaction*, London, 1988.

————, *Roman Bath*, Oxford, 1969.

Daicoviciu, Hadrian, *Dacia de la Burebista la cucerirea romană*, Bucharest, 1972.

Dascalakis, Apostolos, "La déification d'Alexandre le Grand en Égypte", *Studii Clasice*, IX, 1967, 93–105.

Davidson, H. R. Ellis, *Gods and Myths of Northern Europe*, London, 1964.

Dawkins, R. M., *The Sanctuary of Artemis Orthia at Sparta*, London, 1929.

Deonna, W., "Trois, superlatif absolu", *Antiquité Classique*, 23, 1954, 403–28.

Duthoy, Robert, *The Taurobolium: its Evolution and Terminology*, Leiden, 1969.

Duval, Paul-Marie, *Les Celtes*, Paris, 1977.

―――――, *Les dieux de la Gaule*, Paris, 1976.

―――――, *Resumé du Paris antique*, Paris, 1972.

Eckhart, Lothar, "Mars Lauriacensis", *Jahreshefte des Österreichischen Archäologischen Institutes in Wien*, XLVIII, 1966–7, 16–39.

Espérandieu, Émile, *Recueil général des bas-reliefs de la Gaule romain*, Paris, 1907 and later.

―――――― and Rolland, H., *Bronzes antiques de la Seine-Maritime*, Paris, 1959.

Faider-Feytmans, Germaine, *Les bronzes romains de Belgique*, Mainz, 1972.

―――――――, *Recueil des bronzes de Bavai*, Paris, 1957.

Farrer, R. A. H., "Rider Relief from Whitcombe", *Proceedings of the Dorset Natural History Society*, 86, 1964, 103–4.

Fauduet, Isabelle and Pommeret, Colette, "Les fibules du sanctuaire des Bolards à Nuit-St.Georges (C. d'Or)", *Revue archéologique de l'Est et du Centre-Est*, 36, 1985, 61–116.

Faure, Paul, "Les Dioscures à Delphes", *Antiquité Classique*, LIV, 1985, 56–65.

Fleischer, Robert, *Artemis von Ephesos und Verwandete Kultstatuen aus Anatolien und Syrien*, Leiden, 1973.

―――――――, *Die römischen Bronzen aus Österreich*, Mainz, 1967.

Fol, A., Nikolov, B and Hoddinott, R. F., *The New Thracian Treasure from Rogozen, Bulgaria*, London, 1986.

Fontenrose, Joseph, *Python: a Study of Delphic Myth and its Origins*, Berkeley, 1980.

Frankfort, Henri, *The Art and Architecture of the Ancient Orient*, Baltimore, 1954.

Gerster, Ernest, *Mittelrhenische Bildhaurwerkstätten im 1. Jahrhundert n. Chr.*, Bonn, 1938.

Giacchero, Marta, "Santuari indigeni dell'impero romano: i cavalieri danubiani e il cavaliere trace", *Contributi dell'instituto di storia antica dell'Università del Sacro Cuore*, IX, 1973, 168–95.

Gilles, Karl-Joseph, "Die römische Münzstätte Trier von 293/4 bis zur Mitte des 5. Jahrhunderts", *Trier: Kaiserresidenz und Bischofssitz*, Mainz, 1984, 49–59.

Glaser, Franz, *Die römische Stadt Teurnia*, Klagenfort, 1983.

Gončeva, Zlatozora, "Le culte d'Apollon en Thrace", *Pulpudeva*, I, Plovdiv, 1974, 221–4.

―――――――― and Oppermann, Manfred, *Corpus Cultus Equites Thracii, I: Monumenta Orae Ponti Euxini Bulgariae*, Leiden, 1979.

―――――――――, *Corpus Cultus Equites Thracii, II: Monumenta inter Danuvim et Haemum Reperta*, pt. 1, Leiden, 1981.

―――――――――, *Corpus Cultus Equites Thracii, II: Monumenta inter Danuvim et Haemum Reperta*, pt. 2, Leiden, 1984.

Gose, Erich, *Der gallo-römische Tempelbezirk im Altbachtal zu Trier*, Mainz, 1972.

Gough, Michael, *The Origins of Christian Art*, London, 1973.

Grabar, Andre, *Christian Iconography and a Study of its Origins*, London, 1969.

Green, Miranda, A Corpus of Religious Material from the Civilian Areas of Roman Britain, *BAR* no. 21, 1976.

―――――――, *The Wheel as a Cult Symbol in the Romano-Celtic World*, Brussels, 1984.

Greenfield, E., "The Roman-British Shrines at Brigstock, Northants.", *Antiquaries Journal*, XLIII, 1963.

Gschwantler, Kurt, "Donaureiter Reliefs in Österreich", *Römisches Österreichen Jahreschrift des Österreichischen Gesellschaft für Archäologie*, XI–XII, 1983–4, 107–43.

Gualandi, Giorgio, "Marte" in *Enciclopedia dell'Arte Antica*, Rome, 1961, 884 ff.

Gudea, N., "Un relief al cavalerului trac la Pojejena", *Studii și Cercetari de Istorie Veche și Arheologie*, XXII, 1971, 345–9.

Gury, Françoise, "Dioscuri", *Lexicon Iconographicum Mythologicae Classicae*, III.

Gutherie, W. C. K., *The Greeks and their Gods*, Cambridge, 1950.

Hampartumian, Nubar, *Corpus Cultus Equites Thracii IV: Moesia Inferior (Romanian Section) and Dacia*, Leiden, 1979.

Hannestad, Niels, *Roman Art and Imperial Policy*, Aarhus, 1986.

Harris Eva and Harris, John, *The Oriental Cults of Roman Britain*, Leiden, 1965.

Hatt, J.-J., "Les cadres historiques de l'évolution de l'art celtique" in *L'art celtique de la période d'expansion IVe et IIIe siècles avant notre ère*, eds., P.-M. Duval and V. Kurta, Geneva, 1982, 25–34.

―――――, *Celts and Gallo-Romans*, London, 1970.

―――――, "Les monuments gallo-romaines de Paris et les origines de la sculpture votive en Gaule romaine", *Revue archéologique*, 6 ser., XXIX, 1952, 68–83.

―――――, *La tombe gallo-romaine*, Paris, 1951.

Hattatt, Richard, *Ancient and Romano-British Brooches*, Dorset, 1982.

Henig, Martin, *A Corpus of Roman Engraved Gemstones from British Sites*, Oxford, 1974.

―――――――, *Religion in Roman Britain*, London, 1984.

――――――― and Ambrose, Timothy, "A New Roman Rider-Relief from Stragglethorpe, Lincolnshire", *Britannia*, XI, 1980, 135–8.

―――――――, Webster, Graham and Wilkins, Robert, "A Bronze Dioscurus from Wroxeter and its Fellow from Canterbury", *Antiquaries Journal*, LXVII, 1987, 360–2.

Hermary, Antoine, "Dioscuri" in *Lexicon Iconographicum Mythologicae Classicae*, III.

Herrmann, Ariel in *The Search for Alexander: an Exhibition*, New York, 1980.

Hildyard, E. J. W., "Another Roman Bronze Statuette", *Antiquaries Journal*, 38, 1958, 245–6.

Hinz, W., *Altiranische Funde und Forschungen*, Berlin, 1969.

Hoddinott, R. F., *The Thracians*, London, 1981.

Holloway, R. Ross, *The Archaeology of Early Rome and Latium*, London, 1994.

Jacobsthal, Paul, *Early Celtic Art*, Oxford, 1944.

Jenkins, Frank, "The Finds, Nor'nour", *Archaeological Journal*, CXXIV, 1967, 19–21.

Joffroy, René, *Vix et ses Trésors*, Paris, 1979.

Johns, Catherine, "A Roman Bronze Statuette of Epona", *British Museum Quarterly*, XXXVI, 1971–2, 37–41.

Kazarow, Gawril, *Die Denkmäler des thrakischen Reitergottes in Bulgarien*, Budapest, 1938.

Kenner, Hedwig, *Die Götterwelt der Austria Romana*, Sonderdruck des Jahreshefte des Österreichischen Archäologischen Institutes, XLIII, 1956–8.

Kirk, G. S., *Homer and the Epic*, Cambridge, 1965.

_____, *The Nature of the Greek Myths*, Harmondsworth, 1974.

Kitzinger, Ernst, *Byzantine Art in the Making*, London, 1977.

Klindt-Jenson, Ole, "Foreign Influences in Denmark's Early Iron Age", *Acta Archaeologica*, XX, 1950, 119–57.

Kraiker, Wilhelm, *Die Malerei der Griechen*, Stuttgart, 1958.

Krüger, Emil, "Die gallischen und die germanischen Dioskuren," I, *Trierer Zeitschrift*, XV, 1940, 8–27.

_____, "Die gallischen und die germanischen Dioskuren," II, *Trierer Zeitschrift*, XV, 1941–2.

Kruta, Venceslas, "Aspects unitaires et faciès dans l'art celtique du IVe siècle avant notre ère: l'hypothèse d'un foyer celto-italique" in *L'art celtique de la période d'expansion IVe et IIIe siècles avant notre ère*, eds., P.-M. Duval and V. Kurta, Geneva, 1982, 35–49.

Kurtz, Donna and Boardman, John, *Greek Burial Customs*, London, 1971.

Lambrechts, Pierre, "La colonne du dieu-cavalier au géant et le culte des sources en Gaule", *Latomus*, VIII, 1949, 145–58.

_____, *Contributions à l'étude des divinités celtiques*, Bruges, 1942.

_____, "Divinités équestres celtiques ou défunts héroïsés", *Antiquité Classique*, XX, 1951, 107–28.

Lattimore, Steven, *The Marine Thiasos in Greek Sculpture*, Los Angeles, 1986.

Lawson, Annabel, "A Fragment of a Life-Size Bronze Equine Statuary from Ashill, Norfolk", *Britannia*, XVII, 1986, 333–8.

Leech, Roger, "The Excavation of a Romano-Celtic Temple on Lamyatt Beacon", *Britannia*, XVII, 1986, 259–328.

Le Gall, Joel, *Alésia*, Guides archéologiques de France, 1985.

Leibundgut, Annalis, *Die römischen Bronzen der Schweiz*, II, Mainz, 1977.

Lewis, M. J. T., *Temples in Roman Britain*, Cambridge, 1966.

Linduff, K. M., "Epona: a Celt among the Romans", *Latomus*, XXXVIII, 1979, 817–37.

Ljubenova, Venecia, "Ein thrakisches Heiligtum aus der römischen Epoche beim Dorf Daskalovo, Bezirk Pernik", *Thracia*, III, Sofia, 1974, 369–78.

Maaskant-Kleibrink, Marianna, *Catalogue of the Engraved Gems in the Royal Coin Cabinet, The Hague*, The Hague, 1978.

MacKendrick, Paul, *Roman France*, London, 1971.

Mackintosh, Marjorie, "Roman Influences on the Victory Reliefs of Shapur I of Persia", *California Studies in Classical Antiquity*, VI, 1973, 181-203.

_____, "The Sources of the Horseman and Fallen Enemy Motif on the Tombstones of the Western Roman Empire" *Journal of the British Archaeological Association*, CXXXIX, 1986, 1–21.

Magnen, René and Thevenot, Émile, *Epona, déesse gauloise des chevaux*, Bordeaux, 1953.

Maier, Ferdinand, "Quelques éléments stylistiques des bronzes animaliers des Celtes" in *L'art celtique de la période d'expansion IVe et IIIe siècles avant notre ére*, eds., P.-M. Duval and V. Kurta, Geneva 1982, 85–99.

Mallory, J. P., *In Search of the Indo-Europeans*, London, 1989.

Marién, M. E., "Tribes and Archaeological Groupings of the La Tène Period in Belgium: Some Observations" in *Studies in Honour of C. F. C. Hawkes*, eds. J. Boardman, M. A. Brown and T. G. E Powell, London, 1971.

Mattingly, Harold, *Coins of the Roman Empire in the British Museum*, I, London, 1923.

Mazarov, Ivan, "Sacrifice of a Ram on the Thracian Helmet from Coţofeneşti", *Pulpudeva*, III, 1978, 81–101.

Meates, G. W., *The Roman Villa at Lullingstone, Kent*, I, Kent Archaeological Society, 1979.

Megaw, J. V. S., *The Art of the European Iron Age*, Bath, 1970.

Menghin, Wilfried, *Kelten, Romer und Germanen: Archäologie und Geschichte*, Munich, 1980.

Merlat, Pierre, *Jupiter Dolichenus*, Paris, 1960.

_____, *Repertoire des inscriptions et monuments figurés du culte de Jupiter Dolichenus*, Paris, 1951.

Merrifield, Ralph, *The Archaeology of Ritual and Magic*, London, 1987.

Merten, Hiltrud, "Der Kult des Mars in Trevererraum", *Trierer Zeitschrift*, 48, 1985, 7–113.

Metropolitan Museum of Art, *Greek Art of the Aegean Islands*, New York, 1979.

Mócsy, András, *Pannonia and Upper Moesia*, London, 1974.

Moreau, Jacques, *Das Trierer Kornmarktmosaik*, Cologne, 1960.

Morris, John, *Londinium*, London, 1982.

Naumann, Friederike, *Die Ikonographie der Kybele in der phrygischen und der griechischen Kunst*, Tubingen, 1983.

Nicolini, Gerard, *Gallia*, XXXIII, 1975, 381–2.

Nilsson, Martin, *The Mycenaean Origin of Greek Mythology*, New York, 1963.

Ochsenschlager, Edward, "Lead Plaques of the Danubian Horseman Type at Sirmium" in Edward Ochsenschlager and Vladislav Popović, *Sirmium* II, Belgrade, 1971.

Ogilvie, R. M., *Early Rome and the Etruscans*, London, 1976.

_____, *The Romans and their Gods*, London, 1969.

Olmstead, Garrett S., *The Gundestrup Cauldron*, Brussels, 1979.

Oppermann, Manfred, "Thrakische und danubische Reitergötter", *Die orientalischen Religionen in Romerreich*, Leiden, 1981, 510–36.

_____, "Zu einigen Weihdenkmälern mit der Darstellung des thrakischen Reitergottes aus der

SR Rumänien und der VR Bulgarien", *Klio*, LV, 1973, 199–214.

——————, "Zum Kult des thrakischen Reiters in Bulgarien", *Thracia* III, Sofia, 1974, 353–62.

Paliadeli, Chrysa et al., *The Search for Alexander*, Boston, 1980.

Papinot, J.-Cl., *Gallia*, XLIII, 1985, 507–8.

Peyre, Christian, "Y a-t-il un context italique au style de Waldalgesheim?" in *L'art celtique de la période d'expansion IVe et IIIe siècles avant notre ère*, eds., P.-M. Duval and V. Kurta, Geneva, 1982, 51–82.

Picard, Gilbert, "Imperator Caelestium", *Gallia*, XXXV, 1977, 89–113.

Piggott, Stuart, *Ancient Europe*, Edinburgh, 1967.

——————, *The Druids*, Harmondsworth, 1968.

Pippidi, D. M., "Note de Lectură: Peşti şi pescari la Istros şi la Odessos", *Studii Clasice*, VII, 1965, 324–29.

—————— and Popescu, E., "Les relations d'Istros et d'Apollonie du Pont à l'époque hellenistique", *Dacia*, III, 1959, 235–58.

Pliny, *Natural History*, Loeb Classical Library, IX, trans., H. Rackham, 1952.

Powell, T. G. E., "From Urartu to Gundestrup", in *Studies in Honour of C. F. C. Hawkes*, eds. J. Boardman, M. A. Brown and T. G. E Powell, London, 1971.

Price, Martin, *Coins of the Macedonians*, London, 1974.

Reich, John, *Italy before Rome*, Oxford, 1979.

Reinach, Salomon, "Epona", *Revue Archéologique*, XXVI, 3, ser., 1895, 163–95, 309–35.

——————, *Répertoire des reliefs grecs et romaines*, Paris, 1909.

Richmond, Ian, "Roman Legionaries at Corbridge, their Supply-Base, Temples and Religious Cults", *Archaeologia Aeliana*, 4 ser, XXI, 1943, 127–224.

—————— and Wright, R. P., *The Roman Inscribed and Sculptured Stone in the Grosvenor Museum, Chester*, Chester, 1955.

Richter, G. M. A., *Attic Red-Figured Vases*, London, 1958.

Robert, Louis, *Antiquité Classique*, 1973.

Roes, Ann, "Animal au signe solaire", *Revue archéologique*, 6 ser, XII, 1938, 153–82.

Rolland, H., *Bronzes antiques de Haute Provence*, Paris, 1965.

Roques de Maumont, Harald von, *Antike Reiterstandbilder*, Berlin, 1958.

Rowland, Benjamin, "Rome and Gandhara", *East and West*, IX, 1958, 199–208.

Ross, Anne, *Pagan Celtic Britain*, London, 1967.

Rouvier-Jeanlin, Micheline, *Les figurines gallo-romaines en terre cuite au Musée des Antiquités Nationales*, Paris, 1972.

Rose, H. J., *Ancient Roman Religion*, London, 1948.

Saalburgmuseum, *Saalburg Roman Fort*, Saalburg-Kastell, 1984.

Salway, Peter, *Roman Britain*, Oxford, 1981.

Sanders, N. K., *Prehistoric Art in Europe*, Harmondsworth, 1968.

Schachermeyr, Fritz, *Poseidon und die Entstehung des griechischen Götterglaubens*, Bern, 1950.

Scheers, Simone, *Les monnaies gauloises de la collection A. Danicourt à Peronne (Somme)*, Brussels, 1975.

Schilling, Robert, "Les 'Castores' romaines" in *Rites, cultes, dieux de Rome*, Paris 1979, 338–353.

——————, "Romulus l'élu et Rémus le réprové" in *Rites, cultes, dieux de Rome*, Paris, 1979, 103–20.

Schleiermacher, Mathilde, *Römische Reitergrabsteine*, Bonn, 1984.

Schleiermacher, Wilhelm, "Studien an Göttertypen der römischen Rheinprovinzen", *23 Bericht der Römisch-Germanischen Kommission*, 1934, 109–43.

Schutz, Herbert, *The Prehistory of Germanic Europe*, New Haven, 1983.

——————, *The Romans in Central Europe*, New Haven, 1985.

Schweitzer, Bernhard, *Greek Geometric Art*, London, 1971.

——————, "Späthellenistische Reitergruppen", *Jahrbuch des Deutschen Archäologischen Instituts*, LI, 1936,159–74.

Schwertheim, Elmar, Die Denkmäler orientalischer Gottheiten im römischen Deutschland, Leiden, 1974.

Schwinden, Lothar, "Der Tempelbizirk am Irminenwingert", *Trier: Augustusstadt der Treverer*, Mainz, 1984, 243–4.

Scorpan, Constantin, *Cavalerul trac*, Constanţa, 1967.

Selem, Petar, *Les religions orientales dans la Pannonie romaine*, Leiden, 1980.

Seure, Georges, "ΝΕΟΣ ῾ΗΡΩΣ, ΚΟΥΡΟΣ ῾ΗΡΩΣ", *Études grecques*, XLII, 1929, 241–54.

Siedentopf, Heinrich, *Das hellenistische Reiterdenkmal*, Waldsassen/Bavaria, 1968.

Smith, David, "Mosaics" in *A Handbook of Roman Art*, M. Henig, ed., London, 1983.

Speidel, Michael, *The Religion of Iuppiter Dolichenus in the Roman Army*, Leiden, 1978.

Stern, H. and Blanchard-Lemée, M., *Recueil général des mosaiques de la Gaule*, II, 2, Paris, 1975.

Stewart, Andrew, *Skopas of Paros*, Park Ridge (New Jersey), 1977.

Strong, D. E., *Greek and Roman Gold and Silver Plate*, London, 1966.

Tacheva-Hitova, Margarita, *Eastern Cults in Moesia Inferior and Thracia*, Leiden, 1983.

——————, "Wesenzüge des Sabazioskultes in Moesia Inferior und Thracia", *Hommage à Maarten J. Vermaseren*, III, Leiden, 1978.

Tarn, W. W., *The Greeks in Bactria and India*, Cambridge, 1951.

Taylor, H. M and Taylor, J., *Anglo-Saxon Architecture*, II, Cambridge, 1965.

Taylor, M. V., "A Roman Bronze Statuette from Northamptonshire", *Antiquaries Journal*, XXXVII, 1957, 71–2.

——————, "Statuettes of Horsemen and Horses and Other Votive Objects from Brigstock, Northants", *Antiquaries Journal*, XLIII, 1963, 264–8.

Thevenot, Émile, *Divinités et sanctuaires de la Gaule*, Paris, 1968.

——————, "L'interprétation 'gauloise' des divinités romaines: 'Mars' gardien des calendriers celtiques", *Hommages à Albert Grenier*, Brussels, 1962, 1476–90.

——————, "Les monuments de Jupiter à l'anguipède dans la cité des Eduens", *Mémoires de la Commission des Antiquités du Départment de la Côte d'Or*, XXI, 1936–9, 427–98.

_____, "Les monuments et le culte d'Epona chez les Eduens", *Antiquité Classique*, XVIII, 1949, 385–400.

_____, *Sur les traces des Mars celtiques*, Bruges, 1955.

Todd, Malcolm, "Margidunum Rider" *Britannia*, II, 1971, 232.

Toynbee, J. M. C., *Art in Britain Under the Romans*, Oxford, 1964.

_____, *Art in Roman Britain*, London, 1962.

_____, *Some Notes on Artists in the Roman World*, Latomus Collection, VI, Brussels, 1951.

_____, *The Roman Art Treasures from the Temple of Mithras*, London, 1986.

Tran Tam Tinh, *Isis Lactans*, Leiden, 1973.

Tudor, Dumitru, *Corpus Monumentorum Religionis Equitum Danuuinorum*, Leiden, 1976.

Vasilescu, Mihail, "Les Thraces dans les épopées homeriques", *Actes du IIe Congrès International de Thracologie*, I, Bucharest, 1980, 151–64.

Venedikov, Ivan, *Thracian Treasures from Bulgaria*, London, 1976

Vermaseren, Maarten J., *Corpus Cultus Cybelae Attidisque*, III, Leiden, 1977.

_____, *Cybele and Attis*, London, 1977.

Vermeule, Emily, *Greece in the Bronze Age*, Chicago, 1964.

Vian, Francis, *Répertoire des gigantomachies figurées dans l'art grec et romain*, Paris, 1951.

Vlad, Licia Borrelli, Fogolari, Giulia and Toniato, Anna Guidi, "The stylistic problem of the Horses of San Marco", *The Horses of San Marco*, trans J. and V. Webster-Ely, Milan, 1979, 15–44.

Vries, Jan de, *La religion des Celts*, Paris, 1977.

Vulpe, Radu, "Ex-voto au cavalier trace provenant de Callatis", *Dacia* n.s., VIII, 1964, 335–43.

Wacher, John, *The Coming of Rome*, London, 1979.

Ward, Donald, "The Separate Functions of the Indo-European Divine Twins", in *Myth and Law Among the Indo-Europeans*, 1970, 193–202.

Weber, Wilhelm, *Die ägyptische-griechischen Terrakotten*, Berlin, 1914.

Webster, Graham, *The British Celts and their Gods under Rome, London*, 1986.

_____, *The Roman Imperial Army of the First and Second Centuries AD*, London, 1969.

Webster, T. B. L., *Hellenistic Art*, London, 1967.

Weiller, Raymond, "Die Treverer-Munzpragung am Beispiel des Titelberges", *Trier: Augustusstadt der Treverer*, Mainz, 1984.

Weitzmann, Kurt, *Illustration in Roll and Codex*, Princeton, 1947.

Wheeler, Hazel, "Two Roman Bronzes from Brigstock, Northants", *Antiquaries Journal*, LXI, 1981, 309–11.

Wightman, Edith, *Gallia Belgica*, London, 1985.

_____, *Roman Trier and the Treveri*, London, 1970.

Will, Ernest, *Le relief cultuel gréco-romain*, Paris, 1955.

Wilson, D. R., "Temples in Great Britain", *Caesarodunum*, 8, 1973, 24–44.

Woysch-Meautis, Daphné, *La répresentation des animaux et des êtres fabuleux sur les monuments funéraires grecs de l'époque archaïques à la fin du IV siècle av. J. C.*, Lausanne, 1982.

Yalouris, Nikolaos, "Athena als Herrin der Pferde", Museum Helveticum, 1950, 19–101.

Youroukova, Yordanka, *Coins of the Ancient Thracians*, BAR Supplementary Series, 4, 1976.

Zadoks-Josephus Jitta, A. N., Peter, W. J. T. and van Es, W. A., *Roman Bronze Statuettes from the Netherlands*, Groningen, 1967.

Zahn, Eva, *Europa und der Stier*, Wurzburg, 1983.

Zotović, Ljubica, Les cultes orientaux sur le territoire de la Mésie Supérieure, Leiden, 1966.

_____, "Les éléments orientaux dans le culte des cavaliers danubiens et quelques nouveaux aspects de ce culte", *Hommages à Maarten J. Vermaseren*, III, Leiden, 1978, 1351–78.

Zwierlein-Diehl, Erika, *Die Antiken Gemmen des Kunsthistorischen Museums in Wien*, I, Munich, 1973.

Figures

Figure 1. Ares Borghese, after Boardman, *Greek Sculpture: The Classical Period,* fig. 223, h. 212 cm., Louvre.

Figure 2. Axehead with horseman from Hallstatt, after Schutz, *The Prehistory of Germanic Europe,* fig. 172.

Figure 3. Detail of horseman from bronze cult wagon from Strettweg (Austria), after Sanders, *Prehistoric Art in Europe,* fig. 321, Graz, Landesmuseum Johanneum.

Figure 4. Detail of horseman from the Gundestrup Cauldron, after Schutz, *The Prehistory of Germanic Europe,* fig. 228.

Figure 5. The Todi Mars, after Reich, *Italy Before Rome,* 93, h. 123 cm., Vatican Museum.

Figure 6. Terracotta horseman from Altbachtal, after Gose, *Der gallo-römische Tempelbezirk der Altbachtal zu Trier,* fig. 38.13, h. 17.5 cm.

Figure 7. Dioscuri or Martes from La Horgne-au-Sablon, after Espérandieu, *Recueil général des bas-reliefs de la Gaule romain,* no. 4359, h. 61 cm., Metz Museum.

Figure 8. Bronze rider from Brigstock, Northants, after Taylor, *Antiquaries Journal,* XLIII, pl. XXXIXb, h. 9 cm.

Figure 9. Bronze rider from Westwood Bridge near Peterborough, after Taylor, *Ibid.,* h. 8 cm.

Figure 10. Bronze rider from Canterbury, after Green, *A Corpus of Religious Material from the Civilian Areas of Roman Britain,* pl. IIIc, h. 14.5cm.

Figure 11. Bronze rider from Tigring, after von Roques de Maumont, *Antike Reiterstandbilder,* fig. 10, Klagenfort, Landesmuseum für Kärnten.

Figure 12 Bronze rider from Rouen, after Espérandieu and Rolland, *Bronzes antiques de la Seine-Maritime,* no. 107, pl. XXXV, h. 10.5 cm. incl. base.

Figure 13. Bronze statue of Marcus Aurelius, after von Roques de Maumont, fig. 29, Rome.

Figure 14. Stone Altar from Bisley, Glos., after *Archaeological Journal,* XX, 186.

Figure 15. Bronze horse from Frocester Court, Glos., after photograph lent by Mr. E. Price of Frocester Court.

Figure 16. Gold coin from SE England, after Megaw, *The Art of the European Iron Age,* no. 306c, dia. 1.65 cm.

Figure 17. Coin from Gaul, after Duval, *Les Celtes,* no. 390.

Figure 18. Coin from Gaul, after Duval, *Ibid.,* no. 389.

Figure 19. Rider relief from Nottingham, after Green, pl. IIIa, Nottingham University Museum.

Figure 20. Mars from Yardhope, after Charlton and Mitcheson, *Britannia,* XIV, pl. 14A.

Figure 21. Rider brooches, after Hattatt, *Ancient and Romano-British Brooches,* nos. 159–60.

Figure 22. Details of Gaulish coins, after Allen, *An Introduction to Celtic Coins,* nos. 55–6.

Figure 23. Rider relief from Whitcombe, Dorset, after Farrer, *Proceedings of the Dorset Natural History and Archaeological Society,* 86, 103, h. 58 cm.

Figure 24 Arras Medallion, after *Trier: Kaiserresidenz und Bischofssitz,* pl. 26b.

Figure 25. Detail of gold medallion of Justinian, after von Roques de Maumont, fig. 36b.

Figure 26. Rider relief from Stragglethorpe, Lincs., after Henig and Ambrose, *Britannia,* XI, pl. VI.

Figure 27. Reconstructed Jupiter and giant column from Ehrang, after Espérandieu no. 5233.

Figure 28. Rider and giant from Altripp, after Espérandieu, no. 5999, h. 75 cm., Speyer Museum.

Figure 29. Lower section of rider and giant from Hommert, after Espérandieu, no. 4557, total h. 104 cm., Nancy Museum.

Figure 30. Detail of Jupiter from Épinal, after Espérandieu, no. 4768.

Figure 31. Engraved gem, after Maaskant-Kleibrink, *Catalogue of the Engraved Gems in the Royal Coin Cabinet, The Hague,* no. 401.

Figure 32. Terracotta horseman from Egypt, after Weber, *Die ägyptische-griechischen Terrakotten,* no. 336, h. 12.8 cm., Berlin.

Figure 33. Artemis and Iphigenia, after Bieber, *The Sculpture of the Hellenistic Age,* fig. 268, Copenhagen, Ny Carlsberg Glyptotek.

Figure 34 a, b. Menelaos and Patroclos, after Bieber, figs. 274–5.

Figure 35. Dismounting Dioscurus from Locri, after Lattimore, *The Marine Thiasos in Greek Sculpture,* fig. 3.

Figure 36. Detail: Alcyoneus from the Great altar at Pergamon, after Bieber, fig. 460.

Figure 37 a, b. Remains and reconstruction of sailor from Scylla group found at Sperlonga, after Conticello, *Alessandria e il mondo hellenistico-romano,* fig. 1, photo lxxxvi.

Figure 38. Aphrodite and Triton, after Adriani, *Repertoria d'arte dell'Egitto greco-romano,* II, no. 75, Dresden.

Figure 39. Amazon and enemy, after Bernhard Schweitzer, "Späthellenistische Reitergruppen", *JDAI,* LI, fig. 3.

Figure 40. Amazon fighting two foes, after Schweitzer, fig. 4.

Figure 41. Giant from Lichtenau, after Espérandieu, no. 480-1931 Supp., h. 40 cm., Carlsruhe Museum.

Figure 42. Giant and rider from Pforzheim, after Espérandieu, no. 383-1931 Supp., h. 66 cm., Carlsruhe Museum.

Figure 43. Detail of giant and chariot group from Weissenhof, after Espérandieu, no. 407-1931 Supp., total h. 120 cm., Stuttgart Museum.

Figure 44. Head of Alcyoneus from the Great Altar of Pergamon, after Bieber, fig. 462.

Figure 45. Head of giant from Erhang, after Espérandieu, no. 5246, total h. 96 cm., Trier Museum.

Figure 46. Giant and rider from Diedelkopf, after Espérandieu, no. 6090, h. 54 cm., Speyer Museum.

Figure 47. Relief of Epona from Fontaines-les-Chalon (Saône-et-Loire), after Magnen, *Epona,* no. 83.

Figure 48. Epona from Reims, after Magnen, no. 411. h. 14.6 cm.

Figure 49. Epona from Poitiers, after Papinot, *Gallia,* 43, fig. 26.

Figure 50. Epona from Rome, after Reinach, *Répertoire des reliefs grecs et romaines,* no. 72.

Figure 51. Engraved gem from Naples, after Brandt, *Antike Gemme in Deutschen Sammlungen,* no. 842, 1.28 x 1.67 cm.

Figure 52. Epona from Allerey (Côte-d'Or), after Magnen, no. 96, h. 53 cm.

Figure 53. Cybele riding a lion, after Vermaseren, *Cybele and Attis*, fig. 74, Cologne, Rheinisch-Germanisches Museum.

Figure 54. Engraved gem with Europa riding the bull, after Maaskant-Kleibrink, no. 551.

Figure 55. Europa and the bull from Pompeii, after Charbonneaux, Martin and Villard, *Hellenistic Art 330–50 BC*, fig. 179.

Figure 56. Nereid riding a hippocamp, after Zwerlein-Diehl, *Die Antiken Gemmen des Kunsthistorischen Museums in Wien*, no. 255, 1.44 x 1.14 cm.

Figure 57. Mosaic from Ostia with Nereid riding a sea creature, after Clarke, *Roman Black-and-White Figural Mosaics*, fig. 48.

Figure 58. Relief of Epona from La Horgne-au-Sablon, after Espérandieu, no. 4351 (Magnen, no. 187), h. 53 cm., Metz

Figure 59. Standing Epona from Poitiers, after Nicolini, *Gallia*, 33, fig. 25.

Figure 60. Epona from Néris-les-Bains, after Magnen, no. 201, h. 29 cm., Musée St-Germain.

Figure 61. Selene and Phosphorus, after Espérandieu, no. 1608, h. 62 cm., Clermont Museum.

Figure 62. Cybele seated with her lions, after Vermaseren, *CCCA*, no. 248, Rome Capitoline Museum.

Figure 63. Cybele with lions, detail from relief plaque, after Vermaseren, *CCCA*, III, no. 350, Rome.

Figure 64. Epona from Köngen, after Magnen, no. 211, h. 48 cm., Stuttgart Museum.

Figure 65. Reconstruction of horse and standing figure from Athens, after von Roques de Maumont, fig. 5.

Figure 66. Relief from Athens of horseman approaching altar, after Reinach, fig. 27.3.

Figure 67. Altar from La Graufesenque, after Krüger, *Trierer Zeitschrift*, XVI, no. 37a.

Figure 68. Relief of Dioscurus from Dielkirchen, after Krüger, no. 58.

Figure 69. Detail of Dioscuri from a sarcophagus found at Arles, after Espérandieu, no. 169, total h. 53 cm., Arles Museum.

Figure 70. Detail from a votive plaque from Heddernheim: one of the Dolichene Castores, after Speidel, *The Religion of Iuppiter Dolichenus in the Roman Army*, pl. 6.

Figure 71. Relief of Dioscurus and anguipede, after Espérandieu, no. 5758, h. 107 cm. Mainz Museum.

Figure 72 Dioscurus from Corbridge, after Toynbee, *Art in Roman Britain*, fig. 95.

Figure 73. Dioscurus, after Richmond, *Archaeologia Aeliana*, XXI, pl. 7, fig. 1.

Figure 74. Dioscuri (?) from Bonn, after Espérandieu, no. 6231, h. 85 cm., Bonn Museum.

Figure 75. Dioscuri from Sparta, after Chapouthier, *Les Dioscures au service d'une déesse*, no. 21, Sparta Museum.

Figure 76. Dioscuri from Sparta, after Chapouthier, no. 22, Sparta Museum.

Figure 77. Triple Dioscuri from Kerdylion (Macedonia), after Chapouthier, no. 12, h. 42 cm.

Figure 78. Dioscuri from *Histria*, after Pippidi and Popescu, *Dacia*, III, fig. 1.

Figure 79. Thracian Rider from Constanţa, after Hampartumian, no. 19, h. 22 cm., Constanţa, Archaeological Museum.

Figure 80. Thracian Rider with Cybele from Constanţa, after Hampartumian, *Corpus Cultus Equitis Thracii: Moesia Inferior (Romanian Section) and Dacia*, no. 37, h. 45 cm., present whereabouts unknown.

Figure 81. Thracian Rider from Arsa, after Hampartumian, no. 5, h. 31 cm., Constanţa, Archaeological Museum.

Figure 82. Thracian Rider from Celeiu-Corabia (*Sucidava*), after Hampartumian, no. 142, h. 24 cm., Corabia Museum.

Figure 83. Rider with bear from the Letnitsa Treasure, from Venedikov, *Thracian Treasures from Bulgaria*, no. 280., h. 5 cm., Lovech District Museum.

Figure 84. Single Danubian Rider from *Apulum*, after Tudor, *Corpus Monumentorum Religionis Equitum Danuuinorum*, no. 1, h. 37.5 cm., Romania, Brukenthal Museum.

Figure 85. Detail of single Danubian Rider plaque from *Potaissa*, after Tudor, no. 9, total h. 17 cm., Budapest Museum.

Figure 86. Detail of single Danubian Rider plaque (provenance unknown), after Tudor, no. 183, total h. 15.5 cm., Nitra (Czechoslovakia), Museum of the Archaeological Institute of the Slovak Academy.

Figure 87. Detail of double Danubian Rider plaque (provenance unknown), after Tudor, no. 47, total h. 18 cm., Bucarest Museum.

Figure 88. Lead double Danubian Rider plaque, after Gschwantler, *Römisches Österreichisches Jahreschrift des Österreichischen Gesellschaft für Archaölogie*, XI–XII, 130.

Figure 89. Danubian Rider gem, after Tudor, no. 188.

Plates

Plate 1. Alexander with a Lance (possibly Renaissance copy of late 4th century BC type) h. 12 cm, bronze. Courtesy of the Arthur M. Sackler Museum, Harvard University Art Museums. Gift of Mr. C. Ruxton Love, Jr.

Plate 2. Bronze rider from Willingham Fen, (Cambridge University, Musuem of Archaeology and Anthropology) Reproduced with permission.

Plate 3. Mosaic depicting Dionysus riding a panther, British Museum (Reproduced by courtesy of the Trustees of the British Museum).

Plate 4. Bronze Epona from Wiltshire, h. 7 cm., British Museum (Reproduced by courtesy of the Trustees of the British Museum).

Plate 5. Double Danubian Rider roundel found in London, dia. 11.1 cm. (Museum of London) Reproduced with permission.

Maps

Map 1. The provinces of Gallia Belgica, Germania Superior and Inferior, Raetia, Noricum and Pannonia Superior and Inferior — adapted from Schutz, *The Romans in Central Europe*, 18.

Map 2. Main sites at which representations of Epona have been found in Gaul and Germania — adapted from Magnen, *Epona*, 65 and Hatt, *Celts and Gallo-Romans*, endpaper.

Map 3. Important sites in the Danube and Black Sea region — adapted from Berciu, *Daco-Romania*, endpaper.

FIGURES

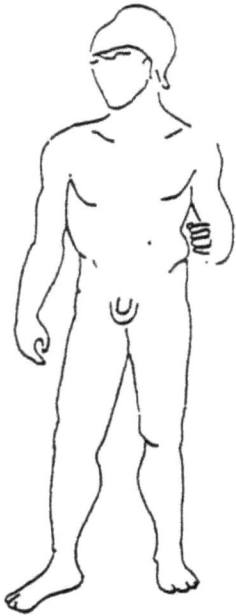

Figure 1
Ares Borghese

Figure 2
Axehead from Hallstatt

Figure 3
Detail from Stettweg Wagon

Figure 4
Detail, Gundestrup Cauldron

Figure 5
Todi Mars

Figure 6
Terracotta horseman from Altbachtal

Figure 7
Dioscuri/Mars from
La Horgne-au-Sablon

Figure 8
Bronze rider from Brigstock

Figure 9
Rider from Westwood Bridge

Figure 10
Bronze rider from Canterbury

Figure 11
Bronze rider from Tigring

Figure 12
Rider from Rouen

Figure 13
Bronze statue of Marcus Aurelius

Figure 14
Stone altar from Bisley

Figure 15
Horse from Frocester Court

Figure 16
Gold coin from SE England

Figure 17
Coin from Gaul

Figures

Figure 18
Coin from Gaul

Figure 19
Rider relief from Nottingham

Figure 20
Mars relief from Yardhope

Figure 21
Rider brooches

Figure 22
Gaulish coins, details

Figure 23
Rider from Whitcombe

95

Figure 24
Arras medallion, detail

Figure 25
Medallion of Justinian, detail

Figure 26
Rider relief from Stragglethorpe

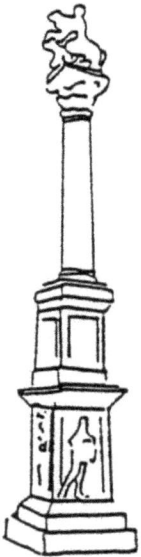

Figure 27
Reconstructed Jupiter and
Giant Column from Ehrang

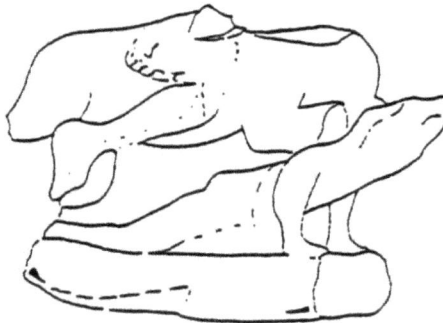

Figure 28
Rider and Giant from Altripp

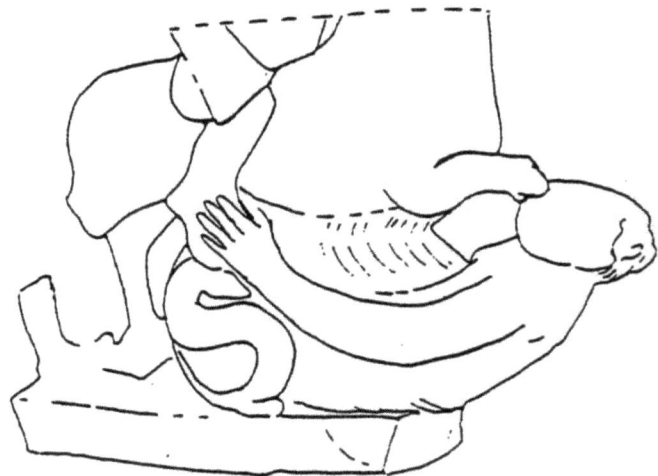

Figure 29
Rider and Giant from Hommert, detail

Figure 30
Jupiter from Épinal, detail

Figure 31
Engraved gem

Figure 32
Terracotta horseman from Egypt

Figure 33
Artemis and Iphigenia

Figure 34a

Figure 34b

Menelaos and Patroclos

97

Figure 35
Dismounting Dioscurus from Locri

Figure 36
Detail: Alcyoneus from the Great altar at Pergamon

Figure 37a   *Figure 37b*
Remains and reconstruction of sailor
from Scylla group, Sperlonga

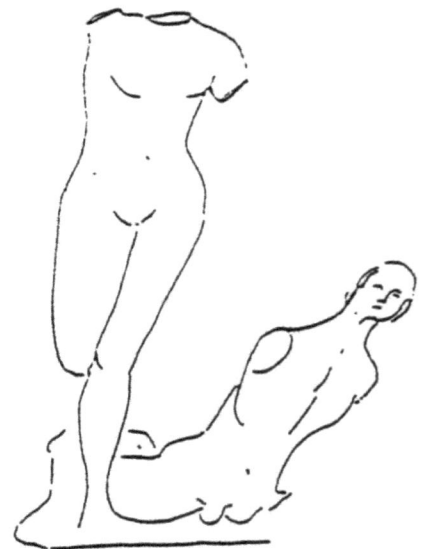

Figure 38
Aphrodite and Triton

Figure 39
Amazon and enemy

Figure 40
Amazon fighting two foes

Figure 41
Giant from Lichtenau

Figure 42
Giant and Rider from Pforzheim

Figure 43
Detail of giant and chariot
group from Weissenhof

Figure 44
Head of Alcyoneus from the
Great Altar of Pergamon

Figure 45
Head of giant from Erhang

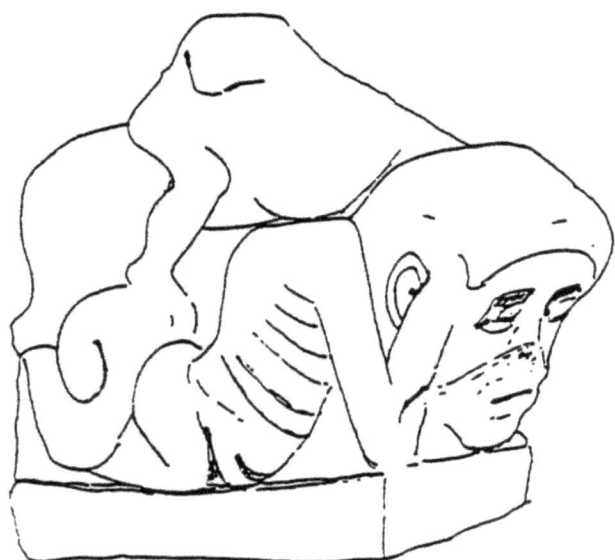

Figure 46
Giant and rider from Diedelkopf

Figure 47
Epona from Fontaines-les-Chalon

Figure 48
Epona from Reims

Figure 49
Mounted Epona from Poitiers

Figure 50
Epona from Rome

Figure 51
Engraved gem from Naples

Figure 52
Epona from Allerey

Figure 53
Cybele riding a lion

Figure 54
Gem with Europa riding the bull

Figure 55
Europa and bull from Pompeii

Figure 56
Nereid riding a hippocamp

Figure 57
Nereid riding a sea creature

Figure 58
Epona from La Horgne-au-Sablon

Figure 59
Standing Epona from Poitiers

Figure 60
Epona from Néris-les-Bains

Figure 61
Selene with Phosphorus

Figure 62
Cybele seated with her lions

Figure 63
Cybele with lions

Figure 64
Epona from Köngen

Figure 65
Reconstruction of horse and
standing figure from Athens

Figure 66
Horseman approaching altar

Figure 67
Altar from La Graufesenque

Figure 68
Dioscurus from Dielkirchen

Figure 69
Sarcophagus from Arles: detail of Dioscuri

Figure 70
Detail from votive plaque from Heddernheim

Figure 71
Dioscurus and anguipede

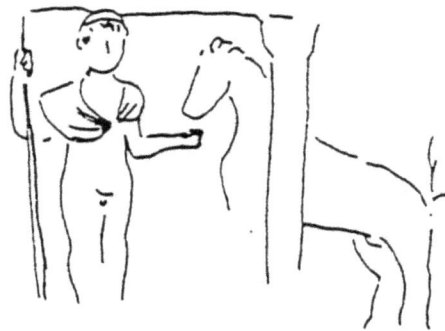

Figure 72
Dioscurus from Corbridge

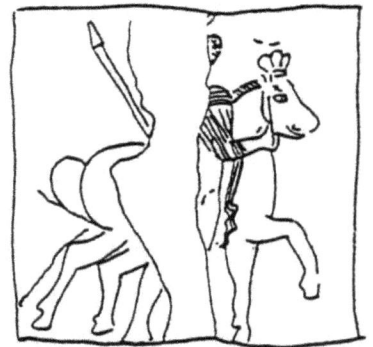

Figure 73
Dioscurus

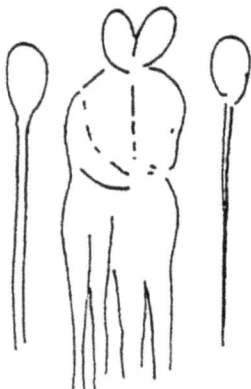

Figure 74
Dioscuri (?) from Bonn

Figure 75
Dioscuri from Sparta

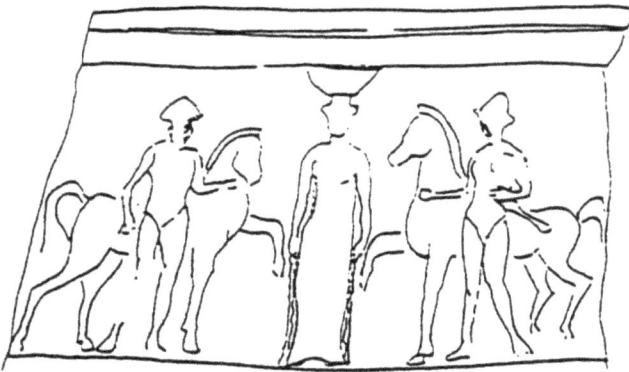
Figure 76
Dioscuri from Sparta

Figure 77
Triple Dioscuri from Kerdylion (Macedonia)

Figure 78
Dioscuri from Histria

Figure 79
Thracian Rider from Constanţa

Figure 80
Thracian Rider with Cybele from Constanţa

Figure 81
Thracian Rider from Arsa

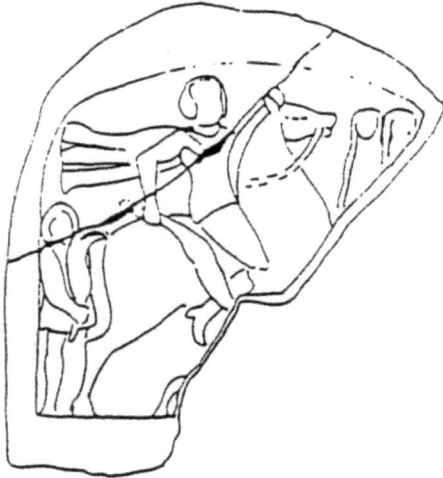

Figure 82
Thracian Rider from Celeiu-Corabia

Figure 83
Rider with bear from Letnitsa

Figure 84
Single Danubian Rider from *Apulum*

Figure 85
Danubian Rider plaque from *Potaissa*, detail

Figure 86
Detail of single Danubian Rider plaque (prov. unk.)

Figure 87
Detail of double Danubian Rider plaque (prov. unk.)

Figure 88
Lead double Danubian Rider plaque

Figure 89
Danubian Rider gem

Plate 1
Alexander with a Lance (possibly Renaissance copy of late 4th century BC type)
Photo: courtesy of the Arthur M. Sackler Museum, Harvard University Art Museums

Plate 2
Bronze rider from Willingham Fen
Cambridge University, Musuem of Archaeology and Anthropology
Photo: Cambridge University, Museum of Archaeology and Anthropology

Plate 3
Mosaic depicting Dionysus riding a panther
Reproduced courtesy of the Trustees of the British Museum

Plate 4
Bronze Epona from Wiltshire
Reproduced courtesy of the Trustees of the British Museum

111

Plate 5
Double Danubian Rider roundel found in London
Photo: Museum of London, reproduced with permission

Danube

Pannonia inferior

Sirmium

Pannonia superior

Carnuntum

Danube

Vindobona

Poetovio

Lauriacum

Sorviodurum

Noricum

Castra Regina

Danube

Augusta Vindelicum

Raetia

Altmühl

LIMES

LIMES

Lake Constance

Arae Flaviae

Vindonissa

Germania superior

Rhine

Neckar

LIMES

Main

Mogontiacum

Confluentes

Lahn

Moselle

Augusta Treverorum ('Treveri')

Maas

Belgica

Ara Agrippinensium

Colonia Claudia

Bonna

Novaesium

Vetera

Noviomagus

Germania inferior

Rhine

Lippe

Ruhr

Ems

Weser

Elbe

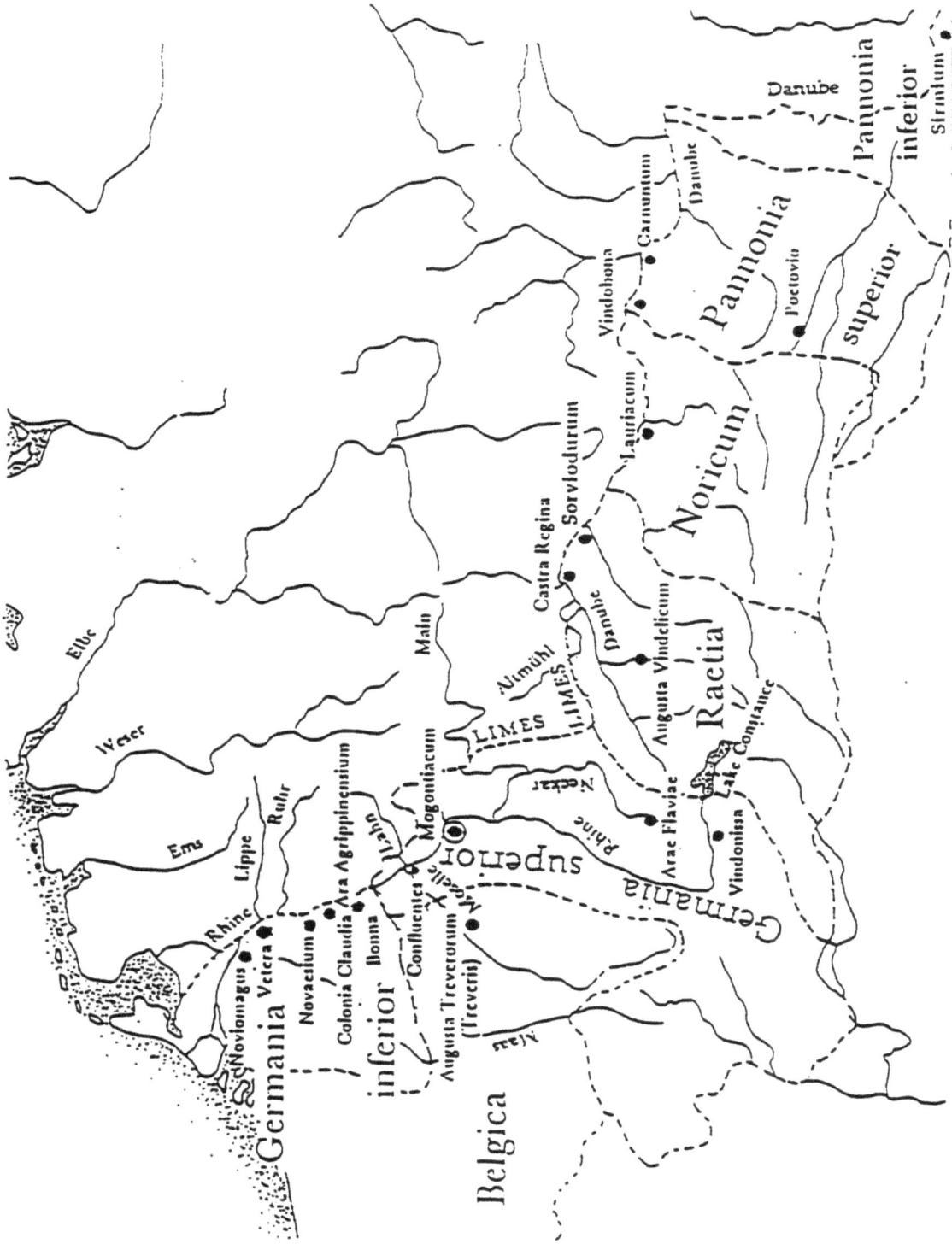

Map 1
The provinces of Gallia Belgica, Germania Superior and Inferior, Raetia, Noricum and Pannonia Superior and Inferior

113

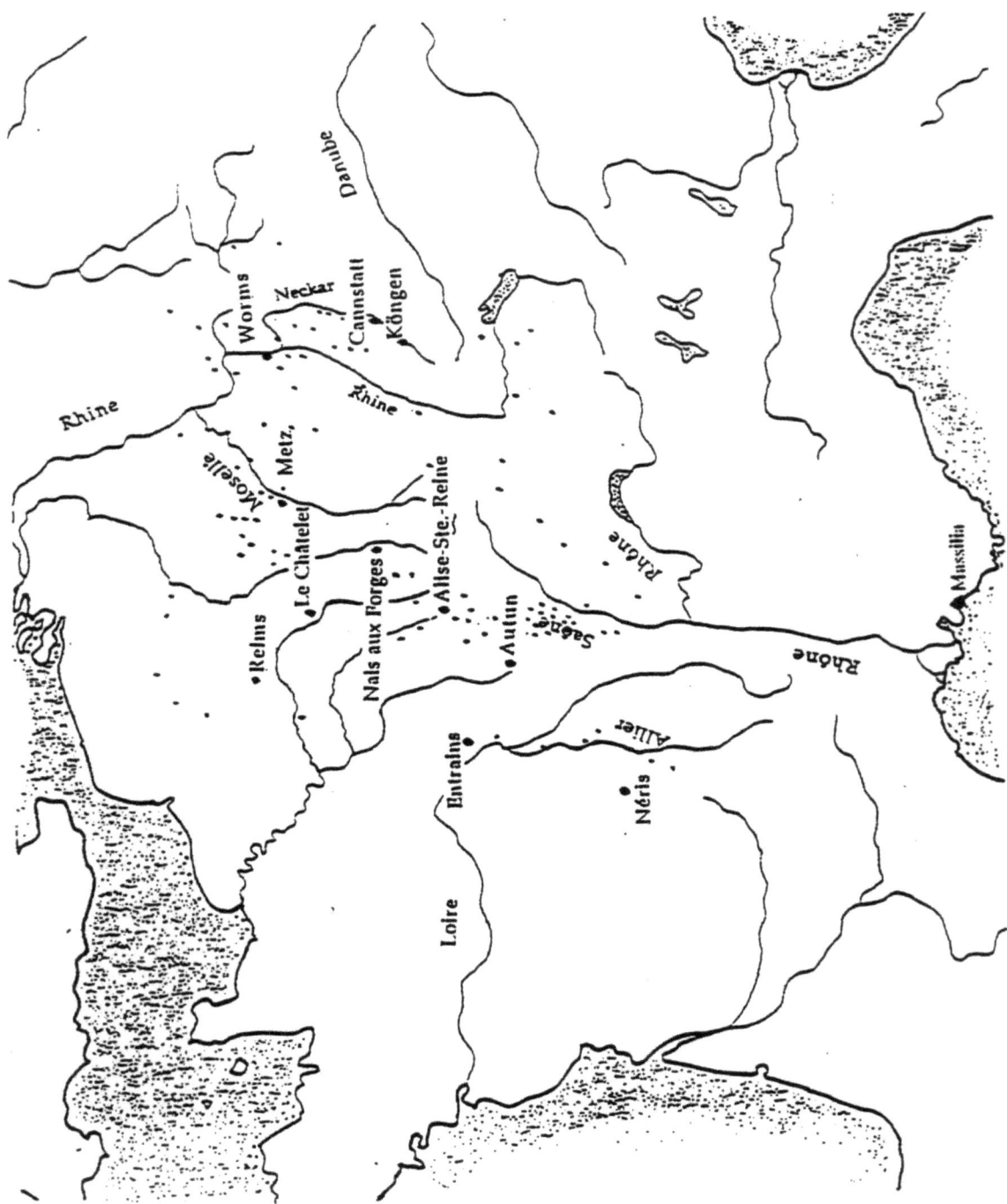

Map 2

Main sites in Gaul and Germania at which representations of Epona have been found

114

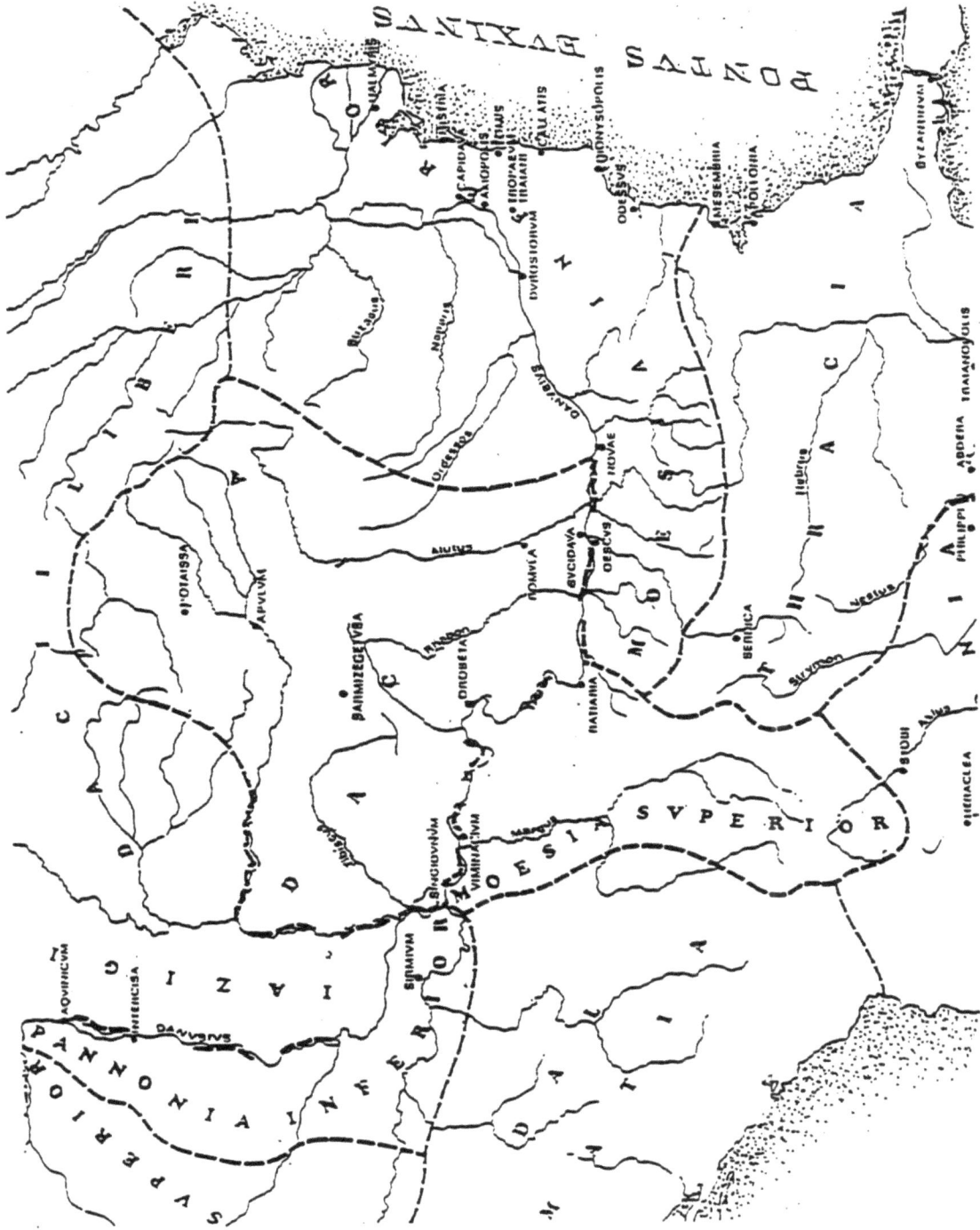

Map 3
Important sites in the Danube and Black Sea region